THEUNTOUCHABLES

Ireland's Criminal Assets Bureau and its War on Organised Crime

Other books by Paul Williams:

THE GENERAL

GANGLAND

EVIL EMPIRE

"Courageously frank and very detailed…This is the best book on Irish organised crime to date and a tribute to a murdered colleague."
The Irish Times

"Evil Empire, exhaustingly researched and chillingly riveting, is traditional crime reporting at its best."
The Sunday Independent

"Each part is meticulously researched and reads more like a thriller than true life. Williams dedicated the book to the memory of Veronica Guerin and the Lucan Investigation Team…He has served both in spectacular fashion."

Evening Herald

CRIME LORDS

"… Paul Williams is the outstanding journalist of his generation."
Joe Duffy, *Liveline* RTÉ

"Williams continues to be a thorn in organised crime's side."
RTÉ *Guide*

"… His work … has made him one of Ireland's best-known journalists and a hate figure for some of the country's most dangerous criminals."

In Dublin

THEUNTOUCHABLES

Ireland's Criminal Assets Bureau and its War on Organised Crime

Paul Williams

MERLIN
PUBLISHING

First published in 2006 by
Merlin Publishing
16 Upper Pembroke St,
Dublin 2, Ireland
publishing@merlin.ie
www.merlinwolfhound.com

Text © 2006 Paul Williams
Editing, Design and Layout © 2006 Merlin Publishing
Except
Photographs courtesy of the individuals and institutions noted on each
page of the picture sections.

10-Digit ISBN 1-903582-64-4
13-Digit ISBN 978-1-903582-64-0

A CIP catalogue record for this book is available from the British
Library.

10 9 8 7 6 5 4 3 2 1

*The publishers have made every reasonable effort to contact the
copyright holders of photographs reproduced in this book. If any
involuntary infringement of copyright has occurred, sincere apologies
are offered and the owner of such copyright is requested to contact the
publisher.*

Typeset by Gough Typesetting Services
Cover Design by Graham Thew Design
Cover Image courtesy of Collins Photo Agency
Picture Research by Gavin McClelland
Printed and bound in Cox and Wyman Ltd., Britain

Dedicated to the memory of
Kevin Stratford, 1972 –
2006, a loyal policeman, son,
brother and friend, who was
so cruelly snatched from life
on June 8, 2006.

We will never forget him.

Acknowledgements

The Untouchables could not be written without the help, trust and assistance of a great many people.

I would like to thank former and current members of the Gardaí, the Revenue Commissioners, Customs and Social Welfare who have worked with the Criminal Assets Bureau over the past decade. Normally I don't name my sources but in this case I couldn't even if I wanted to. They are protected by strict conditions of anonymity which are laid down in the Criminal Assets Bureau Act. Thank you all for your generosity and time. Trying to unravel the money trails and legal complexities involved in this area of law enforcement required a lot of calls and clarifications to these people and I thank them most sincerely for their patience.

My thanks to former Government Ministers, Ruairi Quinn and Nora Owen, whose job it was to introduce the tough legislation that established the CAB, in June 1996. My thanks also to retired Commissioner Pat Byrne, Assistant Commissioner Tony Hickey and the former Bureau Legal Officer Barry Galvin, for their time and shared experiences.

As always I would like to extend my gratitude to my colleagues in the *Sunday World* newspaper where I have been proud to work for the past 19 years. My thanks to *Sunday World* Managing Director Michael Brophy, Editor Colm MacGinty, Managing Editor Neil Leslie and my cranky News Editor John 'Bram/Dot' Donlon for being so understanding about my absences from the newsroom. My thanks also to my Picture Editor Gavin McClelland, researcher Daragh Keany and photographer Padraig O'Reilly. My sincere thanks also to Charlie Collins of Collins Photographic Agency.

I would also like to thank to my long-suffering and extremely hard-working editor at Merlin Publishing, Aoife Barrett. Also to Chenile, Julie, Noelle and Sandra – I was blessed among publishing women! My gratitude also to solicitor Kieran Kelly 'The Consiglieri' of Fanning Kelly and Company, for his legal expertise and friendship.

And my heartfelt gratitude and love to my family who have always been there for me no matter how tough things have got.

Contents

Introduction

Organised crime is one of the biggest and most rapidly expanding 'industries' in the world today. In 2004, a Global anti-money laundering survey estimated that USD$1 trillion is laundered annually by drug dealers, terrorists, arms dealers, human traffickers, smugglers and other criminals. But it is the production, sale and distribution of narcotics that accounts for the largest earnings in the underworld's economy. A report on the illicit drug market by the United Nations Office on Drugs and Crime (UNODC), calculated that in 2003 the industry had a retail value of over USD$322 billion with Western Europe accounting for USD$106 billion of that total. This made drugs and crime the third most profitable world market, after oil and arms.

But these figures are only estimates and many reputable international agencies suggest that the real figures are likely to be much higher. As a result of the clandestine nature of criminal activity, it is notoriously difficult to nail down the true monetary value of the gangland economy. Criminals do not keep company records or audit annual returns. Nor do they report to the stock market or shareholders. The available data is based on the quantities of drugs seized. It is calculated on the hypothesis, internationally accepted by law enforcement agencies, that they manage to intercept an average of one in ten shipments of drugs traversing borders. But the same agencies, including the Customs and Gardaí who have responsibility for the interception of drug supplies in Ireland, accept that this is a "best case scenario and purely aspirational".

Business is clearly booming for the godfathers.

In Ireland we now have one of the highest levels of illicit drug abuse in the European Union. The money being spent on drugs now ranks alongside some of Ireland's most popular consumer goods. Using the same international method of calculation, and basing it on actual drug seizures in 2003, the Irish Health Research Board estimated that the total retail value of the narcotics trade in Ireland was almost €650 million. In just two years, however, that figure had jumped by over 50 per cent. The most recent estimate of the drug trade in this country, based on seizures during 2005, is that it now exceeds €1 billion per year.

Officials, however, who work at the coalface claim that the real cost of the Irish drug trade could be as high as €2 billion per year. Evidence of this can be found in the fact that, despite a growing number of multi-million euro drug seizures in recent years, there were no corresponding shortages of any drug reported on the streets. The sale of cocaine alone, now accounts for between €200 and €400 million per year and the demand for the drug is increasing all the time. A survey published by the National Advisory Committee on Drugs in January 2006 found that one in five adults in the Irish Republic regularly use the Colombian marching powder. One senior official interviewed by this writer put the situation in perspective: "No one believes that we are intercepting one in ten shipments. Sometimes we get a good source of information and catch a gang after just a few shipments or even on their first trip, but that is rare enough. For example, by the time we finally caught up with John Gilligan's operation in 1996 they had already brought in around sixty consignments of hashish, worth about IR£25 million (€32 million). And that operation was small by today's standards."

All this underworld wealth has translated into a continual spiral of more and more serious crime in Ireland. With so much money to play for in the black economy, greed has become the prime motivation of the average hoodlum. And in the underworld, violence and murder are the tools of choice for the greedy godfather. The phenomenon of gangland murders was a direct result of the criminals' move into the drug trade. By the 1990s, the level of gangland violence could be used to gauge the level of activity in the drug world and the godfathers found themselves protected inside a wall of silence. Gangland murders went unsolved because of the fearsome reputations of the people responsible. It was equally difficult to catch and convict the hoods for drug offences. At the same time the criminals were displaying their ill-gotten gains, without fear of anyone taking their money away from them. For a time, it was easy to see why criminals began to consider themselves to be untouchable. But that same greed would ultimately change life for people in the criminal underworld.

* * * *

On June 6, 1996 an IRA gang murdered Det. Gda. Jerry McCabe and seriously injured his colleague and friend Det. Gda. Ben O'Sullivan, as they escorted a postal truck in Adare, County Limerick. The IRA cowards were out raising funds for themselves and for Sinn Féin, the political party that is almost exclusively funded by criminal activity, including extortion, smuggling, armed robbery and even the drug trade. The savagery of the murder shocked the entire country.

But only three weeks later another dangerous criminal gang committed a second atrocity, for the cause of greed and money. On June 26, John Gilligan had decided that he, like Sinn Féin/IRA, was also above the law. In order to protect his thriving drug empire, the diminutive mobster ordered the murder of crime journalist Veronica Guerin. It was the last straw.

The two crimes horrified and subsequently galvanised the people of Ireland. The Government was forced into the realisation that the war against organised crime had to be fought on a whole new front. They would have to use draconian powers to strike at the root of what all criminality is about, money. They had to hit the criminals and terrorists where it really hurt – in their pockets. The murders of Jerry McCabe and Veronica Guerin led directly to the introduction of a package of tough anti-crime legislation, most of which was drafted and passed into law within a month of the Guerin murder. A central principle of these new laws was provision for a revolutionary innovation in law enforcement, which had not been seen anywhere else in the world. This would take the form of a multi-disciplinary agency with wide ranging powers to track down and seize the proceeds of crime. It was called the Criminal Assets Bureau (CAB).

* * * *

In 1996, the international law enforcement community had never seen the likes of the CAB before. The Bureau was a multi-agency unit, consisting of Garda, Customs, Tax and Social Welfare officers, using their combined powers and expertise to target the proceeds of crime on a broad front. For the first time *ever* professional and legislative boundaries, which had prevented co-operation between the various organisations, were taken away. The godfathers could no longer intimidate or attack the civil servants who quizzed them about their tax or social welfare payments. The cops and the tax officials were now all part of the same team.

During the ten years since its establishment, the Criminal Assets Bureau has drastically changed the fortunes of organised crime to become one of the most successful innovations ever in Irish law enforcement. Its success has prompted many other countries, including the Government of the UK, to use the CAB as a template for similar units.

The basic philosophy of the CAB is to relieve criminals of their wealth. The Bureau has the power to seize assets and money, from any target suspected of criminal activity, if that target can not prove the origins of his or her wealth. Once Bureau officers can clearly establish a link with criminal activity and identify assets, an individual can become a target. The legislation, which gave the Bureau its powers, was unprecedented in that it shifted the onus of proof onto the criminal through the civil law process, which requires a lower standard of proof than the criminal law system. In civil law, proof is established on the balance of probabilities, instead of the criminal law requirement of beyond all reasonable doubt. The Bureau was also given powers to search any area where they suspected that evidence could be found which would lead to criminal loot. That meant that, for the first time, the CAB could search the offices of professionals, such as solicitors and accountants. The Bureau could also demand the details of accounts from financial institutions and liaise with the Money Laundering Investigation Unit (MLIU), to take advantage of the statutory obligation on those institutions to report suspicious transactions.

During the Bureau's first decade in operation it exposed the disturbing links between certain professionals and major players in organised crime. Without this partnership, money laundering would not be possible. It was therefore unsurprising that legal advisers and financial consultants protested loudest about what they described as "draconian and unconstitutional powers". But the rest of the public enthusiastically welcomed the CAB.

It was inevitable that this no-nonsense agency would attract the name the Untouchables, after the famous US Treasury Department's Prohibition Bureau which was set up to track down the Mafia's money. It was Elliot Ness and his Untouchables who secured the imprisonment of the notorious Mafia boss, Al Capone, in the 1930s for tax offences. Capone had insulated himself from the law by buying off the cops, the judges and anyone else he needed, to ensure the smooth running of his gigantic criminal empire. In the end, however, it was all the money he had hoarded that won him a one-way ticket to the slammer, where he subsequently died.

The Untouchables tells the extraordinary inside story of the Criminal Assets Bureau, from its establishment in 1996 to its subsequent ten year battle against the crime lords, terrorists and white collar criminals. The book describes the pursuit of some of the most notorious names in Irish criminal history – Martin 'the General' Cahill, John Gilligan, Gerry 'the Monk' Hutch and George 'the Penguin' Mitchell. It also reveals how the Bureau uncovered links between former Government minister, Michael Keating, and organised crime, and tells the story of how they succeeded in securing the imprisonment of Ray Burke, the first ex-minister to be jailed for criminal offences in Irish history.

After a decade in operation the Criminal Assets Bureau has

physically collected almost €100 million in taxes, from drug dealers, armed robbers, terrorists, corrupt officials and smugglers. It has also recovered, and saved, social welfare payments of an estimated €3 million. And in the first six months of 2006 alone, the Bureau had served tax demands of almost €15 million on criminal targets.

The three-letter abbreviation CAB is now a popular household brand name in Ireland – synonymous with exposing gangsters from every walk of life and making them pay.

This is the story of how the tables were turned on organised crime and how the CAB has ensured that the godfathers are no longer untouchable.

Paul Williams
June 2006

One

Thieves' Paradise

In the history of the Irish criminal underworld the year 1996 will forever stand out as a watershed. In the future, if there is ever the equivalent of a retirement home for old villains and drug barons, they will sit around in circles and reminisce about the good old days when they could enjoy their ill-gotten gains without any fear that their money would be taken away from them. They will recall with affection a time when a reputation for violence was enough to prevent the taxman from prying into their business affairs. But then they will spit in anger and remember June 1996 and how a nasty little thug called Gilligan screwed it all up.

In the halcyon days of crime, before the mid-1990s, a gangster could live openly in his luxury mansion and enjoy the life of a high-flying executive, despite having no 'gainful employment' or 'visible means of income'. Once a week he could jump into his top of the range Jaguar or Mercedes and whiz around to the local Labour Exchange to collect his unemployment benefit. Then, later on, if he was feeling energetic or needed some real money, he and his cronies could pick out a bank and make a substantial cash withdrawal – with the help of a sawn-off shotgun. He could then use the cash to buy in several kilos of hash or heroin or cocaine and have his flunkies distribute it for him. All he had to do was sit back and wait for the money to roll in. For most of the latter half of the twentieth-century Ireland *WAS* a thieves' paradise.

The outbreak of the Troubles in Northern Ireland in the late 1960s and the fallout from the Northern conflict ignited a sudden explosion in serious crime in the Republic. Before that there was no such thing as serious crime in Ireland. Terror groups like the Provos (IRA) funded their campaigns by robbing banks in the South. They took the ill-equipped, and under-resourced, Gardaí totally by surprise. Soon petty crooks and burglars began to learn from their terrorist role models. Guns were plentiful and so too were the pickings in a pre-plastic world, when practically all legitimate business was conducted through cash. Armed robbery became the stock-and-trade of a new generation of young thugs with nothing better to do. Families such as the Dunnes, the Cahills, the Cunninghams, the Hutchs and the Mitchells became the new faces on the block. Together they ushered in a new era of organised crime.

In general the State – the Gardaí and Government – was playing catch-up with these criminals when they first emerged. As the mayhem caused by paramilitary groups spilled across the Border throughout the seventies, the Irish police were forced to undergo dramatic changes. In the space of a few years, the ranks of the force swelled from 6,500 to over 10,000 members. The Government deployed a large portion of its security resources to fight terrorism and the perceived threat from Sinn Féin and the IRA, who many believed were plotting to take power in the Republic by force of arms. They were tough times for the police. In the space of five years, from 1980 to 1985, seven Gardaí were shot dead by various subversive groups during armed robberies.

At the same time organised crime was thriving. But Garda Headquarters tended to adopt the ostrich approach to the unfolding crisis – they stuck their heads in the sand hoping it would all go away. In fact during the 1980s Garda management policy was to refuse to even acknowledge the term 'organised crime'. It was the same story with successive governments. One young detective, who had taken a particular interest in the new phenomenon of drug abuse in the late 1970s, had warned his superiors that narcotics were about to hit the country like a tidal wave. Denis 'Dinny' Mullins, the first head of the fledgling Drug Squad, had been largely ignored and even laughed at by his colleagues and superiors. No one had believed him or wanted to know. But by the 1980s Mullins' prediction was coming true. The villains discovered drugs and practically every criminal gang quickly got involved in the action. The gangsters soon realised that one good drug deal could earn them a lot more money, with a lot less risk, than a few bank heists.

In 1979 and 1980, two world events conspired to have another dramatic effect on how the business of crime was conducted in Ireland. In Iran the pro-western Shah was overthrown by fundamentalist Muslims, led by the Ayatollah Khomeini. The country's elite fled in a mass exodus to the West. On the way they converted their mountains of local currency into heroin because it was much easier to transport than diamonds and gold. When the Shah's followers cashed in their assets there was a sudden upsurge in the availability of the drug on the streets of every city in Western Europe and the United States. At the same time Russia invaded Afghanistan, the world's largest opium producing country. In order to buy arms for their war with the Russians, the rebels dramatically increased heroin production. Record levels were for sale in the West and the supply of the drug was guaranteed. As a product it was ideal for the underworld. Supply created a rapid and increasing demand. Soon drug treatment centres in Europe and the United States were recording a substantial increase in the level of heroin addiction.

In any analysis of organised crime in Ireland it is widely accepted that the Dunne brothers, members of a large crime family from Crumlin in south Dublin, were the first in the underworld to realise the huge potential of heroin (smack). The brothers had been part of the first generation of well-organised young hoods with a flair for carrying out armed robberies. They had introduced Martin Cahill to the art of the bank and security van heists. Cahill would later become the country's most infamous godfather, earning the nickname the General because of his unique ability as a criminal mastermind. Another underworld graduate of the time was one George Mitchell from Drimnagh in south Dublin, who later became one of Europe's biggest drug traffickers, known by the nickname the Penguin. Also hanging around with the new brat pack were the Cunningham brothers, John, Michael and Fran, and their pal from Ballyfermot, west Dublin, John Joseph Gilligan. When smack arrived, however, the Dunnes, were the first to decommission their balaclavas and getaway cars. One observer wrote of that awful time: "The Dunnes did for smack what Henry Ford did for the motor car: made it available to the working man and woman, even the kids on the dole, even the kids at school."

Within weeks, heroin took a devastating hold in Dublin's inner-city ghettos, destroying hundreds of families in the process and leaving a legacy of death and despair that still exists almost three decades later. Within months the Dunnes were raking in a fortune from their army of pathetic addicts, who caused a crime wave as they robbed and mugged to get cash to buy their next fix. As the Dunnes increasingly became Public Enemy Number One, politicians, community activists and cops pointed to the obvious wealth the family were making from the misery that had engulfed Dublin. At a time when the country's economy was crumbling under the weight of soaring unemployment and emmigration figures, the flamboyant brothers weren't shy when it came to showing off their new prosperity. In the midst of the depression and hard times they were living the high life. They drove fast cars, wore sharp suits, swilled champagne and enjoyed the charms of the countless women attracted to their bad boy image. People protested, but there was no mechanism, or indeed will, to introduce laws to take the money away from them.

In 1982 the head of the family's drug operation, Larry Dunne, was the first Irish criminal to spectacularly display his ill-gotten wealth. While on bail for serious drug trafficking charges he paid over IR£100,000 (€127,000), a small fortune at the time, for a luxury detached mansion, perched in the foothills of the Dublin mountains in Rathfarnham, south Dublin. Standing on its own grounds, the large split-level villa, quaintly-named Gorse Rock, commanded breathtaking panoramic views of Dublin. "Lar's Gaff", as his cronies preferred to call it, is still one of the cheekiest displays of criminal wealth in over thirty years of organised crime. Dunne bought the house with cash drawn from one of his many bank accounts. At the time it was estimated that he was grossing at least IR£12,000 (€15,000) per week. Dunne had no reason to hide his money. From his high vantage point over the capital, he was telling the world that he was untouchable.

Around this time Dunne was approached by a tax inspector, as he was going into court for a remand hearing relating to his outstanding drug charge. The taxman, who was accompanied by a Garda, asked Dunne how he could afford his mansion in the mountains considering he was not in any kind of legitimate employment.

"Where do you fucking think I got it?" Dunne snapped at the nervous official. "I robbed it of course." Dunne shook his head, almost in disbelief that someone, especially a taxman, could ask him such a stupid question.

In those halcyon days Dunne and his family had major plans for their blood money. Often, in a cocaine-induced haze, the Dunne brothers would take in the spectacular view – a sea of twinkling lights in the city below – and fantasise about building their own little community in the Dublin Mountains. They would ramble on about how the family members would build homes on a site which Henry Dunne, Larry's closest sibling, had purchased higher up in the mountains. They would also invite close friends and associates to build alongside them. Eventually they would create their own little town, walled in and cut off from the hostile world outside. It would have its own shops and even a school. It would have elaborate defence systems to keep the cops out. This new nirvana they would call Dunnesville.

Within two years, however, the dream was abandoned. The Dunnes had become careless. As a result of the work of an undercover unit, nicknamed the Mockies (mock addicts) by the drug pushers they snared, and under the leadership of Dinny Mullins, most of the Dunnes had been busted for drug

offences and jailed for long sentences. The family eventually
self-destructed when they broke the one commandment that
every drug trafficker must adhere to – thou shalt not get high
on your own supply.

* * * *

By the time the reign of the Dunne family had come to an end
drugs were fast becoming the mainstay of organised crime.
Instead of facing it head on, however, the Drug Squad was
allowed to dwindle into an under-resourced and almost
insignificant unit over time. The famous squad of young
undercover Mockies was disbanded because Garda
management deemed such initiatives to be too gimmicky and
dramatic. The Garda top brass had no time for undercover
work. An internal report, colloquially known as the "Three
Wise Men Report", directed a move away from specialist
squads. The theory was that every man and woman in the
force should be able to do any job required.

In the meantime drug traffickers were becoming extremely
wealthy and powerful. In the 1983 Finance Act, Ireland
became one of the only countries in the common law system
with powers to tax the proceeds of crime. Curiously there is
no record of this power ever being used until the establishment
of the Criminal Assets Bureau thirteen years later. Observers
today believe that at the time politicians were actually afraid
to use the legislation because it could be seen as legitimising
criminal activity by making it taxable. But there was another
reason why the available laws were not used. Civil servants
attached to the Revenue Commissioners and the Department
of Social Welfare were afraid to take on the gangsters. In 1989
their fear was justified when they were ordered to confront
the General, Martin Cahill.

In 1988 a high-profile and much-publicised overt Garda
surveillance operation had been launched against Cahill and
his gang. In the previous ten years the General had become
the country's most successful armed robber. In 1983 he had

master-minded the robbery of over IR£2 million (€2.54 million) worth of gold and diamonds from the O'Connors jewellery factory in Harold's Cross in Dublin. The General's gang were also responsible for the robbery of millions of pounds from banks, post offices, security vans and payroll deliveries. Cahill had also displayed his lethal potential when he had a bomb planted under the car of the State's top forensic scientist, Doctor James Donovan in 1982. Dr Donovan's evidence was crucial in several criminal cases before the courts, including one involving Cahill. The brave scientist suffered appalling leg injuries in the act of terrorism but continued his work for another twenty years. In 1986, the General and his mob had also pulled off one of the biggest art thefts in the world when they made off with the Beit art collection of Dutch Masters from Russborough House in County Wicklow. A year later Cahill had even brought his battle to the heart of the criminal justice system when he broke into the offices of the Director of Public Prosecutions and stole the most sensitive crime files in the country.

By mobilising the famous Tango Squad the Gardaí finally went to war with Cahill and his mob. The squad of enthusiastic young officers followed, harassed and cajoled the gangsters over several months. Eventually most of Cahill's men slipped up and were caught for a variety of serious offences, such as possession of firearms and attempted robberies but Tango One, the General, escaped. Cahill, however, had lost his much-cherished anonymity during the months that the Tango Squad was on his case. He had attracted extensive TV and press coverage as a result of the ongoing Garda operation. Overnight the General, an illusive gangster who hid his identity behind balaclavas and *Mickey Mouse*® shorts, had become a household name.

The most striking exposé was broadcast by the *Today Tonight* programme on RTÉ television in February 1988. The programme highlighted the crimes associated with Cahill and his gang. It revealed that Cahill lived between two homes in his native Rathmines in south Dublin. One was a luxury home

in upmarket Cowper Downs which he had bought with
IR£85,000 (€108,000) in cash. The other was a more modest,
semi-detached Corporation house down the road at Swan
Grove. Cahill was filmed as he queued to collect his dole
money and the reporter Brendan O'Brien confronted him on
the street as he left. The programme focused on the obvious
signs of wealth possessed by the masked underworld boss
who, at the same time, was receiving unemployment benefit
from the State.

The programme caused an immediate uproar. It was very
embarrassing for the Government. They were paying society's
new Public Enemy a wage. The Social Welfare Minister
Michael Woods, a member of the Fianna Fail-led Government,
told the Dáil he had ordered the suspension of Cahill's dole
payments.

In the subsequent debate it was a member of the
Progressive Democrats, Mary Harney, who was the first
politician to suggest hitting the mobs by taking their cash and
assets. She told the Dáil she wanted Cahill investigated in the
same way Elliot Ness had targeted and nailed Al Capone.
She wanted the General evicted from his Local Authority
house and said that if the law didn't exist to take action then
the laws should be changed to make it possible to do so. Her
words fell on deaf ears and no such action was taken, or would
be taken, for another eight years. In the meantime Cahill
decided to illustrate his contempt for law and order – again.

Shortly after the *Today Tonight* programme and the
resulting furore, the Department of Social Welfare sent
inspectors to interview Cahill. He politely refused to answer
any questions raised by his claims during the TV programme
that he was a "businessman". He claimed the cars and
motorbikes he owned had been left to him in a will. And he
denied any connection with either the Corporation house at
Swan Grove or Cowper Downs. The inspectors couldn't touch
him.

Some time later a Revenue officer was sent to talk to

Cahill. The General had purposely agreed to meet the official in Cowper Downs because he felt it would irritate the taxman no end. During the meeting Cahill excused himself for a time. When he returned he diverted attention from his tax affairs by complaining about the state of crime in the country. And to emphasis his point he gestured towards the front window. The civil servant's car was engulfed in flames.

Despite these antics, in January 1989, Cahill received a letter from the Department of Social Welfare informing him that his dole payments were to be discontinued. The letter was signed by a Higher Executive Officer named Brian Purcell. Cahill appealed the decision and at the hearing Mr Purcell, who was sitting across a table from the treacherous godfather, outlined the reasons why the payments had been stopped. The General's means clearly showed that he was not entitled to social welfare benefits.

On May 9, the social welfare inspector appeared on behalf of his Department at another appeal hearing, this time for Cahill's sister-in-law and lover, Tina Lawless. Tina, who was mother to the General's second family, was a sister of Frances, Martin Cahill's wife. The two sisters shared the love of the overweight, balding gangster and Tina's social welfare had also been cut off as a result of the Cahill investigation.

Three weeks later, Brian Purcell was abducted from his home by armed and masked men, acting on Cahill's orders. The father of two young children was taken, tied, gagged and blindfolded, to Sandymount where he was left lying near railway lines. The General emerged from the shadows and shot the terrified civil servant once in each leg. Miraculously neither bullet hit an artery or a bone, and Mr Purcell recovered from his appalling ordeal. It was a horrifying crime but it succeeded in achieving what Cahill wanted – to send shock waves through the entire Irish public service. When the civil servant was recovering in hospital he received an anonymous get well card that read: 'The General prognosis is good.' It was suspected that it was another example of Cahill's sick sense of humour. Armed Garda protection was placed on all Department of Social Welfare officials dealing with the Cahill case.

For the second time in seven years the General had sent a chilling message to the Irish State on behalf of Crime Incorporated but yet again no one came up with a legislative solution to the problem. Nobody suggested a way to take the money away from the gangsters. Garda management reckoned that the only way to catch the criminals was to nab them in the act of breaking the law. They could then put them behind bars but nothing could be done about the money resting in the criminals' bank accounts. It was the ordinary cops on the ground who first realised that, in order to take on organised crime, they needed powers to take the money and assets from the godfathers.

In hindsight it would also appear that important members of the Government of the day, under the leadership of Taoiseach Charles J Haughey, had their own agenda when it came to dealing with the proceeds of crime. Many years later it would emerge that Haughey, while leader of the country, had secretly received over IR£10 million (€12.7 million) in corrupt payments and bribes from wealthy business figures. So too had his Minister for Justice at the time, Ray Burke – the minister who had effective control over law and order throughout Ireland. (*See Chapter 9*) He had received at least IR£1 million (€1.27 million) in payments for corrupt planning decisions. His successor in the Department of Justice, Padraig 'Pee' Flynn, would also feature in the plethora of tribunals set up in the late 1990s to investigate allegations of corrupt payments to politicians. In the bigger picture it would have been inconceivable for these men to pass legislation that gave the authorities access to individual bank accounts to track down criminal payments.

Circumstances would have to change dramatically before the thieves lost control of paradise.

Two

Elliot Ness and the Untouchables

In most major investigations in the '70s, '80s and early '90s no emphasis was placed on the monitoring or tracking of assets. No formal protocols existed between the financial institutions and the Gardaí. Even in the ordinary course of searches more emphasis was placed on finding cash than on uncovering financial documents. In the event that evidence was found there was little that could be done with it.

One former Serious Crime Squad officer interviewed for this book summarised the situation: "Every criminal, no matter where he was in the pecking order, was showing signs of increased wealth. In the 1980s and early 1990s you could drive through areas like Crumlin, where a lot of serious criminals were living, and you could easily pick out the homes belonging to the hoods. They had PVC windows and doors before many others, including most of our people, could afford them. They bought the latest colour TVs and sound systems for cash when it cost a small mortgage to do so while at the same time they were officially on the dole. Unfortunately the doors and windows and the odd TV were often 'accidentally' broken during searches but at least it meant that the gouger [criminal] had to spend more drug money to repair or replace them."

The General's terrifying attack on Brian Purcell, an innocent social welfare inspector, had ensured that the criminal's assets, bank accounts and government handouts would be safe for several more years – and he was not the only one. In the following years there was little debate about introducing legislation that would enable the State to pursue the proceeds of crime. But officers attached to the Serious Crime Squad and district detective units all over the country could see that the big crime lords were becoming more powerful – and dangerous with it. The more experienced cops knew that the time had come when the traditional methods of fighting crime were no longer sufficient.

The Serious Crime Squad officer recalls: "After Cahill attacked the social welfare officer there was no way we could get anyone in the relevant government departments to cut these guys off the dole or serve tax assessments on them. The unions who represented them were opposed to pursuing criminals on the grounds of health and safety. No one could blame them because we had guns and they didn't. But we had no powers to look into bank accounts and whenever we seized cash from a criminal, his lawyer could walk into court and have it returned under a Police Property Application. Some people in our job began to seriously question why we couldn't go after the criminal's money but there didn't seem to be the will to do that. We often asked why the legislation could not be changed so that we, the Gardaí, could do the job for the social welfare people. Young Gardaí who have joined since the mid-90s cannot believe that the system was like that. A lot has changed in ten years."

At the time the legislation dealing with the seizure of a criminal's money or goods was archaic. Section 29 of the Dublin Police Act 1842 for example dealt with seizures and it was only applicable within the boundaries covered by the Garda Dublin Metropolitan Region (DMR). Some of the subsections for seizures were time specific – from midnight to 8 am in the morning. This was designed to "counter riotous and indecent behaviour". In 1842 it was probably considered revolutionary but in 1990 it illustrated the utter lack of progress in the area. The 1842 Act was used to combat offences such as "disorderly conduct at a public resort, drunkards guilty of riotous behaviour, riding a carriage without the owner's consent, turning loose cattle or unmuzzled dogs". It empowered an officer to: "stop, search and detain any vessel, boat, cart, or carriage in which he has reason to suspect that anything stolen or unlawfully obtained may be found. It also allowed Gardaí to stop, search and detain, any person reasonably suspected of having or conveying in any manner anything stolen or unlawfully obtained."

But it wasn't enough to give the Gardaí any real power against criminals like Gilligan and legislation was not the only problem in the archaic system. Cost issues were also an important factor. In the conventional policing business it takes a lot of time and resources to catch a professional villain. Several officers, often working round-the-clock, must watch a target's every move in the hope of catching him or her in the act. But the prevailing attitude of Garda management at the time was to cut corners and save money. If a major operation was not producing results within weeks it was often cancelled and the officers were deployed somewhere else. The Tango Squad's operation, targeting the General and his gang, was the exception to the rule and it lasted 18 months. The problem with resources, where cost is put before all other consideration, still often prevails.

And even if the resources and legislation issues were dealt with there was another huge problem – bail. In the days before the emergence of the CAB, suspects, who were actually arrested and charged with serious crimes, found it easy to obtain bail. They enjoyed long periods at liberty, while their lawyers used every trick in the book to delay their trial for as long as possible. In some instances, trials did not come to court for up to three years. In the meantime the criminals made full use of their time on bail to rob enough money to keep their families in comfort while they were inside. Unfortunately some things have still not changed in relation to the highly contentious issue of bail. Despite a Referendum in which the Irish public voted for stricter bail laws, criminal suspects still find it relatively easy to get bail in the High Court and often despite the objections of Gardaí. In a lot of cases criminals can continue to receive bail even though they have been charged with further offences while actually out on bail in the first place! "Letting these guys out just gave us more work because we knew what they would do. It was an awful waste of time when we could have been after other robbers. In the 1980s and early 1990s it was the norm that an armed robber went absolutely berserk robbing. They were like squirrels gathering up as much cash as they could. In those days a criminal could rob a bank, lodge the money elsewhere, and leave it there gathering interest while he was inside and there was nothing we could do. We could not touch the money unless we could physically prove that the actual notes he lodged in the bank were from a heist and that was impossible," recalled the Serious Crime Squad cop.

With so few deterrents, by 1990 organised crime in Ireland had become much more sophisticated and international. The mobsters had gone global. Irish hoods, who already enjoyed close links with their counterparts in the UK, established links with international gangs based in Amsterdam, Holland. Later they began doing business from bases in Marbella and Alicante in Spain, rubbing shoulders with other international players including Moroccans, Colombians and Eastern Europeans. A sinister trend emerged as drug suppliers in Holland and Spain began throwing automatic pistols and machine-guns in with shipments for their Irish customers. It was a bit like a sales incentive scheme for drug traffickers – get a free shooter with every ten kilos purchased. The first time the authorities got proof of this was later that year when a large consignment of hashish washed up on a Dublin shoreline. About 40 kilos were stored in two barrels that were tied together and left floating in the bay. The haul had been dropped off the coast from a ship but the gang waiting to pick it up in a smaller boat missed the rendezvous. Carefully wrapped and hidden among the slabs of cannabis were half a dozen nine millimetre automatic pistols and ammunition.

In another series of searches by the Serious Crime Squad a few years later, a cache of high-powered Heckler and Koch MP5 machine-guns and Glock automatic pistols were found hidden in a bog in County Kildare. The weapons, both of which are preferred by military Special Forces units and specialist police squads, had been smuggled into the country with drug shipments by the Penguin, George Mitchell. In a separate seizure the same Serious Crime Squad found a large amount of ammunition and a number of Armalite rifles. These weapons also originated with the Penguin, who was becoming one of the biggest drug traffickers in Europe. In both cases intelligence sources reported that the guns were intended for delivery to the IRA, as a glorified protection tax. In return anti-drug campaigning Sinn Féin/IRA hard men would turn a blind eye to the drug-peddling taking place on their streets. It was clear that the situation was getting even worse – all over Ireland the godfathers were arming themselves with sophisticated hardware.

The organised crime industry was flourishing. Drug demand, especially, was growing at an alarming rate. The ecstasy craze arrived with the rave disco scene in 1991 and introduced tens of thousands of young Irish teenagers to the drug culture. Use of the drug also contributed to an upsurge in heroin addiction as ruthless hoods sold it to kids to help them come down from the ecstasy high. An indication of the ecstasy market's potential was exemplified in 1994 during an undercover operation against the gang controlled by the Penguin. Members of the newly formed Garda National Drug Unit (GNDU) busted a secret E making factory Mitchell had just set up in a farmyard in North County Dublin. It had the capacity to churn out IR£1 million (€1.27 million) worth of the drug every week.

Frustration continued to mount among the professionals who had first hand knowledge of the worsening situation. A specialised squad called the Anti-Racketeering Unit had been set-up in Garda HQ during the early 1990s with the aim of targeting the money rackets of various crime gangs and the Provisional IRA. The unit was eventually disbanded, however, amid internal disputes between officers.

It appeared that nothing could stop the growing power of the godfathers – the situation was reaching crisis point.

* * * *

By the 1990s Ireland had earned a reputation among Europe's criminal elite as a soft touch, an ideal bolthole from justice. International drug barons such as Dutch trafficker Jan Hendrik Ijpelaar and Englishman, David Huck *(See Chapter 7)* presided over their empires from the safety of luxury homes in Clare and Kerry. International and local intelligence sources were also aware that some of Europe's biggest gangs were using isolated Irish coastal inlets to smuggle in huge quantities of drugs, with the intention of transporting them onwards to the UK and the continent.

This international dimension added insult to injury, but only one man was prepared to risk his reputation, and his own safety, to break with popular convention and demand that action be taken. Anger and frustration at the appalling negligence finally drove him to break his silence and expose the full extent of the scandal to the public. That man was Barry Galvin, the public prosecutor, who would become Ireland's real-life version of Al Capone's crime-fighting nemesis, Elliot Ness.

Soon to play a historic role in Irish law enforcement, the Criminal Justice System had never seen the likes of Barry Galvin before. Driven by a passion for law and order he was described by everyone who ever worked with him as "larger than life and indefatigable". Galvin relished challenging the consensus but he was an unlikely rebel. He was a fourth generation solicitor in one of Cork's oldest and most respected family law firms, Barry C Galvin and Son. His grandfather had received the Law Society gold medal in 1859 when he qualified as a solicitor and members of his family had gone on to fight in the trenches of World War One.

Educated at Clongowes Wood College, the father-of-three had shown a natural flair for the law. He came top of his class in the 1965 bar exams in Kings Inns. He was placed first in the Roll of Honour and was awarded the prestigious Brooke Prize. As a barrister he specialised in the field of corporate, banking and taxation law. He also worked in criminal defence. When he was not in the courtroom, the non-drinker lived an action-packed lifestyle. He was the Munster motorbike scrambling champion nine times and held a life-long passion for sailing. After a short period working as a barrister, he joined the family practice as a solicitor and worked for ten years as a defence lawyer, contesting many landmark cases.

During the late 1980s and early 1990s Galvin was elected to the ruling council of the Irish Law Society, the solicitor's governing body, several times. He also served on the Law Society Compensation Fund committee, the Registrar's committee and the Professional Purposes committee. During his tenure he helped to tackle the problem of rogue solicitors. People remember Galvin as a shrewd and tough "maverick". When he decided to pursue lawyers who had stolen client's money, together with his colleagues and the permanent staff of the Law Society, compensation for malpractice payouts was reduced from IR£6 million (€7.62 million) to practically zero.

In 1983, Barry Galvin was appointed State Solicitor for Cork City. He was responsible for all government work arising in Cork, including the prosecution of criminal cases. Galvin had a reputation for hard work and was widely respected by his peers and by Gardaí. But Galvin was becoming increasingly frustrated with a criminal law system that he felt hampered the investigation of serious crime. He believed that the Criminal Justice System had failed to keep pace with the changing trends in criminal activity – to the public's detriment. He felt that the law favoured the rights of the offender over those of the victim.

Galvin began to take a personal interest in the group of millionaire drug traffickers who were based in the Munster area, including well-known gangsters such as Tommy O'Callaghan, Jeremiah 'Judd' Scanlan, and Paddy McSweeney. He also closely monitored the arrival into Ireland of the likes of drug barons' Huck and Ijpelaar. The more he learned about these ruthless criminals, the more he was angered by the lack of adequate legislation to deal with drug trafficking and the seizure of the proceeds of crime. The State Solicitor quickly realised that it meant that the top godfathers were virtually immune from justice.

Galvin started to campaign for change. One problem at the time was that individuals facing trial for serious crimes in Cork could opt to have their cases heard in Dublin. But there was already a massive backlog in the courts in Dublin. Galvin saw it as a stunt to purposely defer trials for years and successfully campaigned for a change in the rules so those suspects could no longer opt for a Dublin court.

Another achievement was his role in inspiring a change in the law governing search warrants for evidence. These warrants were vital to criminal investigation. Galvin's involvement followed a local case in which two thugs killed a man at a block of local authority flats in Cork. A gas bottle had been dropped on top of the man's head from an upstairs balcony. The culprits had been renting one of the flats and they placed the gas bottle in it before fleeing to the UK. Although investigating Gardaí could actually see the gas bottle through the front door, they had no powers to enter and seize this vital piece of evidence. If they had retrieved it for forensic examination it would have been deemed to be an illegal act and the evidence rendered inadmissible. The Gardaí went to Galvin with their legal difficulty. As a temporary solution Cork Corporation were encouraged to end their tenancy agreement with the absent culprits, take back possession of the flat and change the locks. As the lawful owners of the flat the Corporation could then 'invite' the Gardaí inside to search for the evidence. Galvin subsequently used this case to exemplify the problem, while participating in the Strategic Management Initiative (SMI) set up to review the efficiency and effectiveness of the Gardaí. One of the SMI legal recommendations was for the introduction of an effective search warrant but it was not put in place until 1997.

Galvin was genuinely concerned at the increasing levels of violence in Irish society. In his role as State Solicitor he reviewed Garda investigation files everyday. Evidence of the changing trends in crime was there in black and white. The level of violence involved in attacks and the wanton destruction of property was getting worse all the time. Gardaí were seizing a wider variety of drugs and in much larger quantities than ever before. Through his close working relationship with local police and customs, he realised how hamstrung the officers were if they tried to take on the godfathers. But Galvin soon realised that they had at least one effective weapon – the extensive powers available to the Revenue Commissioners.

Galvin convened an ad hoc, inter-agency group to examine the activities of local hoodlums. He invited officers from local drug squads and Customs to his office at the South Mall in Cork. Sitting around his grandmother's table, at the end of his modest, file-strewn office, they drew up a list of the top ten drug traffickers in the region. The list included the names of O'Callaghan, McSweeney, Scanlan, Ijpelaar and Huck.

Over time they collated information in a dossier. It included details of employment records, criminal records, intelligence on known investments, property and business dealings, lists of known associates, the cars they drove, the holidays they took and the homes they lived in. When it was completed Galvin sent it to the Revenue Commissioners in Dublin, together with a covering report suggesting what existing laws could be used to pursue the ill-gotten-gains of the named mobsters.

Nothing happened.

As a result of the ad hoc inquiry, however, Galvin successfully prosecuted Tommy O'Callaghan for failing to make tax returns contrary to sections of the 1983 Finance Act. Officially unemployed, the high-living gang boss was given a six month jail term which was upheld on Appeal by the High Court. O'Callaghan subsequently appealed his case to the Supreme Court where he won on a technicality.

Galvin was doing everything in his power to encourage the State to take action but when he realised that nothing was going to happen he went to the media and started talking. In 1992 the crusading legal eagle got the nation's undivided attention when he appeared on the *Late Late Show* with Gay Byrne. For the first time, ever, someone from the cutting edge was talking about how it really was out there. Galvin revealed how wealthy foreign villains had been attracted to Ireland, as much by our lax criminal laws as by the beauty of West Cork. He explained that the southern coastline was being used to smuggle in huge amounts of drugs, for transportation onwards to the UK and Europe. He disclosed that the only two customs officers assigned to the region had no boats, no radar and no radios. He criticised the inaction of successive governments against the godfathers. Most significantly, he called for the establishment of a single agency, combining the skills of Customs, Revenue and the Gardaí, similar to the Drug Enforcement Agency (DEA) in the US. He suggested that it would require a staff of around 300 agents, with in-house legal experts like America's District Attorney (DA) system and financial analysts.

It was powerful stuff. The public was astounded at the amounts of money Galvin claimed the mobs were making. But now organised crime bosses were no longer Galvin's only enemy. The Government, which had suffered acute embarrassment as a result of the Corkman's disclosures, was on his case. The Justice Minister of the day, Padraig 'Pee' Flynn took Galvin's criticisms personally. Shortly after Flynn became minister Galvin, as president of the Southern Law Association, was involved in a dispute with the Department. The Southern Law Association solicitors took their names off the free legal aid panel as a form of protest against the Justice Department's refusal to pay realistic fees. The dispute was only resolved after two months of negotiation. After the *Late Late Show* Pee Flynn laughed Galvin off as a publicity-seeking crank, with a hidden agenda of his own. Stories were leaked with the intention of undermining the lawyer, including one that he had been motivated by a political allegiance to Fine Gael. Nothing could have been further from the truth and the reaction spoke volumes about government priorities.

While researching *The Untouchables,* this writer discovered that government officials were instructed to discredit the troublemaker. It is understood that one senior officer attached to the secretive Garda Crime and Security branch – or C 3 as it was then known – was discreetly dispatched to Cork to investigate Galvin. Extensive enquiries were made to find out how many cases Galvin had messed up. The spooks also wanted to know more about the clientele he had represented while working as a defence lawyer. In the end they went back to Flynn empty-handed.

Meanwhile in the Dáil the Minister had made a statement about Galvin's claims. The Justice Minister delivered his rebuff in his own inimitable style – sneering and often patronising. Flynn said Galvin had been "questioned" and his claims found to be exaggerated. There was, he conceded, a drug problem but it wasn't of the scale "suggested by the State Solicitor for Cork".

But Flynn was too late. Galvin had succeeded in his mission. He had firmly placed organised crime on the national agenda. Now it was receiving extensive coverage in the print and electronic media. Not since the 1988 exposé of the General had crime dominated the headlines to such an extent. Galvin's difficult relationship with the Department of Justice subsequently mellowed when Maire Geoghegan Quinn, who was seen as a much more reasonable politician, replaced Pee Flynn.

In the meantime the Cork underworld was becoming more violent as gangs vied for control of the drug trade. Barry Galvin did not have to look very far to prove his point. In April 1995 thirty-five-year-old criminal Michael Crinnion was shot dead at the Clannad bar in the city. Crinnion was a brother-in-law and partner of the notorious O'Flynn brothers. The violent brothers who had been long regarded by Gardaí as dangerous criminals, Donal 'Ducky', Bobby, Christy, Seanie and Kieran, between them ran one of the biggest drug gangs in Munster. The suspects for the murder were members of the gang

controlled by Tommy O'Callaghan. In 1991 the O'Callaghan
mob were suspected of another shooting incident targeting
the O'Flynns in the Acadian bar. A man was injured in the
attack. And a few months before Crinnion's murder the same
rival gang fired a number of shots in another pub, as a warning
to Ducky and Bobby O'Flynn.

Galvin and the local Gardaí were also concerned that
certain pubs in the city had been bought by the crime gangs to
sell drugs and to launder cash. One of those pubs was called
the Screaming Monkey and it was secretly owned by the
O'Flynn family. Using the history of violence at the premises,
Galvin successfully applied to the courts to have the place
closed down. In court the courageous State Solicitor exposed
the pub as a front for the O'Flynn brothers, Bobby and Christy.
The case gained national headlines and succeeded in exposing
one of the country's most dangerous crime gangs.

Galvin and the Gardaí also successfully closed down
another pub that had been bought by Tommy O'Callaghan. In
court Galvin objected to the licence for the premises on the
grounds that it was a front for drug dealing and money
laundering. Gardaí said that they had uncovered evidence
linking O'Callaghan to a front company that owned the pub.
The State Solicitor and the Gardaí were using the few weapons
available to them to make life difficult for the gangsters.

* * * *

One of the senior Garda officers who did agree with Barry
Galvin was Tony Hickey. When Galvin appeared on the *Late
Late Show* Hickey was the Superintendent with responsibility
for drug investigations, attached to Crime Branch in Garda
HQ. Hickey was one of the brightest officers in the force and
would eventually rise to the rank of Assistant Commissioner.
Hickey travelled to Cork to meet Galvin and discuss what he
knew about the growing drug trade. The drug cop was already
keeping discreet tabs on many of the major drug barons Galvin
had referred to, including David Huck. Unknown to Galvin,

Hickey had also been working closely with Scotland Yard. They were sharing intelligence about the movement of drugs and drug traffickers between the two countries. He also started working closely with the Dutch police after Ijpelaar arrived. Hickey agreed with the State Solicitor that legislation was required and also that the drug squads be reformed and redeployed.

Part of Hickey's remit was to attend meetings of the newly established Europol and other EU bodies, set-up to tackle organised crime and drug trafficking on a united front. Ireland had appointed a liaison officer to Europol HQ in The Hague, and others were to be dispatched to London and later to Paris and Madrid. Police forces across Europe were beginning to realise that crime could no longer be fought within national borders.

Less than a year later in July 1993, the Gardaí notched up a major victory when they seized two tonnes of cannabis on board Huck's yacht, *The Brime* at Fenit, County Kerry. But Huck managed to escape the net. He had been arrested and questioned by Gardaí before the Irish Navy located *The Brime* but under the existing legislation they could only hold the drug trafficker for a maximum of twelve hours. Gardaí had no choice but to release him and he immediately left the country.

While the Government was still slow to take action, events were overtaking them in the European Union. In response to mounting international concern over money laundering, the Financial Action Task Force on Money Laundering (FATF) had been established by the G-7 Summit held in Paris in 1989. Recognising the threat posed to the banking system and to financial institutions, the G-7 Heads of State and the European Commission had convened the Task Force from the G-7 member States, the European Commission, and eight other countries. The Task Force had been given the responsibility of examining money laundering techniques and trends, reviewing the actions which had already been taken at a national or international level, and setting out the measures that still needed to be taken to combat money laundering.

In April 1990 the FATF had issued a report containing forty recommendations, which provided a comprehensive plan of action to tackle money laundering. The FATF recommendations included one that every country should have procedures in place for the reporting of suspicious transactions by financial institutions and other bodies. It was further suggested that all countries should have procedures in place for the restraint and confiscation of suspected proceeds of crime. The European Union Directive 91/308, incorporating the FATF recommendations, was issued to member states in 1991.

Ireland finally gave effect to this directive with the introduction on June 30, 1994 of the Criminal Justice Bill 1994. Justice Minister Maire Geoghegan Quinn brought most of the provisions of the Bill into law on November 3, a month before the Government changed.

The most important points of the new Criminal Justice Act included making an offence of money laundering and of handling the proceeds of drug trafficking and other criminal activity. It ordered, "duties of identification" and record keeping on "designated bodies" such as banks, insurance and investment companies. The 1994 Act stated, that institutions and professional advisers, such as accountants and solicitors, could be served with court orders, demanding production of documents and files. The Act obliged the designated financial institutions to report suspicious transactions to the Money Laundering Investigation Unit (MLIU) of the Garda Bureau of Fraud Investigation (GBFI). The MLIU was specially established to process the reports. The new 1994 law also provided for restraint orders against people who had been actually charged, or were about to be charged, with drug trafficking or serious offences.

In addition it provided for confiscation orders against criminals, who had been convicted of drug trafficking and other serious crime. The new Criminal Justice Act applied the civil standard of proof in relation to issues concerning confiscation. It provided for: "The forfeiture of property used, or intended for use, in the commission of an offence and lawfully seized from a convicted person which was in his possession or control at the time of being apprehended or when a summons in respect of the offence was issued." In other words property could only be seized if the person was convicted. If the person was not convicted his assets could not be touched.

But despite these new provisions, and even before the measures in the new Act were fully implemented, it was apparent that the law did not go far enough to combat the rapidly escalating threat posed by drug trafficking and the related activities of organised gangs. By the time the 1994 Act came into force a dangerous criminal was about to illustrate the need for much tougher legislation.

* * * *

In 1994, John Gilligan had no time to waste worrying about a new criminal justice Act. He was preoccupied with building an empire.

In September 1993, Gilligan had been released from prison after serving a sentence for robbing a hardware store. Throughout the 1980s his mob, known as the Factory Gang, had specialised in the systematic plundering of warehouses and factories across the country. By the time he was released he had decided to embark on a new business – drugs. And he had vowed that he would never again serve time in prison.

Gilligan had teamed up with a new business partner and sidekick, John 'The Coach' Traynor, who was also a close associate and confidante of the General, Martin Cahill. The Coach was a life-long career criminal, who specialised in fraud and acted as a 'Mr Fixit' for the General. In 1983 he had helped mastermind the O'Connors jewellery heist. In the early 90s Traynor had done time for receiving stolen goods in the UK where he had made a lot of important contacts in the drug trade. Traynor was also a conniving two-faced hoodlum with a dangerous manipulative side to his character. He was an unnamed underworld source for Veronica Guerin as well as being a Garda informant.

Gilligan's new enterprise also involved some younger hoodlums who had originally encouraged him to get involved in the hash trade, Brian 'The Tosser' Meehan, Paul 'Hippo' Ward and Peter 'Fatso' Mitchell. Meehan and Ward had shared a prison wing with Gilligan in the early 1990s in Portlaoise. They had talked about the huge profits that were there for the taking, in the burgeoning drug trade.

Two months before Gilligan's release, Traynor and Cahill had begun to plot the kidnapping of the family of Jim Lacey the Chief Executive of the National Irish Bank (NIB). The gang's plan was to force Lacey to allow them to load a van full of cash at the NIB's cash holding centre. A gang member, Joseph 'Jo Jo' Kavanagh was supposed to convince Lacey that his family had also been kidnapped and he was being forced to collect the cash for the 'kidnappers'. Traynor told Gilligan that the job would set them up in the drug trade.

The plan went into action in November 1993 but Factory John did not play a prominent role in the stroke. Brian Meehan was recruited instead, to give a helping hand. In the end they got away with just IR£250,000 (€317,500), not the intended IR£7 million (€8.9 million) in cash, when Lacey outsmarted them at the last minute.

The original plan was that Gilligan and Traynor would get a cut of the action from Cahill and use it as seed capital for their new venture. But their share of IR£250,000 (€317,500) wasn't enough money and Cahill's family would later claim that the pair borrowed money from the General to make up the shortfall. Garda intelligence sources have since revealed, however, that the rest of the investment cash was provided from two armed robberies. Gilligan and his new mob carried out two heists in December 1993 and January 1994 when they robbed a security van in Tallaght and a Dunnes Stores supermarket in Kilnamanagh, Dublin. Soon their new investment was paying off and the ruthless gangsters became rich beyond their wildest dreams. And Gilligan was determined that no one would take it away from him.

Even if, as many believed, Gilligan and Traynor had borrowed capital from the General then the issue of repaying him disappeared in August 1994 when an IRA hit man shot Martin Cahill dead. The Provos later claimed that Cahill was murdered because he had provided assistance to a UVF murder gang who had attempted to blow up a Sinn Féin function in a central Dublin pub, a few months earlier. During the attack the UVF had shot an IRA member dead and planted a large bomb that failed to explode. Afterwards the Republicans pulled out all the stops to discover who had provided the Loyalist terrorists with logistical support. Cahill was an obvious suspect because he had crossed swords with the Provos in the past. He had also sold some of the Beit paintings to the UVF. In any event Gilligan and John Traynor were quite happy to oblige the IRA and passed on information confirming that the General had helped the UVF to set up the attack. As a result their debt, if it existed, would have conveniently disappeared.

By the time the General was in his grave the Gilligan gang were on the way to the big time. A week after the murder Gardaí stopped Meehan and Mitchell as they drove through north Dublin. When the officers searched the car they found IR£46,000 (€58,500) in cash which the two hoods had collected earlier for Gilligan. Brian Meehan told the cops the cash belonged to him. Later he changed his story and claimed the money belonged to a friend who he refused to name. The police held onto the money on the grounds that it was suspicious and gave Meehan a receipt. Unless the cops could actually prove that the cash had been stolen or was part of the "instrumentality of a drug trafficking offence" there was nothing they could do with it.

John Gilligan later told the Gardaí the cash belonged to him and that Meehan was a "good friend who has been minding it for me". He said he could prove ownership of the cash. Gilligan produced photocopied cheques he claimed were his winnings from betting on horses, over the previous few weeks. He also produced documents stating that he was a horse breeder. Nevertheless the Gardaí knew who they were dealing with and decided to hang onto the money. But Gilligan wasn't giving up. He promptly applied to the courts, under a Police Property Application for the return of the money. Under the Police Property Act a court could only determine the ownership of the property or cash which had been seized by the Gardaí. The person from whom the money was taken was not required to prove how he or she had come by it. In some cases for example, where property had been stolen and recovered by Gardaí, the person from whom it had been taken was invited to court to seek its return. It was not unusual for a criminal, who may have been cleared of a burglary in court, to have the cheek to seek the return of the stolen property by claiming ownership. It was an example of how ludicrously out of touch with the realities of crimes the existing law had become.

In December, while Gilligan's application was still being processed, customs officers at Holyhead port in Wales seized a parcel containing IR£76,000 (€96,500) in cash. They had found it in an Irish truck. The cash was drug money that Gilligan was sending to Belgium as part of a drug deal. HM Customs seized the cash on the suspicion that it was the proceeds of crime.

Later that day Gilligan rang from Dublin. He demanded the return of the money, claiming that he could prove it was the proceeds of gambling and was intended for investment purposes. He was clearly annoyed at this interference in his business.

The case concerning Gilligan's drug money was passed to Roger Wilson of the Customs National Investigation Service in Manchester. At this stage the police and customs officers were aware of Gilligan, as he had been spotted dealing with a number of UK drug traffickers. Surveillance officers had secretly filmed the Irish hood when he met with the criminals in Brighton. Gilligan was not arrested because he had not been the main target of the undercover investigation. Roger Wilson ordered that the IR£76,000 (€96,500) be confiscated under drug trafficking legislation. When Gilligan was informed of this he flew into a rage.

"He's [Wilson] backed me into a corner... it's not a problem for me to get someone to shoot him... I'm not goin' down that road, I just want me money back. But if someone messes with my family I'll have them fucking shot," Gilligan snarled down the phone at a customs official.

The threat against the officer was taken seriously and he was subsequently placed in a special protection programme. Gilligan meanwhile instructed his lawyers to fight the case at Holyhead Magistrates Court.

A week after the Holyhead incident, on December 22, the Dublin District Court ordered the Gardaí to return the IR£46,000 (€58,500) they had seized from Meehan in August. During the hearing Gilligan claimed that the money was the proceeds of his activities as a professional gambler. Counsel for the State wanted to know why he had entrusted such a large amount of money to a convicted armed robber. Gilligan replied that Meehan was a trusted friend and he had no reservations about leaving the cash in his possession. The State could not prove that the money was from criminal activity and the court ordered its return.

The following day Gilligan strutted into Fitzgibbon Street Garda station, grinning from ear to ear, and demanded his IR£46,000 (€58,500) back.

The following July 1995 Gilligan again exposed the flawed legal system when Holyhead Magistrates Court also ordered HM Customs to return his IR£76,000 (€96,500).

Gilligan and his mob grew more confident by the day. They had no fear of the law and were happy to show off their new-found wealth. Soon Garda units throughout Dublin were making reports to HQ about the gang members' extravagant lifestyles and property acquisitions. But even under the new money laundering provisions of the 1994 Criminal Justice Act there seemed little that could be done about the situation.

One occasion in 1995 summed up how untouchable gang members felt. Peter Mitchell was in Garda custody for questioning about a shooting incident in the city. When the conversation in the interview room changed to the subject of the drug trade, Mitchell began complaining about drug dealers – specifically the ones who worked for him. The problem he had was that he couldn't get them to do any work! "Youse think that drugs is an easy business well it's fuckin' not. I'm payin' fellahs IR£1,000 (€1,270) a week to sell hash and a few Es for me and do you think I can get the bastards to work? You can't get the fuckers out of the pubs or their beds, it's just not fuckin' easy," Mitchell whined to two startled cops.

Fatso then complained about an RTÉ programme, which he claimed had referred to his drug dealing activities. "They [RTÉ] claimed that I was makin' IR£50,000 (€63,500) a week from drugs well that's a fuckin' lie I don't know where they got that figure," Mitchell frowned. "I'll tell ye I don't earn anything like that ... I'd say that I'm only makin' about IR£30,000 (€38,000) a week and nothing more and that's the fuckin' truth lads."

Mitchell was not afraid to talk about his business problems. He knew that the officers sitting across the table from him could do nothing. In any event the cops simply didn't believe the big-mouthed oaf. That was a big mistake.

In another incident Brian Meehan was arrested in the early hours of the morning and brought to the Bridewell Garda Station in north inner-city Dublin for a drug search. While the violent mobster was being strip-searched at the station he began masturbating in front of an officer and asked him: 'Do you like men with big cocks? ...Maybe you fancy me arse instead." (Thus Meehan's nickname the Tosser!)

During the search the cops found over IR£600 (€761) in cash in Meehan's pockets, which they seized for forensic examination.

Meehan sneered at the officers: "Youse fuckers need it more than I do. Give it to the police benevolent fund. Youse are a bunch of fuckin' idiots workin' and payin' tax. I earn more in a week than you earn in a month."

Two years later, the gang's armourer and manager Charlie Bowden who turned State's evidence against his fellow gangsters, told a court that he had personally accumulated between IR£150,000 (€190,500) and IR£200,000 (€254,000) in just over a year. He explained where the rest of his fortune had gone: "I spent a lot of money on cocaine. I bought designer clothes and went on foreign holidays. I would go out. I would live well. I would buy stuff for the kids." He also revealed how handling the bundles of drug cash had been a problem for the gang. "This was a constant refrain throughout the whole time when we were earning this type of money, where to put it. I used to stuff it in a laundry basket. When it was full I got another one. We spoke about offshore accounts and how we would go about doing it. We were thinking about getting the money into bank accounts in the Isle of Man."

John Gilligan, as kingpin of the organisation, seemed to be spending more money than everyone else put together. From the time of his release from prison, Gilligan and his wife Geraldine set about expanding and developing what would become known as the Jessbrook Equestrian Centre. In 1987 the Gilligans had bought seven acres of land with a derelict house at Mucklon near Enfield, County Kildare. Geraldine Matilda Dunne, John's childhood sweetheart, had always loved horses. When she was a teenager she used to take Gilligan out on dates on the back of her piedball pony! Between 1994 and 1996 they went on to buy another 77 acres of land from several locals at a cost of IR£162,000 (€206,000), which they paid in cash.

In November 1994, Gilligan had paid IR£73,000 (€93,000) for a detached house at Willsbrook View in Lucan, County Dublin for his daughter Treacy. And in December 1995 he bought his son Darren a house for his twentieth birthday at Weston Green, also in Lucan, for IR£78,000 (€99,000) cash. At the same time construction began on a magnificent indoor equestrian arena in Jessbrook, with a seating capacity for around 3,000 people, making it one of the largest in Europe. They also built a large luxurious family home next door. In less than a year the Gilligans paid out almost IR£1.5 million (€1.9 million) for the work at Jessbrook. Everyone was paid with wads of cash, stuffed into shoeboxes and plastic bags.

If people didn't take bribes they were threatened and intimidated so things got done the way Gilligan wanted. Gardaí suspected that planning officials at Kildare County Council had been intimidated because Jessbrook was built in blatant contravention of the guidelines laid down in planning permission applications. When the Gardaí finally began investigating Gilligan's wealth in 1996 the planning files in Kildare County Council had vanished, without a trace, from its offices.

In 1995 Gilligan bought a racehorse called Rifawan for IR£60,000 (€76,000). He paid for the horse with cash in a shoebox. Rifawan was put in training in stables owned by renowned horse trainer Arthur Moore, at a cost, between, February 1995 and May 1996, of IR£24,000 (€30,500). The horse won a number of races and the Gilligans often found themselves in the owners' enclosure, swilling champagne with the elite of the racing world. Moore did not know the identity of the horse's real owner and returned the animal when he discovered whom he was dealing with. Rifawan was subsequently sent to an English trainer but broke his leg in the Burns Cottage novice chase at Ayr in Scotland and was put down.

Between 1995 and 1996 Gilligan also splashed out IR£78,000 (€99,000) in cash for new cars and jeeps for Jessbrook and his children. On the same day that he bought a jeep and a car for his son and daughter he also lodged IR£20,000 (€25,500) in cash to each of their bank accounts. Officially Treacy Gilligan's only income was IR£79.10 (€100.50) per week, which she received in the form of Lone Parent's Allowance to look after her baby daughter. According to the State, Gilligan's son Darren was also down on his financial luck and couldn't find a job. The young drug trafficker, who ran his own racket selling ecstasy, was receiving unemployment assistance of IR£64.50 (€81.90) per week even though he had one bank account which contained sums of up to IR£80,000 (€102,000) at any one time.

In May 1994, Treacy Gilligan was called in for an interview with Department of Social Welfare officials, to discuss her allowance. They had been tipped-off by Gardaí who had been monitoring the rise and rise of the Gilligan family fortunes.

During her meeting with the officials Treacy Gilligan was quizzed about her new car. She said it was a present from her father. The officials asked for proof of this and warned that her social welfare money would be cut off if she did not produce the evidence. When Gilligan heard this he flew into one of his life-threatening rages. He made several phone calls to the social welfare officer dealing with his daughter's case and made serious threats, stating that the civil servant was a marked man.

The investigator passed on the Treacy Gilligan file to head office without recommendation. A note in her social welfare file recorded how Gilligan, described as a "very dangerous man", had made "unspecified threats". A further memo by department officials in the file recorded their decision to "drop the subject about the car and continue paying her Lone Parent's Allowance".

The Revenue Commissioners, who were also prompted by Garda reports, wrote to Gilligan asking him to furnish a tax return. The nasty godfather took the letter, wrote the words "FUCK OFF" on the back, and returned it. Gilligan did not hear from the Revenue Commissioners or the Social Welfare again. In light of the General's attack on Brian Purcell the civil servants concerned knew that they had no way of protecting themselves against Gilligan. No one could be forced to take such risks in the line of duty. The civil servants backed off.

With such a growing reputation for wealth and

intimidation, it was only a matter of time before a journalist would hear about John Gilligan's good fortune. Veronica Guerin, a young mother and wife, was the first reporter to approach Gilligan about his sudden wealth and success. Although she had only been in the business for two years, Veronica was already a household name in Ireland as a result of her campaigning newspaper work. She had also survived an assassination attempt, suspected to have been organised by Gilligan's partner, John Traynor, at her home in North County Dublin in January 1995. In a short time she was back at work and had developed a keen interest in the business affairs of little Factory John. It was hard to ignore Gilligan because every cop in Dublin was talking about him.

In September 1995, she wrote to Gilligan inviting him to answer certain questions about his success. Unlike the taxman she got no reply.

On September 14, Veronica decided to drive out to Jessbrook and address her questions to Gilligan in person. When she arrived the gang boss launched a ferocious attack, punching her about the head and body. He repeatedly threatened to kill her, as he continued the terrifying assault. Veronica Guerin made a complaint to Gardaí and Gilligan was subsequently summoned to the District Court on a charge of assault and causing criminal damage to the journalist's clothing. Based on his previous record and the nature of the attack Gilligan was facing at least six months in prison.

Each day, week and month Gilligan was in jail meant that the gang would lose obscene amounts of cash. In six months they were likely to lose millions and a large slice of their market share, which was growing by the week. The godfather and his henchmen decided that no one was going to interrupt their thriving business. Greed ultimately sealed Veronica Guerin's fate. Gilligan ordered his gangsters to murder her.

On June 25, 1996, the assault case against Gilligan was adjourned for two weeks at Kilcock District Court, in County

Meath. That evening Gilligan flew to Holland with his teenage mistress, Carol Rooney.

The following afternoon, June 26, Veronica Guerin was shot dead as she drove back to Dublin from County Kildare. The hit man stepped off the back of a motorbike and fired five shots into the journalist at point blank range, with a powerful Magnum handgun.

The Gilligan gang had inadvertently thrown down the gauntlet and the State now had no choice but to pick it up. Criminals could no longer act as though they were untouchable and above the rules of society. The time had come for a new breed of law enforcement agents – an elite, multi-agency force that would become known as the Untouchables.

Three

Time for Action

The murder of Veronica Guerin caused an unprecedented outpouring of anger, revulsion and emotion. There had never been such a depth of public feeling about a murder in the 74 years since the founding of the State. Her assassination sent a shudder of fear through anyone whose job it was to interfere with the workings of organised crime. Politicians, judges, prosecutors and civil servants were all justified in believing that they could be next. Within 24 hours of the atrocity the Irish public began to place flowers at the gates of Leinster House (Dáil Eireann) in Kildare Street. Soon a virtual wall of floral bouquets was constructed. It symbolised the sentiment of a nation, reeling from the shock of what was the equivalent of a criminal coup.

Thousands of notes and prayers pinned to the bouquets expressed sorrow, demanded action and asked God to mind the woman who overnight had become a heroine in the eyes of the Irish people. A brave young mum who stood up to the cowardly godfathers had been wiped out in the most brutal fashion. To make matters worse, her murder had quickly followed another atrocity a few weeks earlier. In Adare, County Limerick a Sinn Féin/IRA gang had shot dead Detective Garda Jerry McCabe during a botched armed robbery. The leader of the gang, Kevin Walshe, had opened fire with an AK-47 rifle at point black range, as the unmarked Garda car stopped behind the postal truck it was escorting. Jerry McCabe's friend and partner Ben O'Sullivan was also critically injured in the appalling attack. It is still the belief of many of the dead Garda's colleagues and friends that he and his colleague were deliberately targeted for murder.

The politicians inside the railings of Leinster House did not need a tonne of flowers to make them realise that they had to act decisively. Decades of neglect and inaction had created a monster that now threatened the fabric of Irish society. Organised crime had issued a spine-chilling threat – aimed at the very heart of a nation. It would prove to be a huge miscalculation on the part of the murder gang. Society demanded vengeance.

** **

As Guerin's killers sped away from their horrific deed on June 26, another woman was soon to find herself in the public sights, Justice Minister Nora Owen. In the days and weeks after the murder Nora Owen suffered a ferocious onslaught from the media, including from this writer, and from the political opposition. But the deputy leader of Fine Gael did not deserve the mauling. After all she had not pulled the trigger or set up the barbaric crime. In the overwhelming atmosphere of grief and anger the Justice Minister became a scapegoat. The experience was all the more traumatic for Owen, as she had been a friend of the murdered journalist.

During one of the bitter Dáil debates which followed the murder the Taoiseach, John Bruton, the leader of the Fine Gael party, adequately summed up Nora Owen's job: "The office of Minister for Justice is the most difficult and emotionally harrowing job a Minister can hold. Deputy Owen has held that office under sustained and hurtful attack with courage, serenity and continued, fixed purpose, as befits the holder of such an office."

Nora Owen had never held ministerial office before her party went into power with the Labour and Democratic Left "Rainbow Coalition" in December 1994. The new government had formed, without a general election, after the Labour party, under the leadership of Dick Spring, pulled the plug on its coalition partner Fianna Fáil. (The Government partners fell out in a row over the extradition of notorious paedophile priest

Fr Brendan Smith. The Taoiseach Albert Reynolds resigned as leader of the party to be replaced by Bertie Ahern.) The position of Justice Minister is one of the toughest jobs within Government. Justice Ministers tend to find themselves responding to various crises like glorified fire-fighters.

Owen's appointment coincided with a dramatic upsurge in organised crime activity. Her first year in the job as Minister for Justice was a baptism of fire, punctuated by a succession of crises in the criminal justice system. Within weeks of taking the post a well-organised armed robbery gang had stolen IR£2.8 million (€3.5 million) from the Brinks Allied cash-holding depot in Clonshaugh, North County Dublin. The gang was led by an illusive gangland mastermind called Gerry Hutch, aka the Monk. *(See Chapter 6)* At the time Owen told reporters: "The way the Opposition has been going on for the past week or more you would think that I had actually robbed the IR£3 million (€3.8 million)."

Within days of the heist the cops and the Government had been embarrassed when *The Irish Independent* had revealed that Garda units throughout Dublin had been warned that the Monk and his crew were planning a major armed robbery. There was further embarrassment when Liz Allen, the journalist who wrote the story, and Independent Newspapers were subsequently charged under the Official Secrets Act. Both Allen and her employers were later convicted and fined over the story. It was quite scandalous that this was the only conviction that resulted from one of the largest heists in Ireland's history.

The following Sunday, Veronica Guerin had then reported that the Monk had earlier availed of a tax amnesty for his stolen cash. The day after the story was published Veronica had answered a knock at the front door of her home which, coincidentally, was a short distance from the Brinks Allied premises. A lone gunman had shot her at point blank range. Veronica suffered a leg injury in the attack and was lucky to be alive. The would-be assassin's gun had misfired and he fled the scene. Nora Owen and Veronica Guerin had been friends for a number of years and on the night of the shooting Owen had avoided the waiting media and slipped in a side door of the hospital to visit the journalist.

A few weeks later there had been further trouble for Owen. This time senior Gardaí had failed to act on intelligence that a group of professional hooligans were plotting a riot at an international soccer match between the Republic of Ireland and England in Lansdowne Road. The match had to be abandoned when the troublemakers sparked a full-scale riot, causing dozens of injuries. Gardaí were forced to baton charge the miscreants.

In the wake of the Brinks Allied fiasco and the soccer disaster there was more friction between the Justice Minister and Garda Headquarters. Owen had issued an unprecedented instruction to Commissioner Paddy Culligan that she was to receive regular briefings on major Garda operations, no matter how sensitive the information. Relations between the Garda Commissioner and the Department of Justice were already strained when Owen took possession of the poisoned chalice. Culligan had had a less than harmonious relationship with Fianna Fáil Justice Minister, Maire Geoghegan Quinn. In this instance Paddy Culligan stubbornly asserted the independence of An Garda Síochana from Government.

The situation had deteriorated further during 1995 when Culligan refused a request from Owen to attend a Dáil Committee. Culligan, who at the time was busy re-organising the structure of the Gardaí, refused to attend on the grounds that it was a waste of time. The Commissioner felt that Government ministers had had far too much control of the Gardaí in the past and he was anxious to maintain its independence from Government. Justice Minister Ray Burke had been a case in point. He had quietly ensured that certain investigations into allegations about his own involvement in corruption were dropped. *(See Chapter 9.)*

Owen had also inherited a bitter internal feud between the Garda Representative Association (GRA) and a breakaway group called the Garda Federation. Added to this there were tensions in Cabinet between the Minister and her "Rainbow" Government partners, Labour and Democratic Left. Both parties had philosophical problems with the tougher legislation Owen had mooted. Among the changes was a proposal to extend the period of detention for suspected drug traffickers from a maximum of twelve hours to seven days. Fine Gael's partners had also objected to proposals to tighten up the bail laws.

Then in early summer 1995, having been described in one newspaper as the "unluckiest minister in Government", Nora Owen had reportedly threatened to resign when the Labour Finance Minister, Ruairi Quinn, pulled the plug on her department's spending programme. Included in the budgetary cuts had been the construction of a new IR£20 million (€25.5 million) prison at Castlerea in County Roscommon and increased Garda recruitment. After a stand-off, however, Owen had won her Cabinet battle and the projects eventually went ahead.

In November there had been more controversy when a major undercover Garda operation was launched in conjunction with several law enforcement agencies in North America and Europe. The investigation was intended to bust a huge international drug smuggling conspiracy, involving the Penguin, George Mitchell and a Canadian drug gang. In an elaborate sting operation, off the south coast of Ireland, undercover cops, posing as a drug gang, had unloaded over 13.5 tonnes of hashish from a ship, en route from Africa to North America. The shipment had then been brought ashore on a trawler. It was loaded onto a truck, owned by the Penguin's associates, and an undercover detective drove it to Urlingford, County Kilkenny. It was left there, waiting for the real drug traffickers to pick it up. But when it became apparent that the gang had rumbled the plot the Gardaí had had no choice but to officially "seize" the 13.5 tonnes themselves.

At the same time gangland murders were also increasing. In less than 24 hours in December, on what became known as

Bloody Friday, three people were shot dead in two separate gangland attacks in Dublin.

From when she first took office in December 1994, Nora Owen was clearly a Minister under siege but the controversies of the previous 18 months faded into the background in the aftermath of Veronica Guerin's murder.

* * * *

The Minister was in New York attending a United Nations conference on international drug trafficking on June 26, 1996. She had attended a breakfast meeting with Madeline Albright and had returned to her hotel when her private secretary, John O'Dwyer, said he had something urgent to discuss with her. Upstairs in her suite O'Dwyer broke the news.

She recalled: "He told me that Veronica had been shot and was dead. He was certain that the news was accurate. It hit me terribly hard on a personal level. I cried. I rang Graham, Veronica's husband, and we cried together on the phone. I had my secretary arrange for me to fly back to Dublin immediately. Later that morning I addressed the UN meeting and at the end I announced that a few hours earlier one of our best crime journalists had been murdered, possibly by a drug gang. There was a gasp in the conference hall."

In the days that followed the atrocity Nora Owen took the brunt of the public anger and outrage. Owen never forgot the day of Veronica's funeral:

"There were people at the funeral who were so openly hostile and cold towards me. One man actually snarled at me. It was really dreadful. I remember one of Veronica's aunts coming over to me and saying: 'We know that this was not your fault.' To be honest I don't think I would have gotten through that terrible crisis if it hadn't been for Veronica's mother, Bernie, and her husband Graham."

As the news of the murder broke that sun-kissed afternoon it sent a shudder through the Dáil. The sense of shock was palpable as politicians and their staff tried to comprehend the enormity of what had just happened on the Naas road.

A few hours later the Taoiseach, John Bruton, got to his feet and officially informed the hushed Dáil chamber of the terrible news: "Someone somewhere decided to take her life and almost certainly did so to prevent information coming into the public arena. Veronica Guerin was a particularly gifted and professional investigative journalist who has written about the unacceptable face of life. She did so with care and with compassion. In doing so, she made an important contribution to the public life of this country. Without the work she did much of the recent public debate on crime would not have been as informed."

His deputy, the Tanaiste Dick Spring summed up the feelings of the Dáil: "That she should be shot down in this fashion is an attack on all of us and on the values that democracy and democratic politics are based on. It is an outrageous attack on the freedom of the press and the invaluable work that journalists do."

Mary Harney the leader of the Progressive Democrats also made a poignant tribute to the murdered journalist: "The greatest liberty we have is the liberty of free expression and the greatest guarantee we have of that liberty is a free press. Veronica Guerin died because she fearlessly pursued the truth. She was no ordinary journalist. She was a woman apart. Today the criminal underworld decided that in order that they could continue with their activities, she had to be murdered."

The following morning the *Irish Independent* summed up the problem now facing the law-makers with the headline: "We know who killed her – and he's untouchable".

When the tributes were finished, and the politicians had recovered from the shock, they knew that this time they would have to go a whole lot further than mere condemnation.

Outside the Dáil the public were looking for political leadership. Ruairi Quinn was the first Labour Finance Minister in Ireland. A very experienced and capable politician Quinn would soon find himself in the thick of the fight against organised crime. On the day of the murder Quinn was attending the funeral of Adreas Papandreou, a former Greek Prime Minister and the founder of PASOK, Labour's sister party in Greece. The next morning he was in his office when he received a call from John Bruton, who was on his way to address the Dáil. The Taoiseach had also been in discussions with Nora Owen who was returning from New York.

Bruton wanted to know if Quinn had any suggestions on how he should respond to the crisis in the Dáil later in the morning. Quinn told him about an inter-departmental group that had been established with a view to setting up a body to pursue the proceeds of crime.

* * * *

The problems of inter-agency rivalry between the Gardaí and Customs had dogged drug trafficking investigations for years. There was an ongoing, low intensity, turf war raging between the two organisations. It was ludicrous and often descended into farce. This writer recalls one story about a Garda Drug Squad investigation in the early 1990s when detectives went to Dublin airport to monitor a suspected drug trafficker, who was due to get off a flight from Europe. The undercover cops wanted to follow the target to his intended destination and bust him along with the drug trafficker for whom he was working. They informed Customs of their plan and then went into an office where they could watch for their man through a one-way mirror in the arrivals hall. But when the suspect got off the plane the Customs men moved in and searched him. They found several kilos of drugs in his luggage and made an arrest. The Customs agents then walked out past the astonished, and extremely angry, Drug Squad officers. The incident almost escalated into a punch-up, as the two agencies literally squabbled over the bust. In any event the Garda operation was ruined.

On another occasion there was a major investigation after a detective turned up in Dublin airport to meet an underworld

informant, the notorious drug trafficker Declan 'Decie' Griffin.
Customs were also watching out for Griffin and caught him
with a large haul of heroin, as he walked through the arrivals
hall. It was claimed that the Garda left the airport in a hurry
when he saw what was going on. The incident was the source
of a bitter war of words and false allegations between the two
agencies for years. In the meantime Griffin walked away a
free man. (Griffin was subsequently shot dead in a Dublin
pub by an assassin he had hired to kill someone else.) Then,
in the most recent incident, when the Urlingford sting
operation had ended in a staged "seizure", Gardaí had blamed
Customs for leaking details of the operation to the media.

There had been several attempts by Government and
Department of Justice officials to broker peace between the
two organisations. Justice Minister, Maire Geoghegan Quinn,
had sat down with the warring parties, but despite finalising
various undertakings and a memorandum of understanding
to work together, the rivalry had continued.

Nora Owen had also been doing her bit to break down
the professional barriers between the two agencies and to force
them to work together: "There had been some nasty spates
and unnecessary bickering between Customs and the Gardaí
and I was angry about it and I spoke to the Commissioner
about it. The lack of co-operation between the Customs,
Gardaí, Social Welfare and Revenue was a huge hindrance to
progress and it tended to cancel out the good work individual
agencies were doing on their own."

In June 1995, Owen had attended a meeting with several
senior Garda officers, including Commissioner Culligan and
Deputy Commissioner Pat Byrne. "The purpose of the meeting
was to tell them that I didn't want to hear that they were being
hampered by a lack of legislation when something goes wrong.
I told them I wanted to know what were the long-term
annoyances in the system and I would do my best to have
them solved because I intended doing housekeeping legislation
every year while I was in office," the former Minister recalled.

The officers present were frank in their replies. The

Revenue Commissioners, who also controlled Customs, needed to be brought into the investigation of criminals and their wealth. Without them on board nothing could be done about the criminals' loot.

Owen had agreed. She wanted the Revenue people to take a proactive stance against the criminals by auditing them for undeclared and inexplicable wealth and to take advantage of the progress that had been made in Europe.

The issue of how to deal with the proceeds of crime and money laundering had been at the centre of the law enforcement debate in the European Union for several years. The forty recommendations, produced by the Financial Action Task Force (FATF) on money laundering in 1990, had set the ball rolling but the 1994 Irish Criminal Justice Act did not go far enough. It only catered for the seizure of assets and cash from a criminal if they were convicted. Many well-known drug traffickers had walked from the criminal courts on mere legal technicalities, and taken their money with them. Legislation was clearly needed to make it possible to seize money from the mobs, even when they were not convicted. Another problem was that although the 1994 Act meant that the financial institutions now had a legal obligation to report all suspicious transactions, it took most of 1995 before they had staff suitably trained, and the procedures in place, to comply with the new legislation.

In July 1995, Nora Owen and Ruairi Quinn had organised a meeting in the Sycamore Room in Government Buildings to discuss the drug trafficking problem and to encourage greater co-operation; ministers, members of the Garda Síochana and officials from the various departments had attended. Deputy Commissioner Pat Byrne gave what Quinn later described in his memoirs as a "virtuoso performance" on what should and could be done within the existing structures. Byrne had been given the job of co-ordinating the different state agencies, especially Customs, Revenue and Social Welfare.

As a result of the two meetings in the summer of 1995 a

working group had been set up between the Gardaí and the Revenue Commissioners. Their brief was to devise a structure by which revenue powers and sanctions could be applied to tackle proceeds of crime investigation. Commissioner Paddy Culligan had nominated Pat Byrne and two of his officers, Detective Chief Superintendent Kevin Carty and Detective Superintendent Fachtna Murphy, to take part in the discussions between September and November. Their task was to produce a position paper on what would be required.

Detective Chief Superintendent Kevin Carty and Detective Superintendent Fachtna Murphy had several meetings with Sean Moriarty, an Assistant Secretary, and Paddy Donnelly, a Principal Officer, with the Revenue Commissioners. The group had agreed that every avenue of sanction was necessary in order to hit back at organised crime. The most effective way for the two agencies to work together was through the exchange of information.

Carty and Murphy were experts in their respective fields of law enforcement. Carty had been head of what was then classified as the Central Detective Unit (CDU), having come from the Garda Special Branch. He was considered a hardworking and innovative investigator who believed in using every tool at his disposal to catch the bad guys. Carty had been given the responsibility of setting up a new Garda National Drug Unit (GNDU) and the Urlingford "seizure" had been his operation. He also had extensive knowledge of developments in the international drug trafficking scene. Fachtna Murphy was the most experienced white collar and economic crime investigator in An Garda Síochana, having worked in the Fraud Squad for much of his career. Murphy was the Garda representative on the OECD and on the Government steering committee, set up to agree the guidelines for the implementation of the EU directive on money laundering.

During discussions, Revenue had made it clear that they required legislative change in order to be in a position to exchange information with the Gardaí. They were barred by

statute from officially disclosing anyone's personal tax records
to a third party. And if the Gardaí were to obtain tax records
unofficially, they could not use that information in any
subsequent proceedings because it had been obtained illegally.

The talks continued and by January 1996 the group had
been ready to present their agreed position paper to Owen
and Quinn.

This paper had resulted in the establishment of an inter-
departmental working group on June 5, involving senior
officials from the Departments of Justice, Social Welfare,
Finance and the Gardaí. The purpose of the group was to
remove legal obstacles to co-operation between the agencies
by identifying necessary legislative changes. The group would
then report back to Ruairi Quinn, who as Finance Minister
would be responsible for the drafting of any new legislation
concerning the Revenue or Customs. However there was no
clear timetable and the prospect of establishing a multi-agency
body at the end of the process was vague. There was a risk
that institutionalised professional barriers, and proprietary
interests, would render the group a glorified bureaucratic
talking shop. Change is anathema to the conservative culture
of many public servants and as a result the machinery of State
grinds tortuously slow. Despite the best wishes of government
ministers, recommendations from the working group were
likely to have taken several months to emerge. Then it could
have taken years before those recommendations became law.
Many of the people interviewed for this book, Gardaí,
politicians and civil servants, concede that, in truth, little would
have been achieved were it not for the events on the Naas
road exactly three weeks later. With a conflict of such vested
interests still reigning supreme, there would never have been
an effective Criminal Assets Bureau.

The Guerin murder crisis brought urgency to the situation.
The establishment of a multi-agency body, and the legislation
giving it adequate powers, was now 'a must' on the political
agenda. In such an atmosphere there was suddenly no room
for professional rivalries. The wealth of experience and

knowledge between the dozen or so senior civil servants and Gardaí had to be shared. They needed to come up with a solution, and fast. Staff from the Attorney General's office and parliamentary draftsmen would also be on hand to work with the group. The inaugural meeting was hurriedly scheduled to take place two days after the murder, on the morning of Friday, June 28, in the Department of Justice on St Stephen's Green.

Nora Owen suggested to Ruairi Quinn that they should both attend the first meeting as the two ministers with responsibility for the proposed anti-crime legislation. They were aware of the sluggish pace of the bureaucratic world and needed to impress on everyone involved the absolute priority the Government had attached to the project. If the ministers didn't create the right impetus the initiative could be lost in red tape.

At the meeting Owen and Quinn sat either side of the Chairperson Frank Dunne, a hard-working Assistant Secretary in the Department of Justice. The ministers addressed the assembled group and wished them well in their deliberations. Time, they emphasised, was of the essence. They needed the groups' findings and proposed legislation by mid-July. When the two ministers had said their piece Frank Dunne thanked them for their attendance. When interviewed for this book, and as mentioned in his memoirs *Straight Left: A Journey in Politics,* Ruairi Quinn had a clear recollection of what happened next: "Frank Dunne thanked us and continued to say that if the working party came to the conclusion that a new body such as that proposed was required, then they would proceed to develop the concept. Before he had finished, however, I erupted. 'Excuse me. You will fucking come to that conclusion. The decision has already been made, If you don't fucking understand that, then we'll get someone else who does. Is that clear?'"

Ruairi Quinn was shocked by his own outburst. It clearly indicated the sense of urgency in the matter. He and Nora Owen then left the meeting.

Said Quinn: "I was surprised at how I reacted that day because that is just not my style. But I was passionate about this problem. I knew that this legislation had to go ahead and I was determined that it would happen and I wanted to make that clear to everyone. Small time drug dealers were strutting around working-class neighbourhoods showing off their money and this got up the noses of decent people trying to give their children a better life. Most normal people are embarrassed and shamed by being sent to jail. But sending criminals to prison was like sending them to Trinity College. We needed to impoverish them because they are greedy bastards and taking their money was the only way to hurt them. We needed to take their money and assets over to our side of the table. But it was clear that we could no longer rely on the Customs and Gardaí to work closer by simple agreement so it was vital to make co-operation a statutory obligation."

* * * *

The day after the murder John O'Donoghue, the Justice spokesman of the Fianna Fáil party, had produced a Private Members Bill. He had first published it in February 1995 but had done nothing with it since. The Organised Crime (Restraint and Disposal of Illicit Assets) Bill had been drafted with the help of Eamon Leahy, a brilliant criminal lawyer who would later work as one of the State's two lead counsels in the criminal trials of the Gilligan gang members. The proposed legislation would reduce the standards of proof required to seize a criminal's assets. An individual claiming ownership of assets would have to prove that they had been legitimately acquired. There was also provision for making interlocutory/ restraining orders to freeze properties and bank accounts. O'Donoghue had not pushed the Bill any further at the time as he was waiting for a general election before producing it again – in the hope of winning votes. Now he could use this Bill as a powerful public relations tool.

On July 2, Nora Owen announced to the media the

intention to introduce a wide-ranging package of laws and measures to tackle organised crime. The measures included extra Gardaí, a new prison building programme and the appointment of extra judges and administrative staff for the courts and her department. There was to be six pieces of legislation designed to aid the tracing and sequestration of criminal assets. For the first time, the public heard of the Government's commitment to establish a "special unit" which would combine the services of the Gardaí and the Revenue Commissioners.

The next day in the Dáil, Owen announced that the Government would accept John O'Donoghue's Private Members Bill in principle. In the midst of an unprecedented crisis it was a pragmatic decision. Owen's department, however, needed time to further examine the legislation because of fears that sections were unconstitutional and erroneous in law. She later recalled: "We in the Government knew that we really needed to have legislation up and running within a month or so. The Private Members Bill did give us a framework from which to work and we would need the full support of everyone in the Dáil or else we could not move forward."

The large legislative package had to be ready in time for July 25, when the Dáil was to be recalled for a special debate on organised crime. The weeks that followed would be the most productive in the history of the Irish House of Parliament. The result was what became known as the "anti-crime package". *The Irish Bar Review* described it as "the most wide ranging proposals for change in Irish criminal law and procedure since the foundation of the State".

On July 9, the charges against John Gilligan, arising from his assault on the murdered journalist, were struck out in Kilcock District Court in County Kildare. The grounds were that the complainant could not proceed with the case – she was dead.

On the same day Nora Owen announced the appointment of Deputy Commissioner Pat Byrne to the rank of

Commissioner to replace Paddy Culligan who had retired. Assistant Commissioner Noel Conroy was promoted to the rank of Deputy Commissioner in charge of operations. Both men were vastly experienced officers. Conroy had spent most of his career as a serious crime investigator and Byrne, who had trained with the FBI and Scotland Yard, had been mostly involved in anti-terrorist operations and national security. A few months earlier, Byrne had greatly impressed the Cabinet and Nora Owen when he addressed them on the subject of drug trafficking and organised crime in preparation for Ireland's presidency of the European Union.

As the inter-departmental working party continued their deliberations, it appeared that the Revenue Commissioners in particular wanted to retain control of the proposed agency. But Pat Byrne was concerned that if the agency was left in the hands of the civil servants, it would not work. It wasn't that the Revenue people hadn't the ability or willingness to do the job, it was that the crime lords would prevent them from functioning. In a number of private meetings the new Commissioner advised Nora Owen, John Bruton and Ruairi Quinn, that Gardaí should run the new agency. The police had a huge database of criminal intelligence going back decades and a wide range of resources to choose from. They had several specialised investigation units, including Special Branch, the National Drug Unit, the Bureau of Fraud Investigation, the Money Laundering Investigation Unit (MLIU) and the newly established National Bureau of Criminal Investigation (NBCI). The Gardaí also had surveillance teams, technical teams and armed back-up squads in case situations got dangerous. The organisation had stations and personnel in every city, town and village in the country to call on, if required. And they were the only body in the State with powers under the criminal law. In any event if a civil servant was attacked or threatened it would be the job of the Gardaí to investigate that crime and to provide protection. The Taoiseach and the Ministers agreed and the decision was conveyed to the working group.

Byrne explained his reasoning: "Our experience always showed that criminals were more ruthless with those who were not members of An Garda Síochana because they had no fear of civil servants. They knew that we were not afraid of them. When a man or woman joins the Gardaí they know that they may have to risk their own lives in the course of their duty. They are trained for it and have the back up of 12,000 colleagues. I said that it would be wrong to expect civil servants to take on these dangerous individuals. That had already been illustrated when the General shot a social welfare inspector in 1989. John Gilligan had also openly threatened other public servants and there were many other cases of intimidation that we had been aware of for years but were powerless to do anything about. I advised the Taoiseach and the Ministers that if they didn't put the agency in the control of the police then a year down the road they would come back and admit they had made a mistake."

In the meantime the inter-departmental working group had come back with its recommendations and suggested legislative changes. They had completed their findings in record time, after only two weeks of intense work. They proposed two pieces of legislation: the Disclosure of Certain Information for Taxation and other Purposes Bill which would allow for the exchange of information between the various agencies. The second Bill would establish a multi-agency body with the powers to pursue the proceeds of crime. Both pieces of legislation would be the responsibility of the Department of Finance.

The Criminal Assets Bureau was about to go into business.

****

In July 1996, the working group recommended that the new unit be set up with immediate effect on a non-statutory basis. It would be an operational body of thirty staff with specialists from the four agencies. The Disclosure of Certain Information for Taxation and Other Purposes Bill, and the second Bill which would later become the Criminal Assets Bureau Bill, would provide the necessary powers to enable the officers from Revenue, the Gardaí and Social Welfare to become operational. (A Bill is proposed legislation that is presented to parliament for approval before being passed into law. It then becomes an Act of parliament.) The plan was that while the Bill was still being drafted at Dáil Committee stage the unit would become operational using existing legislation and Garda powers. During the interim period, the officers in charge of the new unit would have an opportunity to identify any deficiencies or requirements in the proposed legislation. They could then refer these back to the Government for inclusion in the finished Act.

A Chief Bureau Officer (CBO), who would be a Garda of the rank of Chief Superintendent and who in turn would report to the Garda Commissioner, would need to be recruited immediately. The CBO's responsibilities would include the organisation of personnel, resources, strategy and direction of operations.

The inter-departmental agency's recommendations also provided for the appointment of a Bureau Legal Officer (BLO) who would answer to the CBO. The legal officer would have responsibility for providing legal expertise to the unit and participate fully in its work. He would have a "proactive and central role" and have input in the formulation of strategy.

Barry Galvin was well-known to the Government of the day. Through his friendship with former minister, Hugh Coveney from Cork, he had been invited to a number of meetings with Nora Owen and had discussed various proposals for reform in the criminal justice system. When it came to finding a suitable candidate for the job of Ireland's own Elliot Ness style Chief Legal Officer, there was no competition. "When it came to the multi-agency approach we knew we needed a legal adviser who cared passionately about what he was doing," Owen said. Galvin had also been recommended to Ruairi Quinn as a likely candidate for the job. Quinn's wife Liz had, like so many others, remembered Galvin's powerful

performance on the *Late Late Show* four years earlier. The
outspoken State Solicitor for Cork was about to make his mark
on history.

Ruairi Quinn was attending a meeting in the European
Parliament in Strasbourg on July 17 when he asked his
Programme Manager, Ciaran O'Mara, to make contact with
Galvin. O'Mara had also been impressed by the legal eagle's
TV appearance and agreed that he was the ideal candidate for
the job. The Programme Manager dialled Galvin's office
number in Cork and passed the mobile phone to Quinn, as
they stood in a corridor in the parliament building.

Quinn came straight to the point. He told Galvin the
Government wanted to set up a specialist agency along the
lines of what he had originally suggested back in 1992. Galvin
was all ears and said he welcomed the move. Then Quinn
asked the lawyer one question: "Would you be interested in
running the legal side of the new organisation?"

Galvin expressed an interest and agreed to meet Quinn
the following day. He caught the early commuter flight from
Cork to Dublin and attended a meeting in the Department of
Finance with Hugh Coveney, Ruairi Quinn and Ciaran
O'Mara. Also present was the Attorney General, Dermot
Gleeson, and a group of senior civil servants from the various
departments, including Finance and Justice. They had retrieved
a number of documents Galvin had drafted in which he had
outlined his concept of a multi-agency approach and the
legislative changes required to make this a reality. Galvin was
presented with a draft of what would become the Criminal
Assets Bureau Bill, giving statutory powers to the new
specialised unit in a file stamped "strictly secret". He was
asked for his suggestions and help in drafting it.

Galvin's first problem was the proposed title for the new
organisation. The unit was to be called the Agency for Tracing
and Targeting the Assets of Crime or ATTAC for short. Galvin
suggested that such an abbreviation might prove to be
unfortunate in the long run and it was eventually changed to
the Criminal Assets Agency or CAA.

But later when Pat Byrne was informed of the proposed name for the unit he also had a difficulty. He argued that calling the new organisation the Criminal Assets Agency would result in his officers being referred to as "agents" and that would conjure up images of the FBI. The Commissioner did not want the criminal community to perceive that this was an agency outside the realm of the Gardaí. "There had to be no doubt in the criminal's mind that he was dealing with the police because ultimately he would know the rules of the game," Byrne revealed a decade later. The Criminal Assets Bureau or CAB was proposed instead and no one had a problem with the name change.

As the first meeting continued, Quinn then asked Galvin what he thought of the legislation. The straight-talking solicitor candidly remarked that it was "utterly useless…pure window dressing, which will not work." Galvin agreed to take the sensitive document back to Cork and work on it. He spent over eighteen hours redrafting the Bill and inserted fifty new points.

Over the following weeks there were several high-powered meetings between Galvin, senior civil servants from all the departments involved, the Attorney General's office and the Gardaí, as the legislation for the new Bureau was teased out. In the meantime Barry Galvin accepted the job as the Bureau Legal Officer of the new Criminal Assets Bureau.

Meanwhile there were other legislative changes that had to be in place so that the CAB could get going as soon as possible. On Tuesday July 23, the Dáil Select Committee on Legislation and Security met to discuss and make amendments to John O'Donoghue's Organised Crime (Restraint and Disposal of Illicit Assets) Bill, before sending it back to the Dáil for approval two days later. Several changes were made to O'Donoghue's Bill, including the name. It became known as the Proceeds of Crime Bill.

The Bill would enable CAB to apply to the High Court for orders freezing assets believed to be the proceeds of crime and to also appoint a Receiver to dispose of the property. Cash and property would remain frozen for a period of seven years before it could be transferred to the State's coffers in the Department of Finance. Under the Criminal Assets Bureau Act the CAB is the only body with the powers to prosecute the provisions contained in the Proceeds of Crime Act.

The Junior Justice Minister, Pat Rabbitte, said he was concerned that there was a danger in limiting the Proceeds of Crime Bill to particular crimes. This approach left it wide open for somebody to legitimately argue that his or her assets represented the proceeds of a crime not listed in the Bill. He felt that the new definition of proceeds of crime would bring all offences within the scope of the Bill, regardless of whether they were committed alone or with another person. He added: "They constitute drafting changes, a tidying-up exercise aimed at making the definitions as comprehensive and foolproof as possible and are in keeping with the intent of the Bill."

At every opportunity O'Donoghue had made a party political speech about how Fianna Fáil had given birth to the legislative equivalent of a panacea for all ills. When John O'Donoghue addressed the Committee he commented: "The amendments proposed by the Minster are acceptable to our party because all the amendments put forward by the Government are in keeping with the broad spirit, intent and principle of our legislation. This Fianna Fáil legislation removes that final obstacle. It brings the criminal underworld into the spotlight of the High Court and makes them account for their lifestyles, assets and wealth. In introducing this legislation in the Dáil, on behalf of Fianna Fáil, I said that it represents the will of the people, that it is an example of democracy in action and of society moving against an evil within. I believe those sentiments to be as true today as they were when the Bill was first published."

The Kerry lawyer could not resist putting the boot in and scoring more political points. "It appears that the Government has decided to wax eloquently about this Fianna Fáil legislation. I always welcome and admire eloquence provided it is not used the same way as one would produce a rabbit out of a hat, with a view to obfuscating the public view and suggesting that the legislation is not Fianna Fáil legislation."

Tony Gregory, an independent TD who represented the north inner-city, one of the areas worst affected by crime and drugs, was in no doubt why the legislation was being introduced with such urgency. For years Gregory had been a lone voice, fighting in vain to force Government to take action against the godfathers who were destroying his neighbourhood. He stated: "I have a strong feeling that if Veronica Guerin had not been murdered in broad daylight on a main thoroughfare, we would not be here today debating amendments to this Bill. That is an indictment of the Legislature. For a number of years many of us said these powers were required to go after the most unscrupulous drug dealers. It had to reach the stage where a journalist was murdered in this city before the powers, which may be effective in the fight against drug dealers, were introduced."

Before the discussion ended Pat Rabbitte rebuffed John O'Donoghue's point scoring in typically acerbic style: "As somebody who has not been concerned with the Bill up to now, I compliment Deputy O'Donoghue on the instigation of this legislation and his tenacity in pursuing it. I hope the Deputies on the other side will forgive me if I do not argue about the paternity of the Bill as it now stands. The public is not concerned about demeaning the legislative process by arguing like children as to whose lollipop it is now. The people are concerned only that the Bill is effective."

Two days later the showdown continued. The Dáil chamber echoed to a barrage of heated, bitter exchanges between the Government and the Opposition. John O'Donoghue was at his abusive best. He went straight for Nora Owen's jugular: "She has, at this stage, promised so many measures that her long finger resembles Pinocchio's nose. Realising that she has become an object of political derision, she now seeks, in a political hop, skip and jump, to transform herself from a Minister who did not introduce any legislation to the Minister who introduced the most legislation on the one day."

Owen fought her corner and refused to back down. She reminded O'Donoghue and his colleagues that is was their successive neglect of the problem, while in Government, that had left Irish society with the current state of affairs.

But when the bluff and bluster died down the politicians had done a good day's work. By the end of July, four weeks after Veronica's murder, the Government had put together its anti-crime package. It centred on six Bills: the Courts Bill; the Criminal Justice (Miscellaneous Provisions) Bill; the Proceeds of Crime Bill; the Criminal Justice (Drug Trafficking) Bill, the Disclosure of Certain Information for Taxation and other Purposes Bill and the Criminal Assets Bureau Bill. The whole package was tailor-made to provide statutory mechanisms for identifying the proceeds of criminal activity and granting greater powers for the investigation of serious crime, particularly drug trafficking.

Practically all the legislation laid down was passed into law during a bruising ten-hour session. Ruairi Quinn revealed that they had taken every care to ensure that the new laws were constitutional and would stand up to challenges in the courts. He commented: "After that I felt that we should let the criminals test the law because we had done as much as we could. When there is consensus in this place [Dáil] it can actually work pretty well."

Four

Fighting Back

By the time the lights went out in the Dáil on July 25, 1996 the politicians had done their jobs. The legislation enabling the Criminal Assets Bureau to pursue the ill-gotten proceeds of crime was in place. The Bill giving the organisation its statutory powers would be enacted within months. The media gave the CAB an enthusiastic welcome with front-page coverage and the public were reassured that action was being taken. It was the first good news story since Veronica Guerin's murder four weeks earlier. After the fuss died down, however, it was time for the most difficult and challenging job in the history of Irish law enforcement to begin. The men and women of the Criminal Assets Bureau, who quickly became known as the Untouchables, were about to embark on a task that had all the hallmarks of a punishing, record-breaking mountain marathon.

The task of mobilising the CAB was going to be a mammoth undertaking. Within days, the frenetic pace of the previous month would seem like a leisurely stroll in the park. In the week before the various laws were enacted Barry Galvin was still the sole member of the Untouchables. The rest of the organisation had to be built from scratch. As one officer later recalled: "We were moving onto a green field site and we didn't have a selection of construction plans to chose from. There was no one we could consult to ask how this should be done. We were on our own."

The real drama would unfold behind closed doors away from the gaze of the media and the public.

Finding a Chief Bureau Officer (CBO) was now the top priority. As soon as the Government had agreed that the Bureau

would be under the command of a Garda Chief
Superintendent, Commissioner Pat Byrne and his Deputy, Noel
Conroy had begun assessing who was best qualified for the
job.

In January, Fachtna Murphy had been officially promoted
to the rank of uniformed Chief Superintendent and sent to
Dun Laoghaire as the officer in charge of the Eastern Division
of the Dublin Metropolitan Region (DMR). The Eastern
Division is considered to be one of the quietest in Dublin,
with a high density of upper-middle-class neighbourhoods that
are home to the elite of the Irish business and professional
communities. The region is dotted with embassies, gleaming
corporate HQs and upmarket hotels. In comparison with
Murphy's earlier career it didn't present much of a challenge.
But that was about to change.

When Conroy and Byrne drew up their list Fachtna
Murphy's name was at the top. He was their most experienced
officer in the area of economic crime. A native of Timoleague,
County Cork, Murphy joined the Gardaí in 1967 and spent
his entire career in Dublin, most of it in the Fraud Squad. He
had previously worked closely with other Irish civil servants
on the steering committee to implement EU Directives to
tackle international money laundering. He had also worked
with other European agencies, including the Financial Action
Task Force (FATF) and had his finger on the pulse of what
was happening throughout the rest of Europe. As the Dáil
debate was still raging Murphy received a phone call from
Noel Conroy. The job of Chief Bureau Officer (CBO) was on
offer. Murphy, who loved a challenge, jumped at the
opportunity. Within 48 hours he had packed his briefcase and
left his office at Eastern Division HQ. All he had to start the
new Bureau with was a mobile phone.

On the morning of Tuesday, July 30, Nora Owen and
Ruairi Quinn met with Commissioner Pat Byrne, Barry Galvin
and Fachtna Murphy for a press photo on the steps of
Government buildings. They officially announced that the
Criminal Assets Bureau would start operations the following

morning. The Ministers gave the press brief comments about their confidence in the CAB's potential. When the cameras had gone the five retired to an office for a discussion about the enormous task ahead. Both Quinn and Owen outlined their hopes for the future of the Bureau. Both impressed on Galvin and Murphy that they should use their new powers to hit the drug gangs – hard.

Galvin and Murphy were to establish the Bureau on an ad hoc basis until the Criminal Assets Bureau Bill came into law. When the Bill came into law all Gardaí, Revenue officials, from both Tax and Customs and Social Welfare Inspectors would be certified as Bureau officers with all the powers provided for in the Act. The Bureau Legal Officer (BLO) was a separate appointment by the Minister for Justice. Section four of the Bill set down the common, statutory objectives of the CAB:

A. The identification of the assets, wherever situated, of persons which derive, or are suspected to derive, directly or indirectly from criminal activity.

B. The taking of appropriate action under the law to deprive or deny those persons of the assets of the benefits of such assets, in whole or in part, as may be appropriate.

C. The pursuit of any investigation or the doing of any other preparatory work in relation to any proceedings arising from the objectives mentioned in A and B.

From then on, criminals like Gilligan would no longer be able to walk into Garda Stations and demand their money back if they were not convicted and the courts would have legislation to take proceedings against them.

In the meantime the plan was to use two of the new Acts which had just been passed, the Proceeds of Crime Act and the Disclosure of Certain Information for Taxation and Other Purposes Act, as the tools of the trade. Another valuable asset was the Money Laundering Investigation Unit (MLIU).

Coincidentally Fachtna Murphy had also been given the responsibility of organising the MLIU when it was established two years earlier, in the wake of the 1994 Criminal Justice Act. The money laundering unit's brief was to process any reports received from financial institutions about suspicious transactions. The MLIU shared all their intelligence with the CAB which helped it to get started. Throughout its existence the MLIU has been a crucial source of financial intelligence for the Bureau. The unit specialises in prosecuting cases of money laundering through the criminal law process.

Murphy and Galvin were well aware that they did not have the luxury of time. From the moment the establishment of a Criminal Assets Bureau was announced the clock was ticking. The mere idea of the CAB had caused panic in the underworld – bank accounts were being emptied at an alarming rate.

Galvin and Murphy had first met in the early 1990s when the Fraud Squad investigated the activities of *Irish Press* lawyer Ellio Mollocco. The rogue solicitor had been embezzling funds from the doomed newspaper group's legal fund. It was the first high-profile criminal prosecution of a lawyer. He was convicted and sentenced to five years in prison. Galvin had been interested in the case because of his involvement with the Law Society Compensation Fund committee. Mollocco's dodgy dealings had cost the fund over IR£2 million (€2.5 million). The two law enforcers did not meet again until two nights before the photo call at Government Buildings. Over dinner they had discussed the enormity of the job ahead.

Their first difficulty was that they were effectively homeless. Apart from their mobile phones they didn't have any equipment, or a base from which to work. At one stage they considered acquiring secure office accommodation in an anonymous, fortress-like building away from Garda HQ. But instead, Murphy decided to use four rooms he had borrowed on the top floor of Block One in the Garda HQ complex, Harcourt Square, on Harcourt Street in central Dublin. The large three-block complex is home to several specialist police units. The residents include officers from the National Bureau of Criminal Investigation (NBCI), the Special Detective Unit (SDU) (comprising anti-terrorist Special Branch and the Emergency Response Unit), the Garda Bureau of Fraud Investigation (GBFI), incorporating the Money Laundering Investigation Unit, the DMR Command and Control radio centre and the DMR HQ. Up to 1,000 cops and support staff work in Harcourt Square. Murphy decided that it was the safest place for his staff, a bit like hiding a tree in a forest. Later the homeless CAB would borrow more office space in a second block. In January 1997, the Bureau was finally allocated its own floor in Block One.

With temporary accommodation organised, Murphy's next job was the most difficult – recruiting a competent team. In order for the CAB to be successful he needed the right mix of people with the skills and the inter-personal abilities to ensure that Revenue, Customs, Social Welfare and Gardaí could work together. The Gardaí would form the single largest component of the staff but there would need to be a balance between detectives with experience in investigating organised crime and detectives with analytical skills who could follow the paper trails. One former Bureau member recalled: "Basically people with a flair for investigation and some cop-on were required. A good detective could adapt to a new form of financial investigation."

The job of selecting suitable candidates from Revenue, Customs and Social Welfare was the responsibility of two men. Dermot Quigley, Secretary of the Revenue Commissioners who control Tax and Customs, and Eddie Sullivan, Secretary of the Department of Social, Community and Family Affairs. The senior civil servants had already played a crucial role in the inter-departmental working group that laid the foundations for the Bureau's legislation. On the Garda side, Murphy consulted with Commissioner Byrne and Deputy Commissioner Conroy to select a Detective Superintendent suitable for the job. They had an ideal incumbent in mind.

Felix McKenna had spent practically all his career investigating organised crime. The tough Monaghan man had been a detective for the majority of the previous twenty-six years and had locked horns with every major gang boss in the Greater Dublin area. McKenna was an original member of the first Serious Crime Squad, better known as the Flying Squad, in the 1970s. He was the officer who succeeded in bringing Larry Dunne's reign to an end when he charged the heroin dealer with drug trafficking. Dunne got over ten years as a result. Later, as a Detective Sergeant, he was one of four team leaders in the famous T or Tango Squad, set-up to target the General and his mob in the late 1980s. After that, McKenna headed up another specialist squad to specifically target armed robbery and firearms. His team had prosecuted ten major gangland figures over an eighteen-month period. McKenna who was nicknamed "Felix the Cat" by some villains, had also targeted Gilligan and his infamous Factory Gang many times. He had the distinction of securing the godfather's last major prison sentence in 1990. The Monaghan man had an intimate knowledge of all the major players in gangland and had built up an impressive collection of underworld informants. He was a tough adversary. Like Murphy, he had been sent away from the action on promotion to Tipperary Town, as a uniformed Superintendent. He had only read about the establishment of the CAB in the newspapers. Then he got a call from an Assistant Commissioner in Garda HQ. McKenna was told to pack his bags and report to Murphy's office in Block One, within a week.

Sources who worked for Galvin, Murphy and McKenna described them as "a perfect mix of three complete opposites". Murphy was cautious and circumspect, McKenna was considered aggressive and Galvin was the maverick lawyer. "I picked Fachtna Murphy because of his tremendous experience investigating white collar crime. We knew that Murphy was careful and very cautious and he would work hard to make the Bureau a success. Felix McKenna was picked because he was a great serious crime investigator and a quintessential tough guy who would not stand back if things got hot. And Galvin was a brilliant lawyer with a good working knowledge of dealing with criminals. As a legal practitioner he was a breed apart. He was prepared to take risks and he had great courage. He actually became like a cop himself. Between the three of them it was a match made in heaven, so to speak. If it had been a different combination it is possible the Bureau might not have been so successful," Pat Byrne revealed in an interview for this book.

Over the next weeks two Detective Inspectors, four Detective Sergeants and eight Detective Gardaí were brought in to form the nucleus of the Untouchables. Detective Inspector Pat Byrne took charge of administration within the new Bureau. He had worked for several years in the fraud squad with Murphy and had been one of the main investigators in the Mollocco case. His colleague, Detective Inspector John McDermott took over the operational side of things. Like McKenna, he came from a tradition of working in serious crime investigation, including the Tango Squad. He was an expert on organised crime. Soon the Criminal Assets Bureau would be armed and ready to come out fighting.

Fachtna Murphy and Barry Galvin also found that they were alone when it came to devising the modus operandi by which the CAB would function. It was agreed that the unit would start small, with a tight-knit group of key people. From the outset the biggest internal challenge was breaking down the cultural barriers between the four agencies. Once that had been achieved, in conjunction with an efficient working system, then staff numbers could be increased.

Before the issue of breaking down cultural barriers could be addressed Murphy had to actually recruit officers from the three agencies. In the atmosphere of intense fear that had prevailed since the murder of Veronica Guerin, Revenue and Social Welfare had found it difficult to get applicants for the job. But the forthcoming CAB Act had been carefully drafted. It catered for the strict anonymity of non-Garda Bureau officers. Revenue and Social Welfare officials could simply sign tax demands in the name of the Criminal Assets Bureau. It would be forbidden by law to identify a CAB officer or to publish his or her picture. Other sections dealt with attempts to assault intimidate or obstruct Bureau officers in the course of their work and the punitive consequences that would follow. Sanctions included maximum cash fines of up to IR£100,000 (€127,000) or a term, not exceeding ten years, in prison. In the meantime, as an incentive, the Department of Finance sanctioned a special annual allowance of IR£1,600 (€2,000) for all non-Garda CAB members.

All these measures paid off. Within days five officers arrived from Customs, Tax and Social Welfare. Secretaries were hired by the Department of Justice to run the offices. All the civil servants received detailed briefings on their personal security and a high-tech security system was installed in the Bureau's offices.

The new Bureau had also experienced difficulties over security fears with the Chief State Solicitor's Office. Armed protection was placed around Barry Galvin and all Garda members of the Bureau were ordered to carry their personal firearms at all times. Some months later the crusading Elliot Ness was provided with a Garda issue Smith and Wesson revolver on the instructions of Commissioner Byrne. He was the first lawyer in Irish history to be officially armed. In Cork, Department of Justice contractors installed elaborate security systems in Galvin's home and office, including bomb-proof walls.

Once security issues had been dealt with, it should have been time to get down to business. In the first weeks, however, there was considerable friction between the new partners. In particular the long history of bitter rivalry and mistrust between cops and Customs was a problem. Here Murphy illustrated his unique abilities as a shrewd strategist. He rejected a suggestion that the people from each agency be effectively segregated, situated in separate offices or in different corners of an open-plan room. Instead he came up with a team-based system that included one sergeant, two gardaí, one tax, one customs and one social welfare officer, working out of the same office. Four teams were set up. In a team-room the officers had no choice but to interact with each other. After a short time the initiative started to work, as people began to trust each other and an atmosphere of mutual respect developed. Murphy, McKenna and Barry Galvin also held weekly meetings with each team and there were regular conferences involving all personnel, to review progress in cases, assess potential targets and share ideas.

At the same time, Murphy appointed Felix McKenna to chair an internal inter-agency committee to devise operational and administrative structures. Security and information technology experts were brought in from the US. Designated phones lines, cars and computers were sourced. An operational system was soon honed, covering every aspect of the CAB process, from selecting targets and serving tax assessments to freezing assets in the courts and disposing of them. Before a target was nominated for investigation there were two crucial questions – "Were there identifiable assets?" and "Could criminality be established?". Once an individual was deemed to be a suitable target the case was passed to a team where all the available information was pooled. Tax, social welfare and criminal records would be collated, along with Garda and Customs' intelligence reports. Then any financial institutions and professional offices involved were identified and served with production orders.

Galvin, Murphy and McKenna, however, soon discovered that they lacked one important weapon in their legislative arsenal – a search warrant. They knew that in order to successfully pursue the money they had to get access to the evidence. The CAB would simply not work if they did not have the power to search wherever they felt evidence could be found. But they knew that provision for a comprehensive search warrant would cause considerable controversy. The Gardaí had known for many years that organised crime could not operate without the involvement of respected professionals, such as solicitors and accountants. These professionals had traditionally been left alone. There was a real concern inherent in serving production orders on the solicitors who represented some of Ireland's most dangerous criminals. Lawyers would have a duty to inform their clients that the CAB was looking for their private files. In certain cases hoodlums could possibly threaten or intimidate solicitors and their staff, forcing them to destroy vital evidence. When Murphy and Galvin went to the Department of Justice with their proposal for a search warrant they met with a wall of opposition. Undeterred Galvin wrote to the law-makers several times, outlining a detailed case for the search warrant and how the Bureau would fail if it could not go after the files in the offices of solicitors and accountants. The Bureau Legal Officer was so adamant about the importance of the warrant that he even offered his resignation if it was not included in the CAB Act. Eventually, after consultation with the Government, the search warrant was included at Section 14 of the Criminal Assets Bureau Act.

During the Dáil debates a few weeks earlier, John O'Donoghue had confidently predicted that, "up to fifty of our biggest criminals will have their assets frozen within weeks". There was no doubt that the CAB were entering a target-rich environment. The dogs on the streets knew who the main targets should be. It was like shooting fish in a barrel. But Murphy decided to exercise caution. His philosophy was that the organisation would have to earn credibility in the courts. He wanted to avoid the CAB getting a reputation as a maverick group, rushing into the High Court with dozens of cases only to lose them later. Murphy wanted to go into court and win. In a case dealing with the proceeds of crime, it is done so under civil law, where the burden of proof required operates at the lower level – on the balance of probabilities – but Murphy urged his staff to aim for the higher level of proof that applies in a criminal prosecution – beyond all reasonable doubt. The Detective Chief Superintendent also had the facility to hire the best legal counsel available. In all other cases Gardaí have to make do with whatever counsel the Chief State's Solicitor hires for them.

As the weeks went by every member of the Bureau put in a huge effort, often working twelve-hour days and most weekends. Galvin, who was living in a hotel, was picked up by his bodyguards each morning around 7 am. He would not return until after 10 pm each night. A shortlist of targets was drawn up and investigations begun. At the same time CAB officers visited Garda Divisions around the country, giving seminars about what the Bureau would be doing and what cases should be referred to them for further investigation. By September, however, it was obvious to Galvin and Murphy that they needed their statutory powers as soon as possible. The sections of the Act covering the anonymity of the Revenue, Customs and Social Welfare officers needed to be in place before they could begin serving tax assessments. Murphy and Galvin met the Attorney General, Dermot Gleeson, and appraised him of the situation.

On October 15, 1996 the Criminal Assets Bureau Bill became an Act of parliament and the Criminal Assets Bureau had officially come into existence.

Following the General Election of 1997, the Rainbow Coalition Government was replaced by a coalition of Fianna Fáil and the Progressive Democrats. Nora Owen's arch nemesis, John O'Donoghue, was about to be passed the poisoned chalice. On her final day in office, June 26, 1997, the first anniversary of Veronica Guerin's murder, Fachtna Murphy invited Nora Owen to visit the offices of the Criminal Assets Bureau, to see for herself the result of all her hard work. By that time the Untouchables were kneedeep in investigations, court orders and affidavits. Together with Galvin and McKenna, the CBO introduced Owen to the staff and showed her an operations room. At one end was a large board that was being used to chart an ongoing investigation. It was a complex diagram with names, addresses, sums of money and lists of banks, with arrows connecting them. On it were four columns, with one each assigned to Garda, Revenue,

Customs and Social Welfare. It was the visible manifestation that the CAB was a fully functioning operation and everyone was working together.

The former politician recalled that day: "When I looked at that board I felt a great surge of satisfaction. There was the physical proof that the walls, which had existed for so long between the different arms of the State, were being broken down. Those walls had effectively protected the criminals for many years. Once the barriers had been smashed the results were spectacular. All the work we had done had finally paid off. I was very proud of what had been done in such a short period of time. Ten years on it [the CAB] has proved to be a very necessary and effective tool. It has stood the test of time."

Five

Public Enemy

By the time the Criminal Assets Bureau was formed on July 31, 1996, the Veronica Guerin murder investigation was over four weeks old. At that stage the largest probe into organised crime in the history of the State was already moving into top gear. Headed by Detective Chief Superintendent Tony Hickey, (Hickey was promoted to Assistant Commissioner a month later) the Lucan Investigation Team had spent their time painstakingly preparing the groundwork for an all-out assault on the underworld. In the weeks following the murder most of the criminals and terrorists in Dublin got a visit from the Lucan team, no matter where they stood in the gangland hierarchy. It was the largest search and arrest operation ever mounted by the Gardaí. The cops' approach was robust and aggressive. Over 330 individuals were arrested, 1,500 were interviewed without arrest and 3,500 statements taken. A large quantity of drugs, guns and cash were also seized.

The Guerin murder investigation turned the criminal world upside down. Villains were afraid of being associated with the crime as they saw the tide of trouble crashing towards them. In the eyes of a dying breed of so-called Ordinary Decent Criminals (ODCs) the murder was an egregious breech of unspoken protocols. The Gardaí began to receive an unprecedented level of co-operation from the underworld. Just like the law-abiding community, the criminals wanted to see Gilligan and his ruthless thugs get their comeuppance. But they were not solely motivated by a sense of outrage – the consequences of the murder were very bad for business.

With so much intense police activity going on, whole drug distribution networks were closed down overnight. Greedy gangsters, who were waiting for the dust to settle so they could go back to 'work', were getting nervous. There appeared to be no sign of a winding down in the investigation. To make matters even worse they were reading about the introduction of a powerful new agency called the Criminal Assets Bureau that could take their money and property away from them. And it was all Gilligan's fault. One gangster, who was particularly agitated by the arrival of the Untouchables, declared to an associate at the time: "Gilligan or one of those fuckers will have to be whacked for this. They've fucked everything up."

The Garda offensive was causing such a sense of panic in the underworld that, at one stage, the international drug trafficker George 'the Penguin' Mitchell, who had fled the country, suggested to Gilligan that he should plot the murder of a Garda to divert the heat. Mitchell advised his old pal that a third high-profile case would stretch the cops beyond their limits. The police were already involved in two massive enquiries, the Guerin murder and the Sinn Féin/IRA murder of their colleague Jerry McCabe in early June. According to a report from a reliable intelligence source at the time, Mitchell advised Gilligan: "Set one [Garda] up and riddle him using machine guns. There'll be so much hassle with that investigation that they'll put all their good men onto the cop murder. The Guerin thing will be forgotten in no time." His 'advice' was never acted upon but when the intelligence was passed to Garda HQ, Hickey and his team were ordered to be extra vigilant and to wear their firearms at all times. Two members of the Special Detective Unit (SDU), armed with Uzi machine guns were also deployed at night, to guard the investigation incident room. Extra SDU patrols were mobilised in and around Lucan village to watch for suspicious activity. The actual station house had to be refurbished to accommodate bomb and fireproof safes, to store evidence in the case.

Hickey summarised what the Gardaí and the CAB were up against during one of scores of court appearances connected with the case: "We know from intelligence that the people concerned [Gilligan gang] have the resources, the money and the firearms and will resort to anything to maintain this wall of silence which they believe is necessary to protect themselves."

While Tony Hickey's initial strategy in the early weeks of the investigation had been to keep an open mind in the case, everyone knew who the prime suspects were. Within 24 hours of the murder the media were writing about John Gilligan and the charges he was facing for assaulting the journalist. The fact that he had disappeared from Ireland, on the eve of the murder, and was currently lying low in Belgium and Holland was seen as a little more than suspect. The public were flabbergasted by the pictures of Jessbrook – owned by a man who hadn't worked in 'gainful employment' for twenty years. In newspaper interviews Gilligan made no secret of the fact that he was a violent, criminal low life and even bragged about moving over IR£15 million (€19 million) offshore. There was a public record of the death threats he made against the journalist and her colleagues. His denials of being involved in Guerin's murder rang hollow. It didn't require the deductive abilities of Sherlock Holmes to uncover his motive either. Within days, John Gilligan had become Ireland's Public Enemy Number One.

From the moment Fachtna Murphy took the job as Chief Bureau Officer he knew that Gilligan would be his number one target. By July 31, when the CAB officially came into existence, the Lucan Team were focusing their undivided attentions on the Gilligan mob. At the first meeting in their cramped offices in Harcourt Square, dubbed the 'Hen House' by one Bureau wag, Murphy, Galvin, McKenna and the senior officers from the four agencies met to draw up a short list of priority targets. Top of the list was the Gilligan mob. Next to them were the Monk, Gerry Hutch, and his gang of successful armed robbers. (*See Chapter 6*) Also on the list were a number of Dublin's biggest heroin dealers and a handful of international drug traffickers, who had made Ireland their bolthole from justice. (*See Chapter 7*) They were the first dirty dozen in a casebook that, over the next decade, would feature several hundred targets.

During that first conference CAB insiders recall the enthusiasm of Barry Galvin and the non-Garda element who believed that this would be an easy job. After all, these were notorious gangsters and the CAB had overwhelming powers to take them on. In many cases the assets were clearly visible – they were simply there for the taking. But Murphy, McKenna and the Garda staff sitting around the table were not so excited. They knew the hoodlums best and they were well aware that the criminals would not give up a red penny without a fight. McKenna warned those present: "They [criminals] and their lawyers will test us at every opportunity and they will make sure that they do not lose face. Gilligan especially uses every legal avenue he can to frustrate the system. It's quite possible that we will be retired by the time we get our hands on the likes of Jessbrook." The underworld was certainly not going to make life easy for the Untouchables.

Despite all the heat the Gilligan gang's drug money was still rolling in, as the godfather continued to control the business from his European safe house. At the height of the intense police activity other drug traffickers had been forced to scale down their operations, which created a dramatic drop in supply. Gilligan's arrogant mob – the people who had created the crisis in the first place – actually took full advantage of the situation to increase their market share. Figures uncovered by the Criminal Assets Bureau a few months later would show that the gang imported over 2,000 kilos of hashish in July and August alone. They had made a staggering profit of IR£2.6 million (€3.3 million) since the journalist's murder. Their only real headache with the onset of the Criminal Assets Bureau was deciding where to stash all the money.

In the days leading up to the Proceeds of Crime Act being made law on July 25, several major crime figures had begun to close down bank accounts and move bagloads of money out of the country. In the space of one week, between July 24 and July 31, Geraldine Gilligan had withdrawn over

IR£200,000 (€254,000) from four Bank of Ireland accounts she held in Lucan Village. In an ironic twist the bank was just across the road from the heavily-protected Garda station where the hunt for her husband's gang was being co-ordinated.

It was no surprise that it was decided that the first major operation of the Criminal Assets Bureau would be to assess John and Geraldine Gilligan for tax, based on their obvious wealth. Using existing Revenue legislation to raise a tax assessment was the only way that the Bureau team could follow the money trail at that stage, as it was still without its statutory powers.

The Bureau Legal Officer, Barry Galvin, and Fachtna Murphy used Section 19 of the Finance Act, as amended by Section 11 of the Disclosure of Certain Information for Taxation and Other Purposes Act, that had passed into law on July 25. Basically the legislation provided for the taxation of "miscellaneous income" or income derived from criminal activity. In order for the CAB to raise an adequate assessment they would first have to build up a comprehensive picture of the Gilligans' cash and assets. The Untouchables needed to know how much the Gilligans had spent on Jessbrook, how much property they owned, how much they had in bank accounts, what cars they drove and any other financial details they could get their hands on. Every penny would have to be traced.

Conferences were arranged between the CAB and Tony Hickey's team. In the first months of the murder investigation the Lucan team had seized over IR£200,000 (€254,000) in cash from members of Gilligan's gang. They had also uncovered a lot of intelligence and documents that would be of little use to them in a criminal court. It was agreed that the two teams would work closely together to hit the Gilligan gang on all fronts. Some important intelligence had already been compiled and it would soon help them to hit the jackpot.

In April 1996, Detective Chief Superintendent Kevin Carty had set up a secret intelligence-gathering operation, codenamed Pineapple to target John Gilligan and his mob.

Carty had recruited twelve officers from the National Drug Unit and the Central Detective Unit to compile all the intelligence available on the gang.

Their main weapon had been the Money Laundering Investigation Unit (MLIU). In 1994 EU Directives had been issued to member states to implement legislation in an attempt to clamp down on money laundering. It was mandatory for financial institutions across the EU to report all suspicious transactions to the specialised police unit set up to receive the information, in Ireland's case the MLIU. Intelligence reports had also been collated from Garda districts across Counties Dublin, Kildare and Meath to build up a picture of the Gilligan mob's activities. It hadn't been a hard job. Units everywhere had been sending in reams of reports to Garda HQ about Gilligan's sudden financial success. There was also a record of the two cash amounts seized from Gilligan in 1994, in Dublin and Holyhead. Carty also had good contacts in other European police forces from his time representing the Gardaí in Europol. Established as a result of the Maastricht Treaty in 1992, the objective of Europol is to pool police resources and intelligence from all the EU member States to tackle organised crime on a pan-European front. His contacts had soon paid off with some interesting information.

In October 1995, the Judicial Police in Antwerp, Belgium had received a suspicious transaction report. It outlined five transactions at the KB Securities bank in which large sums of Irish currency were exchanged for Belgian Francs. As a result convicted drug trafficker, Thomas Gorst, and his wife Mariette were arrested under Belgian money laundering laws. The couple had been working for Gilligan for several months. They were introduced to him by Simon Rahman, Gilligan's Dutch-based drug supplier. During questioning, the couple had admitted that they were exchanging the currency on behalf of an Irish man, 'John Gillon'. They had claimed he was a professional Irish gambler and he used them to get a better exchange rate. In December, the Judicial Police had then sent a request to the Gardaí to help identify the mystery Irish man.

The Untouchables, Det. Chief Superintendent Fachtna Murphy (now Deputy Commissioner), Det. Inspector Pat Byrne (now Superintendent) and former Bureau Legal Officer, Barry Galvin.
© *Photocall Ireland*

Veronica Guerin, her murder led to
the establishment of the Criminal
Assets Bureau in 1996.

Ruairi Quinn, the first Minister for Finance in the
history of the State to be involved in formulating anti-
crime legislation.
© *Sunday World*

Nora Owen, Justice Minister
who introduced the tough anti-
crime package of 1996.
© *Collins Photo Agency*

Garda Commissioner Pat Byrne, (now retired), who oversaw the establishment of the CAB.
© *Sunday World*

Noel Conroy, Deputy Garda Commissioner in 1996, who had overall operational control of the Untouchables.
© *Sunday World*

John O'Donoghue, Fianna Fáil 1996 Justice spokesman, who drafted the Bill that ultimately led to the Proceeds of Crime Act.
© *Sunday World*

Tony Hickey, Assistant Commissioner, (now retired), who led the Veronica Guerin murder investigation.
© *Sunday World*

Det. Chief Superintendent Kevin Carty, who led Operation Pineapple.

Austin McNally who led many operations against the Penguin.

Detective Chief Superintendent Felix McKenna, head of the Criminal Assets Bureau until Autumn 2006. McKenna, who was the first Detective Superintendent to join the CAB, played a key role in the success of the Untouchables.
© *Sunday World*

Det. Chief Superintendent Fachtna Murphy carefully guided the CAB through its first three and a half years in operation.
© *Collins Photo Agency*

'Elliot Ness'. The former State Solicitor for Cork, who risked his life to make organised crime pay. In 1992 he was the first legal expert to reveal how Ireland had become a haven for Europe's most dangerous criminals.
© *Collins Photo Agency*

Larry Dunne, the first major godfather to cash in on Ireland's drug misery. He and his family blatantly displayed their ill-gotten gains. At the time this picture was taken Dunne owned a spectacular mansion in the Dublin Mountains, overlooking the city he dominated.
© *Sunday World*

Martin Cahill, the General, who organised the abduction and shooting of a social welfare inspector in 1989. The case would prove the urgent need for a multi-agency approach to tackling organised crime.
© *Sunday World*

John Gilligan, who organised the murder of Veronica Guerin
to protect his evil empire.
© *Sunday World*

Jessbrook. Gilligan's house and world class equestrian centre
undergoing construction in 1995.
© *Sunday World*

Geraldine Gilligan in the bar of the Judge's Chamber pub *(below)* in Alicante, Spain, which the Criminal Assets Bureau believe was bought with her husband's drug money.

Treacy Gilligan
© *Padraig O'Reilly*

Darren Gilligan
© *Collins Photo Agency*

Eugene Patrick 'Dutchie'
Holland, John Gilligan's
enforcer.
© *Sunday World*

Brian 'the Tosser' Meehan
© *Sunday World*

Paul Ward
© *Collins Photo Agency*

John 'the Coach' Traynor
© *Sunday World*

The Monk comes out to pay. Gerry Hutch, *(2nd from the right)* leaving the offices of the Revenue Appeals Commissioner in Dublin in 1998 where he was fighting a IR£2 million (€2.5 million) tax demand. *From left:* Det. Inspector John McDermott (now Det. Superintendent), Hutch's accountant, John McGrattan, and Det. Superintendent Felix McKenna.
© *Padraig O'Reilly*

Gerry 'the Monk' Hutch
© *Sunday World*

Best pals, Gerry Hutch and Noel 'Kingsize' Duggan, attending the funeral of an old friend.
© *Sunday World*

© *Sunday World*

Buckingham Buildings, the inner-city flat complex built by former armed robber Paddy Shanahan (*left*) in the early 1990s, to launder the proceeds of crime, including the loot from the Marino Mart heist.
© *Sunday World*

© *Padraig O'Reilly*

© *Sunday World*

Matt Kelly *(above)* and his brother Eamon *(right)*. Matt Kelly taught the Monk how to launder his dirty money. He paid the CAB over €7 million.

Noel 'Mr Kingsize' Duggan, 'discussing' his ongoing difficulties with Det. Sgt. Paul O'Brien of the Criminal Assets Bureau.
© *Padraig O'Reilly*

Felix McKenna and Barry Galvin taking possession of Noel Duggan's warehouse and apartments in December 2002. Also in the picture is Det. Insp. John McDermott and Det. Gda. Danny Rice.
© *Padraig O'Reilly*

Gang member, Geoffrey Ennis.
© *Sunday World*

Gang member, Gerry Lee, murdered
in 1996.
© *Sunday World*

Gang member, William Scully.
© *Padraig O'Reilly*

The bundles of cash, totalling over IR£500,000 (€635,000), which Hutch 'lodged' in part-payment of his IR£1.2 million (€1.52 million) tax bill.
© *Sunday World*

The empty-handed Monk.

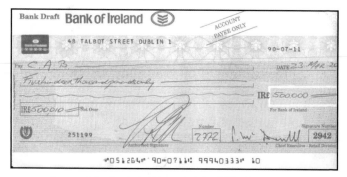

A copy of the bank draft issued to the CAB after the bank took possession of the Monk's cash lodgement.
© *Sunday World*

The Gardaí had replied that there was no man of that name on their records: "There is a person named Gilligan who has numerous convictions for larceny and burglary offences. He is considered dangerous. In order to confirm identity can you supply a set of fingerprints of the subject."

It was only when Operation Pineapple began that Gilligan was positively identified. In the meantime Gorst and his wife were convicted on money laundering offences.

Operation Pineapple also discovered that Gilligan had visited a casino in Scheveningen, Holland on March 18, 1996. With him were Brian Meehan and Derek Baker. Baker, a bookie from Tallaght, was one of Gilligan's most trusted associates and collected drug money to bring to Simon Rahman in Holland. Huge sums of Irish currency were exchanged for Dutch guilders and then given to Rahman. In the casino Meehan had exchanged 250,000 Dutch guilders IR£80,000 (€101,500) into tokens. After a few hours Meehan had gone to the cashier desk and asked to have the tokens cashed in and the money transferred to a Dutch bank account. It would have looked like the money had been won through gambling and was therefore legitimately acquired. But security staff in the casino had been watching the three Irish crooks. They knew that they had not gambled any of the money and immediately recognised a money laundering scam. Staff had refused either to transfer the money to a bank account or to lodge it in the casino account. Meehan had then become typically agitated and aggressive. Under strict money laundering laws, the staff had explained, they could only transfer or lodge sums of money that had been won on the premises. And the casino staff made it clear that they knew the Irish trio had not made any money in the casino. In the end the three thugs had been thrown out, with their wad of cash. The casino later reported the incident to the Dutch Office for the Disclosure of Unusual Transactions (MOT). In turn MOT had passed the information on to the Money Laundering Investigation Unit in Dublin and it ultimately ended up in the Operation Pineapple basket. It was important intelligence that could eventually be used by the CAB in a Proceeds of Crime application before the courts.

On the same day that the Criminal Assets Bureau came into existence, the Operation Pineapple team had raided Jessbrook and seized documentation and banking records. They had also raided Gilligan's accountant and took away all relevant documentation.

By the middle of August Operation Pineapple had uncovered all the bank records of accounts controlled by Geraldine Gilligan and her two children, Treacy and Darren. John Gilligan had no bank account in his name. The research showed that, in less than two years, Geraldine Gilligan, who also used her maiden name Matilda Dunne, had controlled sums of over IR£1.2 million (€1.5 million). As the pieces of the jigsaw started coming together, it appeared that the Gilligans had a lot of questions to answer.

In Garda HQ it was then decided that the Lucan Investigation Team and the CAB would take over the Operation Pineapple investigation. The Pineapple intelligence gave the Lucan team some important leads and the CAB was the only arm of the Gardaí who could use the same intelligence to pursue Gilligan's loot.

Over the following weeks, officers attached to the Louth/ Meath Division of the Gardaí were drafted in to assist the CAB in identifying every landowner who had sold property to Gilligan over the years. Every contractor and supplier who had worked at Jessbrook was also located.

Those who had been paid in cash – most of them – were given unwritten assurances that they would not be pursued by the taxman as long as they co-operated. The officers soon discovered that the people they interviewed were terrified of Gilligan, long before he became a household name. During the probe they heard horror stories about how Gilligan had intimidated and threatened people around Enfield who had been reluctant to sell him parcels of land. In one incident, Gilligan beat up a landowner he had been "negotiating" a deal with. The vicious mobster attacked the man along a country road and then, as the landowner lay there, urinated on him. The deal was done soon afterwards. A builder who had not turned up to finish a job was threatened. He was told that he and his family would be murdered if he didn't turn up the next day. The builder finished the job without delay and Gilligan simply refused to pay him. Suing the crime lord had never been an option.

The Untouchables also interviewed staff in various car showrooms to find out how Gilligan had paid for his fleet of vehicles. The houses the gangster purchased for his children were also identified and the vendors interviewed. The Social Welfare, Tax and Customs Bureau officers also trawled through their department records. The Social Welfare documented every penny the family members had received from the State. Customs accessed intelligence files they had compiled about intercepted drug shipments that they suspected belonged to Gilligan and John Traynor.

The CAB officers went on to make contact with police and customs units in the UK, Belgium and Holland as they continued to build up their dossiers. In September 1996 the Gardaí discovered that for quite some time Gilligan and his henchmen had been travelling to The Netherlands every week. A list of business class flights Gilligan had taken, mainly between Dublin and Amsterdam, was compiled. Between November 29, 1993 and June 25, 1996 they discovered that he had spent over IR£27,000 (€34,000) flying as a member of the Aer Lingus Gold Circle. A Bureau insider recalled: "Everyone knew that Gilligan had a lot of money and that he was a drug trafficker but when we began compiling the list of all the money he was spending everyone was astonished. It was mind-boggling."

The leader of Team One, Detective Sergeant John Naughton, an experienced fraud investigator, was assigned the task of investigating Gilligan's gambling habits. The diminutive godfather had been a life-long gambler but over the previous two years he had apparently hit the big time. He used gambling as an elaborate form of money laundering. A network of couriers, including Derek Baker, would lay bets on a weekly basis in bookies throughout the Greater Dublin area. Sometimes Gilligan would bet on all the horses running in a particular race at up to IR£10,000 ($12,500) a time. Some of the larger bookmakers had conducted discreet inquiries into Gilligan's betting but they could not detect any pattern suggesting a scam. One major bookmaker's chain eventually limited the amount of money he could wager at any one time.

CAB officers painstakingly examined the individual records of Gilligan's dealings with twenty-five branches belonging to the five major betting chains in Ireland. What they found was startling. Between March 1994 and June 1996 Gilligan had bet a total of IR£4,982,590 (€6,326,000). Adding tax at 10 per cent, his gross outlay came to IR£5,480,849 (€6,959,000). His return was IR£4,860,713 (€6,172,000), showing a loss of IR£620,135 (€787,500) or 11.5 per cent of the total. On the surface he appeared to have been unlucky. But when calculated on the lowest standard rate of taxation, Gilligan's money laundering operation was providing superb value for money.

The Bureau officers also suspected that Gilligan had a number of corrupt betting shop employees secretly working for him, either as a result of intimidation or bribes. The mobster would swagger into betting shops and dump bundles of used notes on the counter to cover his bets. But when he won he didn't want cash – he insisted on being paid with a bookmaker's cheque. During the Operation Pineapple search of Gilligan's home in July, officers had found a large framed montage of photocopied cheques from various bookies based in and around Dublin. Everywhere he went he carried copies of the betting shop cheques with him, to account for the large amounts of cash he was carrying. He continued to describe himself as a professional gambler.

By this stage the CAB officers knew that the money they had so far uncovered was only the tip of the iceberg. From the information being collated between the two investigations they suspected the drug operation was bigger than anything they had ever encountered before in the underworld. However a breakthrough in the case was proving illusive. The Lucan team still hadn't actually got a direct line on Gilligan's drug distribution operation. But they were rapidly building up a detailed picture of the gang and had identified up to twenty individuals – including Gilligan's inner-circle – who ran the huge crime empire for the godfather. Detailed analysis of phone records on the day of the Guerin murder had effectively given detectives a picture of who was involved in the crime. The gang members' locations were worked out by identifying the transmission masts the individual phones had used to get a signal on the day. It was the first time that such mobile phone analysis had been used to solve a serious crime.

Apart from Gilligan and Traynor, it was now known that Brian 'Tosser' Meehan, Peter 'Fatso' Mitchell and Paul 'Hippo' Ward were among the main players in the gang. Ward's brother Shay was also a member. The Lucan team identified an ageing convicted armed robber called Patrick Eugene Holland, nicknamed Dutchie, as one of Gilligan's enforcers. The two hoods had done time together in Portlaoise prison. Gardaí in Dublin suspected that Holland had been a gangland hit man for several years. The cops had also established that Derek Baker and his neighbour Russell Warren, a weak-willed coward, were in the gang. Denis 'Dinny' Meredith, a truck driver who grew up with Gilligan in Ballyfermot, had also been identified through Customs' intelligence data. Meredith had driven the stolen trucks used in the Factory Gang heists and had helped Gilligan set up various smuggling routes from Europe, using crooked truck drivers. Former soldier Charlie Bowden, from Finglas, was one of the last gang members to be identified. The ex-infantry soldier, who was a crack shot and a marshal arts expert, was the gang's line manager and armourer. He took care of the day-to-day running of the gang, organising drug deliveries and maintaining the gang's arsenal of lethal pistols and machine guns.

With the most feared members of the gang's inner-circle

still free in Dublin and Gilligan still controlling events from the Continent, people were too terrified to give the cops that final breakthrough to crack the case. In the prevailing climate a tax demand would at least start putting some pressure on Gilligan.

At the same time the CAB began individual investigations into the assets of each of the gang members identified so far. They served production orders on several financial institutions and were given details of bank accounts. In August, Brian Meehan had begun clearing out his cash with the help of his father, Kevin, and his uncle, Thomas. In the same month Meehan and his father had opened two Sterling deposit accounts in the Creditanstalt Bank in Vienna, Austria. They lodged a total of Stg£619,491 (€906,000), over a number of weeks. Another Stg£60,000 (€88,000) was lodged in an account on the Isle of Man. The money had been hurriedly withdrawn from banks and building societies across Dublin. The Meehans signed non-resident statements and produced their passports for identification purposes. They gave the bank specimen signatures and requested that no correspondence be sent to their homes in Ireland. They signed "code word agreements" which allowed them to make withdrawals by simply mentioning the code words.

Using the production orders to demand records from Irish banks the Criminal Assets Bureau started following Meehan's paper trail. They began one of their first international searches, to find out where the money had gone.

The CAB had also identified properties owned by each gang member, in preparation for Proceeds of Crime applications in the courts. In the meantime action could not be taken against the gang until the Criminal Assets Bureau Act gave the Untouchables their powers. As the weeks went by they were becoming increasingly anxious that the law should be passed as soon as possible.

A former CAB insider described the atmosphere in those early days: "There was a huge amount of work being done and you could feel the sense of excitement. There was an absolute belief that something was happening and everyone got stuck in, from Fachtna Murphy and Barry Galvin down. Taxmen, customs, social welfare and Gardaí were all working together, accessing information, typing up reports, preparing legal documents. The attitude was that everyone shared the same rank, we were all in this together, and no one was going home until the job was finished."

In mid-September Fachtna Murphy chaired a conference with his key personnel in Harcourt Square. All the available information was scrutinised and discussed. It was decided that Geraldine Gilligan was a central player in the whole criminal conspiracy. In a subsequent High Court Affidavit, Barry Galvin stated that having studied confidential Garda intelligence documents and financial records he was satisfied: "The plaintiff [Geraldine Gilligan] is, and has been for many years, a full partner with her husband in the conduct of his criminal enterprises."

The Revenue officers attached to the CAB made a detailed assessment of tax and interest due for John and Geraldine Gilligan for the year 1994 to 1995. By the time they put down their calculators John Gilligan owed the Irish exchequer IR£1,766,814 (€2,245,000) with interest of IR£530,044 (€673,000) which brought his total bill to IR£2,296,858 (€2,916,500). Geraldine's tax demand came to IR£882,414 (€1,120,500) with interest of IR£264,724 (€336,000) bringing her total liability to IR£1,147,138 (€1,456,500). Between them the Gilligans owed the State a cool IR£3,443,996 (€4,373,000) in tax for only one year. And interest was being added for every week that the bill remained unpaid.

But there was a new problem. The law stated that an individual tax inspector must sign a tax demand, otherwise it was not legal. But none of the Revenue officials attached to the CAB, or indeed anywhere else in the Department of Finance, were prepared to sign the documents for obvious reasons of personal security. In the prevailing climate of fear and danger no one could criticise their position. Fachtna Murphy and Barry Galvin certainly didn't. If the gangsters could shoot a high-profile journalist dead in broad daylight, then a taxman was fair game. The CAB had a crisis on their hands. It reinforced the crucial need for the provision of airtight anonymity clauses for all non-Garda personnel to be enshrined in the eagerly awaited Criminal Assets Bureau Act. In the meantime they were powerless. As one former member recalled: "It was a bit like having a prize race horse champing on the bit to get out of the stalls and win the Grand National. But the only thing stopping it was that no one would let it lose, it was very frustrating."

A cloud of despondency hung over the Untouchables as there appeared to be no solution in sight. But then Barry Galvin had a clever idea. He had studied the various Revenue and Public Service Acts and discovered that there was no reason why he could not be appointed a temporary tax inspector himself. He told Murphy his plan and the pair immediately went to discuss the proposition with the Attorney General, Dermot Gleeson. The two Bureau chiefs were attending regular meetings with department civil servants, legal advisers and parliamentary draftsmen as they continued to draft the CAB Act legislation.

On the morning of September 16, Galvin put his proposal to the AG. "Make me a tax inspector and I will sign the demand," he bluntly told Gleeson. The Government's most senior lawyer could find nothing in law to prevent this novel approach. The Department of Finance and Minister Ruairi Quinn were also informed. Quinn thought it was a great idea and issued a ministerial order that Barry Galvin be appointed a tax inspector without delay.

Later that day, Murphy and Galvin met with Cathal MacDomhnaill, the Chairman of the Revenue Commissioners in Dublin Castle. In MacDomhnaill's office the indefatigable solicitor swore a statutory declaration and officially added the title of tax inspector to his impressive portfolio. The two men sped back to their "hen house" where Galvin signed the two demands for payment of overdue tax for Ireland's Public

Enemy Number One.

The following morning at 8.45 am Galvin handed two large brown envelopes to Detective Sergeant Kevin Ring and instructed him to personally deliver them to Geraldine Gilligan at Jessbrook. An hour later he and another Bureau officer met Detective Sergeant Des McTiernan from Navan Garda station, near the gates of Gilligan's ranch, outside Enfield. The Detective Sergeant had been involved in the ongoing background investigations for both the CAB and the Lucan Team. McTiernan rang the intercom at the electronic gates and looked up at the security camera so Geraldine Gilligan could see who it was. Just over a year earlier, on September 14, Veronica Guerin had stood in the same spot and pressed the intercom button. The brown envelopes Kevin Ring now clutched in his hand were a direct consequence of the events unleashed that fateful morning in 1995. As the wrought iron gates slowly creaked apart, the three cops no doubt considered the tragic coincidence that had changed a lot of lives and careers, including their own.

The three detectives drove up to the house and met Geraldine Gilligan at the door. She already knew McTiernan and the two Untouchables, dressed in smart suits, identified themselves and showed Gilligan their official identity cards. She was cordial and invited them into the sitting room. At exactly 10.48 am Det. Sgt. Ring wiped the smile from her face when he handed Geraldine Gilligan the envelope with her name on it. In a calm professional tone, Ring informed John Gilligan's 'partner-in-crime' that it contained a notice of assessment for taxes. When he tried to hand her the envelope in her husband's name, she refused to accept it. She claimed that he did not live there. Ring told her that it was his belief that Jessbrook was Gilligan's "most usual place of abode" and placed the large tax demand on the arm of a sofa. Geraldine Gilligan then ordered the Untouchables to leave her home.

When the cops left Geraldine rang her husband. He flew into a murderous rage. Only this time it wasn't a defenceless journalist he was dealing with. He later told an associate who was secretly passing information back to the Gardaí: "Who in fuck do these pricks think they are… Are they fucking mad? It's daylight robbery, that's what it is!" For a while John Gilligan apparently considered having one of the Untouchables shot.

Under the law, the Gilligans had 30 days in which to respond to the tax demand. Geraldine Gilligan sought legal advice from her solicitor. The legal firm wrote to the CAB enquiring how the assessment had been calculated and pointed out that she could not file tax returns or appeal the demand because most of her documentation and accounts had already been seized.

On September 20, Assistant Commissioner Tony Hickey chaired a conference in the Harcourt Street HQ with the CAB and the MLIU, as part of the continuing investigation into Gilligan's financial affairs. It was decided that they needed access to the Gilligans' legal files to proceed with the money laundering probe. Michael E Hanahoe and Company in Dublin represented the Gilligans and the investigation team had the option to serve a production order on the legal firm. But Barry Galvin said that it was the view of the Law Society that if a production order was served on a solicitor then the solicitor would be obliged to inform his client about the order. The problem was that if Gilligan had prior knowledge about the search there was a serious risk he would send his henchmen to intimidate staff in Hanahoes and force them to destroy those files. There was even a possibility that the godfather would order the destruction of the offices in a bid to thwart the investigation. During a subsequent High Court hearing Detective Inspector Terry McGinn gave a candid assessment of what she felt Gilligan would do if he was forewarned of the search: "I think nothing on this earth would have stopped him. He is a very dangerous criminal. It was vital and primary evidence of money laundering."

It was finally decided that the investigators would obtain a search warrant and enter the offices unannounced. The details of the operation were kept strictly secret. But when officers from the MLIU and the CAB arrived at the offices in Parliament Street, on October 3, the media were waiting to record the event. An anonymous caller had tipped them off in advance. It was a big story. Gilligan's legal advisors would be the first solicitors in Ireland to have their premises searched by the police.

The publicity surrounding the raid caused understandable consternation among the legal profession and the Gardaí. It was particularly unfair to the Hanahoes, a respected firm of solicitors, who had done nothing wrong. The Hanahoes later claimed that the public could draw untrue inferences about their firm because of the Garda raid. During the operation the search team removed files relating to the Gilligans' property transactions over several years. Following the incident the Law Society blamed the Gardaí for the leak and demanded a public apology from Commissioner Pat Byrne. But the country's top policeman vigorously resisted, creating a tense stand-off with the Attorney General's office in the process.

In the meantime the Hanahoes issued proceedings seeking a judicial review to have the original warrant overturned. The District Judge who had issued the warrant, Gillian Hussey, the Gardaí and the State were cited as defendants. Behind-the-scenes Byrne refused a request from the Government's lawyer that he issue an apology over the leaks to the media, on behalf of An Garda Síochana. If the High Court quashed the search warrant it was argued that the crisis over the Hanahoes search could have damaging implications for the fledgling Criminal Assets Bureau and how it went about its business. But Byrne stood his ground. He argued that if he apologised it was an admission that the police had been responsible for the leak. There was no evidence that any of his officers had leaked the information and he was not about to apologise for something that could have come from someone outside the police. He pointed out to the State's legal advisers that if the legal profession was in a similar situation they would not, in the absence of proof, issue an apology either.

He would, however, have no problem issuing a statement clarifying that the firm had no connection with criminal activity.

Privately Byrne and his senior management were furious at the leak and conducted unofficial investigations to discover if it had originated within the Gardaí. The secret mole was never identified, although several suspects were nominated, both inside and outside the ranks of the Gardaí. The Hanahoe case was potentially very damaging for the CAB who were due to receive their statutory powers twelve days later. The incident had caused considerable resentment among members of the legal profession, with whom the Untouchables would have extensive contact.

In the meantime the CAB officers immediately began to examine the files on the Gilligan's vast financial empire.

* * * *

Meanwhile, there had been dramatic developments in the murder investigation. Russell Warren and members of his family were arrested about the murder on Oct 1, 1996 two days before the raid on the solicitor's offices. During interrogation Warren admitted to being Gilligan's bagman. Since his introduction to the gang Warren had effectively taken over the job from his pal Derek Baker. He collected and counted millions of pounds on behalf of the gang. He also travelled on a regular basis to Holland where he exchanged the Irish currency for Dutch guilders in a Bureau de Change near Central Station in Amsterdam. The money was then given to Simon Rahman or Rahman's assistant, Martin Baltus. In a statement he told officers: "When I started collecting money for Gilligan there used to be IR£20,000 (€25,500) or IR£30,000 (€38,000) in it. This figure would be the lowest amount; it would go as high as IR£160,000 (€203,000) sometimes but most of the times it would be around IR£70,000 (€89,000)."

Warren's parents, sister and brother-in-law also admitted

that they had been counting Gilligan's drug money and were paid for it. Warren was too terrified to speak about the murder and claimed he knew nothing about it. The money was as far as he would go. The disclosure that the Warrens had been collecting and counting money for Gilligan meant that they were liable to be charged with money laundering offences. The cases were handed over to the CAB and the MLIU and files were prepared for the Director of Public Prosecutions.

In the meantime Warren and his family were released without charge. (Warren and his family were all subsequently jailed for terms ranging from one to five years, after pleading guilty to money laundering charges.) The cops had made a connection with Warren and they knew he was a weak link in the gang. They planned to stay in touch.

On October 5, Charlie Bowden, his girlfriend, brother and a number of associates were arrested for questioning. Over the next two days the former soldier underwent a conversion that would have dire consequences for his former cronies. At first he refused to say anything while he was being interrogated. He would later claim that his sudden desire to tell the truth was prompted when Det. Sgt. Des McTiernan slammed down the photographs of the journalist lying dead in her car on the Naas Road. Either Bowden wanted to save his own skin or he had genuine remorse over his role in the murder of Veronica Guerin. Whatever the motivation the former soldier was about to blow the Gilligan gang apart.

At first he told a mixture of lies and truth. Bowden showed Det. Insp. John O'Mahoney and Detective Garda Bernie Hanley a friend's apartment, where he had stashed IR£100,000 (€127,000). He admitted working as a drug distributor for the rest of the gang but denied involvement in the murder. Eventually his interrogators, O'Mahoney and Hanley, convinced him to come clean. As a result of what they learned from some of the other gang members arrested with Bowden the Lucan Investigation Team went to a lock-up in Greenmount Industrial Estate in Harold's Cross which the gang had used as its central depot. They found a huge amount of evidence, including 49 kilos of hashish. When he was told the cops had found Greenmount, Bowden told them everything he knew. It took him three hours to tell the astonishing story of life inside the Gilligan gang.

The following evening he brought the same officers to the gang's hidden arsenal of automatic weapons, concealed in a Jewish cemetery near Tallaght. Two days later he was charged with drug trafficking offences and remanded in custody.

Through Bowden and Russell Warren the Gardaí finally pieced together the plot to murder Guerin. Bowden told them about conversations in the gang discussing Gilligan's intention to do something about Guerin because of his pending assault charges. John Traynor, Veronica's underworld source, knew that she was due to appear in Naas District Court on the morning of June 26 to face speeding charges. It was an ideal opportunity to ambush her. Bowden admitted oiling and loading the murder weapon, a.357 magnum revolver, and leaving it for Brian Meehan to collect in the Greenmount lock-up. He claimed Dutchie Holland had been picked as the assassin and Brian Meehan drove the motorbike used in the attack. On the day of the attack Peter Mitchell had been driving around the area keeping a watch out for Garda patrols and was waiting to pick Meehan up after the outrage. Russell Warren shadowed the journalist from Naas and informed the killers of her exact location. Warren later admitted to the Gardaí that he had actually witnessed the murder. Gilligan co-ordinated the whole nefarious plot from a hotel room in Amsterdam. After the murder, Meehan and Holland went back to Paul Ward's house in Walkinstown and left the bike and murder weapon with him for disposal. Ward later got rid of the weapon. He and John Foy, a customer of the gang and a former member of the General's mob, cut up the motorbike and dumped it in the River Liffey.

Most of what Bowden and Warren told the Gardaí had checked out through analysis of the mobile phone traffic between the various gang members on the day of the murder.

Other witnesses also gave vital statements that corroborated the testimony of the men who would become Ireland's first supergrasses and cause the establishment of a witness protection programme. But as a result of fear and intimidation many of these other crucial witnesses refused to testify in court despite their earlier assurances. Bowden's revelation that Paul Ward and Brian Meehan had attempted to assassinate, Martin 'The Viper' Foley, the previous February, also emphasised the terrifying power of Gilligan and his gang of thugs.

Within days of Bowden's arrest the Lucan Team finally had a detailed description of how Gilligan's drug operation worked. The gang would order drugs and guns from Simon Rahman in Holland. He would then instruct his assistant Martin Baltus to load the stuff in boxes marked as machine parts. They would then be shipped from Rotterdam port to the Seabridge shipping company in Cork Harbour, where John Dunne was operations manager. Dunne, who was originally from Dublin, had been introduced to Gilligan by Dinny Meredith. Before each shipment members of the gang would arrive in Amsterdam where they exchanged large quantities of Irish and UK currency for Dutch guilders. The cash was then handed to either Rahman or Baltus. In Cork, John Dunne would collect the crates of 'machine parts' and load them into a van driven by a trusted associate. Dunne's associate would then deliver the load to the car park at the Ambassador Hotel on the outskirts of Dublin, just off the Naas Road, where gang members collected it. Dunne was paid IR£1,000 (€1,270) per delivery. The crates were taken to Greenmount where Bowden checked the load and divided it into individual orders. Bowden and other members of the gang delivered the drugs to customers in a van bought specially for the job – it was dubbed the 'dope mobile'. When the Gardaí raided the drug depot they found checklists which included the initials of each customer and the quantities he bought and money due. Most of the gang's clients were subsequently identified after exhaustive Garda enquiries and over the following months each of them were arrested. Some of them were later convicted of drug offences. Their files were also sent on to the CAB with a view to identifying any assets that could be seized.

As Charlie Bowden was spilling the beans in Lucan, John Gilligan was making his way to the departures lounge of Heathrow Airport, with a case full of IR£330,000 (€419,000) in cash. A friend, convicted kidnapper Michael Cunningham, had dropped the money off to him from Ireland. In order to keep the drug business running and with his couriers compromised back in Dublin, Gilligan had to pick up the cash himself.

Unknown to the dangerous thug, the Lucan Investigation Team and the CAB had been working closely with their colleagues from police and Customs in the UK and Holland. The godfather had been secretly watched in both countries. Through intelligence sources they knew Gilligan would be carrying a large amount of drug money with him that day. It was time that he was taken out of the picture. HM Customs investigator Roger Wilson, the man Gilligan had threatened nearly two years earlier, was waiting in his Manchester office for a call – the call that would concern Gilligan's arrest.

Customs officers at Heathrow asked Gilligan what was in the bag. He brazenly replied it was cash for investment purposes in Holland. He produced photocopies of bookmakers' cheques, a copy of a receipt for the return of the money seized in 1994 by Roger Wilson and a bizarre IR£4 million (€5 million) "loan agreement" from a mysterious Lebanese businessman who turned out to be involved in international arms and drug trafficking. A Customs' officer at Terminal 3 phoned Wilson and told him what they had found. "Arrest him now. Don't let him out of your sight. I'm on my way," Wilson answered, as he headed towards London.

At the same time Felix McKenna and Det. Garda Bernard Masterson were dispatched on the afternoon flight to Heathrow to liaise with their colleagues. The two men would brief their counterparts on the murder investigation and the CAB's probe into Gilligan's ill-gotten gains. The information from the

Untouchables would prove to be vital in sustaining criminal charges against the godfather in the UK.

Gilligan was arrested on suspicion of laundering the proceeds of drug trafficking under Section 49 (1) of the (UK) Drugs Trafficking Act 1994. A few hours after his arrest Roger Wilson, the man who received protection because of death threats Gilligan had issued, walked into the interview room. The mobster realised he was in a bind. Wilson sat across the table from the godfather and reminded him of their little spat two years earlier. When Factory John then saw Felix McKenna strolling past the door the penny finally dropped. McKenna waved at his old adversary and gave him a smile that had "gotcha" written all over it. It was the first time the cop and the robber had seen each other since McKenna's evidence got the hood a four-year stretch in November 1990. The last time 'Felix the Cat' had smiled at Gilligan was when the gangster was being taken away to prison from the Special Criminal Court.

Sitting in the holding room at Heathrow Airport Gilligan tried to put on a brave face but deep down he knew he had been out-manoeuvred. The cops in Ireland were no longer tied behind their own borders. Gilligan was trapped, but he smirked and told one of the Customs officers holding him: "Tell Felix I said hello".

A few minutes later McKenna popped his head around the door and with a wide grin on his face, addressed his old enemy: "How are you John? I'll see you in about 14 years if you're lucky."

The following Monday, McKenna met with the Crown Prosecution Service and HM Customs to brief them on the findings of the CAB case back in Dublin. He explained about finding the drug distribution centre in Dublin, earlier statements by Russell Warren connecting Gilligan with the drug money and, that at that moment, Charlie Bowden's statement was also being typed up in Lucan station. The Untouchable also shared the details of the rest of the CAB investigation into Gilligan's money laundering activities, including his gambling rackets and the amount of cash he had spent on property.

The following day, Tuesday, October 8, Gilligan was formally charged with money laundering offences before Uxbridge Magistrates Court in London. HM Customs' agent Roger Wilson was granted an application to seize the cash when he informed the court that Gilligan could not offer a legitimate explanation for its origins. He said that Gilligan had been associated with two UK-based drug traffickers and that he was linked with the seizure of 50 kilos of cannabis at the lock-up in Greenmount, Dublin. Gilligan was remanded in custody to Belmarsh maximum-security prison where he was classified as a Category A prisoner. This category is assigned only to the most dangerous criminals and terrorists.

As Gilligan spent his first night behind bars, the Lucan Team turned their attentions to Paul Ward and his connection with a corrupt Garda called John O'Neill. On October 16, the cop and the drug dealer were arrested. Meehan, Mitchell, Shay Ward and Dutchie Holland had already fled Ireland on false passports which O'Neill had helped them to obtain. As a result of his own admissions, and the evidence of the supergrasses, Paul 'Hippo' Ward became the first member of the gang to be charged with the murder. He was convicted of the murder in the Special Criminal Court in 1998 but that conviction was overturned four years later. By that stage, however, the CAB had sold his house and emptied his bank accounts.

John O'Neill was charged with sixteen counts of accepting bribes from the Gilligan gang. He later pleaded guilty and was jailed. During his interrogation, the once decorated cop revealed that he had also been on the pay roll of two other notorious drug dealers, Tony Long and Derek 'Dee Dee' O'Driscoll from Ballyfermot. The two hoods were subsequently convicted for corruption. O'Driscoll got one year but Long paid a IR£45,000 (€57,000) fine instead. As a result, the Criminal Assets Bureau hit Long with a tax demand for almost IR£250,000 (€317,500). The drug dealer had walked himself into trouble by actually paying the fine. Officially he was supposed to be unemployed!

As the drama continued to unfold back in Lucan, Russell Warren told Hickey's team that he was prepared to testify along with Bowden against his former gang members. Then on October 25, John Dunne was also arrested. Before he was inside the door of a police station he had begun to talk. "I was driven by pure greed and nothing more. After the murder I was too scared to get out," he said. Dunne also joined Warren and Bowden. The evidence was piling up.

Detectives from the CAB and the Lucan Investigation Team went to the shipping company in Cork to analyse their records. They were trying to find out how much cannabis the gang had smuggled into the country, using that route. Other officers from the MLIU and the CAB were sent to Holland to examine records from the Dutch shipping companies and Bureau de Change. Records of cash transactions were also uplifted from a number of casinos in Holland.

Using all this information, the Untouchables later compiled an in-depth analysis of the gang's activities. The document included records of the date of every flight made by the different gang members, the amounts of money they each exchanged and the weight of the shipments arriving in Cork. The figures were staggering. In two years Gilligan's mob had exchanged IR£11.5 million (€14.5 million) alone at the Bureaux de Change in Amsterdam. From an analysis of the shipping records it was conservatively estimated that 21,000 kilos of hashish had been smuggled into the country between April 1994 and September 1996. The gang had paid a total of just over IR£25 million (€32 million) for the hashish. With an average sale of IR£2,000 (€2,500) per kilo Gilligan had made a profit of IR£16,800,000 million (€21,331,500 million). The rest of the gang made an estimated IR£8.5 million (€10.8 million) in profit. But these were conservative figures and did not include a number of other large consignments of cocaine, ecstasy and cannabis that had been smuggled through other routes. The CAB document was the first official evidence of the real monetary value of organised crime in Ireland.

* * * *

Soon after the CAB got their statutory powers towards the end of October 1996, they went after the rest of the gang. On November 6, they began the process of obtaining High Court injunctions freezing properties and bank accounts belonging to Traynor, Meehan, Mitchell and Ward. Vehicles, including high-performance cars and jeeps were also lifted. Barry Galvin was appointed Receiver to the properties for the purpose of selling them off.

Meehan had been letting a number of his apartments and after he fled the country, his drug dealing pal, Robbie Harrison collected the rents. CAB officers contacted Harrison and told him he was fired – from now on the Untouchables would be collecting the rent. When one of the officers turned up to collect the rent money due, however, one female tenant informed him that she didn't actually pay Harrison in cash. Their transaction had been of a more physical nature. The lady began paying in hard cash after that!

The international investigation to track down Brian 'the Tosser' Meehan's cash was still ongoing and the Untouchables were issuing tax demands on other criminals involved with the gang.

The time the Gilligans had to respond to the tax demand had expired. In early November Geraldine Gilligan, her children and several close associates had been arrested and questioned about the murder but were released a few days later without charge. In the meantime Geraldine Gilligan's solicitors had informed the CAB that they could not contact John Gilligan to take instructions. On November 14, the CAB served a final demand on Geraldine Gilligan, requiring payment of over IR£3.5 million (€4.5 million). When no payment was forthcoming it was decided to send in the County Sheriff, to seize property to offset the sum demanded.

On the morning of November 20, Felix McKenna launched the Bureau's first high-profile operation. Sheriff Frank Lanigan, a team of bailiffs and armed Gardaí, hit Jessbrook at dawn. The bailiffs and some of the CAB staff wore balaclavas and scarves to conceal their faces and protect their identities. There was very tight security in the entire area. The Sheriff's staff removed the number plates from their vehicles to avoid identification. TVs, video recorders, furniture, riding equipment, industrial washing and drying machines, anything of value was loaded into a convoy of vans and taken away. The CAB also seized ten ponies and horses, valued at more than IR£100,000 (€127,000), a luxury all-terrain vehicle, a new JCB digger, a site dumper and horse trailers. When the CAB had finished Geraldine Gilligan was left with the bare essentials to live on.

The dramatic raid received extensive coverage from the media, only this time no one was complaining about leaks. Ruairi Quinn's request that the bad guys be exposed and shamed had certainly been honoured. Over the previous six months Geraldine Gilligan had continued to build Jessbrook into one of the finest equestrian centres in Europe. By the time the last CAB officer drove away, it was desolate and empty.

Standing at the gates Geraldine told reporters: "I couldn't answer the tax assessment because the police have all my documents of returns and everything else, so I didn't have any documentation to answer with. Me demand has gone from IR£882,000 (€1,120,000) to IR£1,292,000 (€1,640,500). I can prove the source of my income."

She never did.

* * * *

The raid on Jessbrook sparked a myriad of legal actions in the following months, which have continued to the present day. The day after the raid, Fachtna Murphy obtained a High Court order under the Proceeds of Crime Act freezing

Jessbrook and the homes of Treacy and Darren Gilligan. Cars belonging to the children were also impounded. In an Affidavit Fachtna Murphy said it was his belief that the property forming the subject matter of the application – Jessbrook, three houses and several cars – was, directly or indirectly, the proceeds of crime. He said his belief was supported by Gilligan's long history of involvement in crime and his accumulation of very substantial assets in a short period, without "enjoying any apparent lawful source of income". Murphy also stated the belief by Gardaí that Gilligan had a significant involvement in the importation of narcotics. The Social Welfare officials attached to the Bureau also moved to cut off Treacy and Darren Gilligan's State benefits.

In response Geraldine Gilligan's lawyers immediately sought a High Court injunction restraining the CAB from advertising for sale, or taking any steps to dispose of, the property that had been seized, while she appealed the tax demand. The application was refused.

A few days later, the case was appealed to the Supreme Court which sent it back to the High Court. The particular issues concerning whether Geraldine Gilligan was a chargeable person under the relevant tax acts had to be addressed first. The proceedings named the defendants as the Criminal Assets Bureau; Barry Galvin, Frank Lanigan, and the Revenue Commissioners.

In the High Court hearing, Geraldine Gilligan's counsel, Adrian Hardiman SC, said that for the relevant tax period Geraldine Gilligan was a married woman and it was her husband who should have been charged. In the case of a married couple, it was the husband, and the husband alone, who was the chargeable person.

Richard Nesbitt SC, for the defendants, argued that she was liable for the tax demand. During the chargeable period she had bank accounts in her own name and this was her own income. He argued that under the Act, chargeable persons were identified as persons "receiving or entitled to the income in respect of which tax is to be charged".

On February 25, 1997, Geraldine Gilligan won her case. The High Court ruled that, under the Income Tax Act 1967, she was not liable for the CAB tax bill and that her husband was obliged to make the tax return. Mr Justice Morris said the first issue had been to establish if she was a chargeable person for the chargeable period, the 12 months ending April 5th, 1995. The judge said that Section 19 of the Act contained words which were clear and unambiguous. It provided that the husband was to be assessed and charged for tax in respect of his wife's total income. The Act provided that, for income tax purposes, a wife's income was deemed to be her husband's and not her own.

Mr Justice Morris said it was clear "that significant consequences" might flow from his determination of the issues but it was no part of his function to consider any such consequences. He confined his judgement to the issues before him, which were matters of law arising out of a consideration of the income tax code.

Two days later the Criminal Assets Bureau told the High Court it would be taking further legal action against Geraldine Gilligan. The CAB's counsel, Richard Nesbitt SC, said there were matters outstanding but revealed that his clients would not be appealing the judgement. He submitted that costs should be reserved and said the judge had "some indication of the wider picture". He said Gilligan's victory was only a "temporary respite". The question of the tax was still outstanding and there were also questions about the source of the monies which were undoubtedly in her name and in her possession.

Mr Justice Morris said he should make it clear that his only interest in the matter was confined to the determination of two issues of law dealing with the interpretation of the tax code. It appeared to him that this was but one step in the overall case being pursued between the parties. He proposed that the costs of the case be reserved until the outcome of the broader and general issue between the parties was resolved.

Geraldine Gilligan was delighted with her victory. She

told *The Irish Times* she was determined to stay at Jessbrook: "This is my home and I'm staying put."

The Untouchables had suffered their first setback but it was a learning exercise. Internally there was a feeling among some of the Bureau officers that they should have been more circumspect about landing a tax demand on Geraldine Gilligan. It was argued that the action could have potentially finished the CAB off before it even got started. But those fears proved to be unfounded. The Untouchables had only lost a skirmish in the overall war. The legal wrangle with Geraldine Gilligan made little difference to the CAB's overall strategy. In the words of Ruairi Quinn, the criminals were getting their chance to test the new anti-crime powers. Two years later the tax laws were amended so that the same situation would not arise again.

Around the same time the CAB made their move against Dutchie Holland. They obtained a freezing order preventing him from selling his luxury country home near Brittas Bay in County Wicklow. Sixteen officers from the Bureau and the Lucan Team raided the house and arrested his wife Angela and a close family friend. Holland was subsequently arrested on April 9, 1997, as he returned to Ireland in disguise, on a ferry from the UK. There was more controversy when, a few hours later, officers from the Criminal Assets Bureau arrested Dutchie's solicitor, Jimmy Orange, under the Drug Trafficking Act in connection with the attempted sale of Dutchie's home in County Wicklow a month earlier. Jimmy Orange later told a court that his arrest had been "a circus and a charade".

When Holland was brought back to Lucan Garda station detectives discovered that he had elaborate bugging devices specially built into the heels of his shoes. It emerged that one of Holland's associates had also placed sophisticated listening devices at two locations near Lucan and Tallaght Garda stations to record transmissions from the bugs. Dutchie had spent over Stg£20,000 (€29,250) buying the equipment before he returned to Ireland. The Lucan team had been tipped off by their counterparts in Scotland Yard, who had secretly watched Holland visiting a spy shop in London. During his interrogation Holland admitted to being involved in drug trafficking with Gilligan but denied any involvement with the murder.

Three days later Holland was charged with drug trafficking offences and remanded in custody. There was not enough evidence, however, to sustain a murder charge.

In November 1997, Holland was convicted and sentenced to 20 years by the Special Criminal Court. The sentence was later reduced to 12 years on appeal and Dutchie Holland was released from prison in April 2006.

In February 1998 auctioneers acting for the Criminal Assets Bureau sold Dutchie's country home for IR£120,000 (€152,500).

Over the following months houses and apartments owned by Paul Ward, Brian Meehan, Peter Mitchell and John Traynor were also auctioned off by the Untouchables.

* * * *

Behind bars John Gilligan was living up to Felix McKenna's prediction that the criminals would use every legal tool possible to thwart the system. In the UK he had begun a series of challenges attacking every aspect of his detention and extradition, going as far as the House of Lords. His legal manoeuvres successfully held up the system for over four years. It wasn't until February 2000 that he was eventually extradited back to Ireland to face charges for murder, drug trafficking and possession of firearms.

In March 1997, John Gilligan made his first attempt to have the Criminal Assets Bureau abolished. His Irish legal team mounted a challenge to the constitutionality of the Proceeds of Crime Act which gave the Criminal Assets Bureau its powers.

It was the first major test of the new legislation and the Bureau's survival depended on the outcome. Barry Galvin and the CAB's legal team worked long hours to prepare for the case. A lot was at stake. If Gilligan succeeded it would have serious consequences on the CAB's freedom to pursue the ill-gotten gains of organised crime.

During the four day hearing, Gilligan's counsel claimed that the powers allowing Gardaí to confiscate and dispose of an individual's assets meant that "we are on the slippery slope towards the creation of a police state". Through his counsel, Gilligan argued that he was only part owner of many of the properties the Bureau wanted to seize. He stated that they were bought with gambling money and a IR£4 million (€5 million) loan from a foreign businessman.

Counsel for Gilligan, Brian Langwallner SC, also claimed that the Proceeds of Crime Act "masqueraded as a civil statute when it was a criminal law which circumvented the criminal process". He said: "We are approaching a situation where a police officer can stop a man in the street and warn him that his property was being confiscated unless he could prove it was not the proceeds of crime. It is a slippery slope and it is not endorsed or acceptable in any civil jurisdiction." He described as "Kafkaesque" the fact that the word of a Chief Superintendent or Revenue Official could have an individual's assets frozen, put in receivership and disposed of, on the basis of assumed criminality, without charge, trial or conviction. There was a provision in the Criminal Justice Act, 1994, which related to the proceeds of criminal activity. But within that structure there was also an adherence to civil liberties. A person had to go through the process of criminal law and then be sentenced before his assets could be confiscated. He likened the Proceeds of Crime Act to emergency legislation, which had been transferred from an emergency powers regime to deal with a difficult international problem. Such legislation was appropriate where the courts were deemed to be inadequate to protect the public and preserve public order. But Ireland, he claimed, was not in a state of emergency and had one of the lowest crime rates in the world.

The Gardaí and the Government were determined to fight for the CAB and the new powers they represented. It was decided that Felix McKenna and Deputy Commissioner, Noel Conroy, would give unequivocal evidence on money laundering to the court. It was seldom that such senior and experienced Gardaí got an opportunity to publicly explain how organised crime operated.

On the third day of the hearing, Felix McKenna told the court that over the previous eight months, one of the effects of the Proceeds of Crime Act had been to "force criminals above ground". Before the Act, a lot of money had also been taken out of bank accounts and moved abroad and several criminals had also moved their money into legitimate businesses. "Over the last six to seven months, one major criminal gang has put millions of pounds into apartment blocks and licensed premises, principally in Dublin," he said.

Under cross-examination McKenna said the Bureau's function was to establish that there was criminal activity, apart from the identification of the person believed to be involved. He said the British police force had prepared a document on the operation of the Proceeds of Crime Act for the British Home Office. Other police forces in Europe were also interested in the legislation because it allowed the CAB powers that were not available to similar investigative bodies in other countries.

Donal O'Donnell, counsel for Ireland and the Attorney General, argued that there were protections built into the Proceeds of Crime Act. The court could refuse an application made by the CAB for confiscation if it felt there was a risk of a serious injustice. In addition an application for a disposal order could not be made until after a period of seven years. Seven years was an extensive period that allowed for the discharge of the confiscation orders made by the court, if it was proved that the assets were not accumulated from the proceeds of crime.

Deputy Garda Commissioner Noel Conroy gave a frank assessment of how organised crime had evolved in Ireland over the previous 10 years. He revealed that criminals had switched from armed robbery and used that money to get involved in supplying drugs on a grand scale. They used runners or "couriers" so that they could remove themselves completely from the operation. They could command respect and fear within the criminal community, he said, so that the runners would not inform on them and in turn some of them had also become wealthy. He testified that if major criminals were not stopped, people would become frustrated and disillusioned with the criminal justice system and be less likely to come forward as witnesses or informants.

Conroy said that the Bureau was a success. He revealed that since the Proceeds of Crime Act came into force "major criminals are being forced to work on the shop floor" of their activities and were therefore running the gauntlet of being charged with criminal offences. The Act had also resulted in major criminal figures attempting to leave the jurisdiction with their cash and trying to dispose of properties. He believed that the legislation was important for public confidence in the judicial system.

Counsel for the CAB, Frank Clarke SC, argued that there was nothing in the Proceeds of Crime Act which allowed "an impermissible interference with the good name of any person involved". He said the legislation's objective, which concerned the amassing of wealth as a result of criminal activity, was of the highest importance. There were provisions in the legislation, he added, which entitled a person to challenge the evidence against him, to have hearings in private and to be compensated if confiscation orders were discharged.

On March 20 the court reserved its judgement.

It wasn't until the first anniversary of Veronica Guerin's murder that the future of the Untouchables was assured. The High Court ruled that the Proceeds of Crime Act was indeed constitutional. In her eighty-page ruling Mrs Justice Catherine McGuinness, said that the question was if the Act, within the framework of the Constitution, was a proportionate response to the threat to society posed by the operations of the type of major criminals described in evidence by Felix McKenna and Noel Conroy. She said it appeared that as a matter of proportionality, the legislature was justified in enacting the Act and restricting certain rights through the operation of it. She said the two Garda officers had "painted a picture of an entirely new type of professional criminal who organised, rather than committed crime and thereby rendered himself virtually immune to the ordinary procedures of criminal investigation and prosecution". The Judge said: "Such persons are able to operate a reign of terror so as effectively to prevent the passing on of information to the Gardaí. At the same time, their obvious wealth and power cause them to be respected by lesser criminals or would-be criminals."

Justice Catherine McGuinness said she would accept that certain elements of the media, both written and broadcast, tended to exaggerate the comparative level of crime in this State and "to create in regard to crime an undesirable form of hysteria which has its own dangers". Nevertheless, in the context of a relatively small community, the operations carried out by major criminals had a serious and worsening effect. This was particularly so in regard to their importation and distribution of illegal drugs, which, in its turn, led to a striking increase in lesser crimes carried out by addicts seeking to finance their addiction. Mrs Justice McGuinness continued: "In theory this type of threat to public order and the community at large may seem less obvious than the threat posed to this State by the operation of politically motivated illegal organisations. In practice major and minor drug related crime is probably perceived by ordinary members of the community as more threatening and more likely to affect the everyday lives of themselves and their children."

The staff at the Bureau had good cause to celebrate. They had survived the first major attempt by organised crime figures to shut them down by using the law. But more challenges would come.

* * * *

In April 1997 there was a major breakthrough in the

international hunt for Brian Meehan's hidden loot, when the Criminal Assets Bureau tracked it to Austria. The Irish Director of Public Prosecutions issued an international rogatory order on behalf of the Untouchables, seeking assistance from the Austrian authorities under money laundering laws. Officers from the CAB visited the Creditanstalt Bank in Vienna with officials from the Federal Ministry of the Interior. As a result the Superior Court for Criminal Cases in Vienna ordered that the six accounts held in the names of Brian and Kevin Meehan be frozen on the grounds that the money was the proceeds of organised crime. Brian 'the Tosser' Meehan was in for a big surprise.

On May 7, the Tosser strolled into the Vienna bank and gave his secret code to access his account. John Traynor and Peter Mitchell were waiting for him outside. The assistant asked Meehan to wait a moment. Half an hour later the assistant returned with bad news. As a result of a court order the accounts had been seized. Meehan broke out in a sweat and began to scan the other customers in the large bank building. If they had found the accounts then the Gardaí could easily be standing around waiting for him. Meehan ran out of the building.

Five days later, the High Court granted the Criminal Assets Bureau an order preventing Brian and Kevin Meehan from disposing of the bank accounts in Austria and the Isle of Man. Peter Charleton SC, counsel for the CAB, told the court that while Kevin Meehan was in court for the hearing, the whereabouts of his son were not known. He claimed that both the father and son had gone to considerable lengths to disguise the whereabouts of the cash. Kevin Meehan told the judge that he would not be able to send a copy of the documents served on him to his son.

In October 1997 Brian Meehan was arrested in Holland, on foot of an international warrant issued by the Special Criminal Court in Dublin. The Tosser was to face charges for possession of firearms, drug trafficking and the murder of Veronica Guerin. Meehan and John Traynor were both lifted after being ambushed by undercover Dutch police on a street in the centre of Amsterdam. Undercover Gardaí, working with their Dutch colleagues, had secretly followed one of Meehan's girlfriends who flew from Dublin to meet him for a dirty weekend. Traynor was released from custody because the DPP back in Dublin felt there was still insufficient evidence with which to charge him for murder, drugs or firearms' offences. Meehan was remanded in custody and began a legal attempt to prevent his extradition. Exactly a year after his arrest he was flown back to Ireland to stand trial. In July 1999 he was convicted on all charges, including the journalist's murder.

Kevin and Thomas Meehan were both subsequently charged with money laundering offences as a result of the CAB investigation. Kevin Meehan was jailed for five years in 2000, after being found guilty of six counts of money laundering. But in 2002 the Court of Criminal Appeal overturned his conviction and he walked free. In the meantime his brother, Thomas, had pleaded guilty and was given two years inside. In the Meehan family there was not much respect for blood ties. It was revealed that Thomas Meehan was living in fear that his own nephew was going to have him murdered as a result of his decision to co-operate with Gardaí.

* * * *

On Wednesday July 16, 1997, Michael Hanahoe and Company began their judicial review proceedings in the High Court against District Judge Gillian Hussey, the Garda Commissioner and the State. The lawyers sought an order from the court to quash the original search warrant granted by Judge Hussey to the Money Laundering Investigation Unit in October 1996. The State denied there was an error in law or that it had acted in excess of jurisdiction. The State also denied it had alerted the media about the raid.

Counsel for Hanahoes, Donal O'Donnell SC, described the raid as "unprecedented in the history of the legal profession in this State". The Managing Partner of the firm, Tony

Hanahoe, told the court of murder threats and "outrageous damage" to his firm's reputation as a result of the publicity surrounding the Garda search. Mr Hanahoe said that colleagues had told him that being the recipient of a warrant was not that serious. But the ordinary 'Joe Soap' on the street, who happened to be the firm's client, took a certain view and believed that "a raid was a raid". Clients had asked him what he had done; there was a stigma attached. His father and mother had received calls talking about someone being wiped out or about a son being killed. People had come in and run up and down the stairs in the firm's premises shouting "effing drug barons" and "effing murderers". His own kids had been told at school that the firm only represented drug barons. There had been murder threats he said, which had been passed on to the Gardaí. He had also been worried about the health of one of his brothers who was also a solicitor; there were a lot of dangerous people about and a lot of dangerous 'leaks', and he was afraid his brother was going to get caught up in this.

There was a heightened interest in anything relating to Veronica Guerin and the court also heard evidence that an anonymous caller had tipped off the news desks of a number of daily newspapers a short time before the raid began.

Detective Inspector Terry McGinn, of the MLIU, told Mr Justice Kinlen that Gilligan was involved in drugs and criminal activity, had access to unlawful firearms and would do whatever he could to prevent her obtaining evidence. She said he was a very dangerous criminal. The officer said she had been involved in Operation Pineapple since April 1996, investigating money laundering and drug trafficking. John and Geraldine Gilligan were among the main targets. DI McGinn stated that if she had served an order seeking the production of the documents on Hanahoes, the solicitors' firm would have been obliged to look for instructions from its clients. Gilligan would have then become aware she was trying to obtain documents. She felt that Gilligan would have frustrated her efforts in any way he could – by the time she got a search warrant, the documents would be gone.

When asked about the leak, Det. Insp. McGinn said that, apart from the people at the September 20 meeting in Garda HQ, the only person to whom she spoke was a Garda Inspector on October 2 about computer information. The search team was not briefed until noon on October 3, when she had explained that this was a very sensitive search of the offices of prominent Dublin solicitors, and therefore the Gardaí wanted to keep it secret. No one had made a telephone call during the meeting.

In his evidence Assistant Commissioner Tony Hickey said that the leak could have come from an individual eavesdropping on his investigation centre. Hickey gave the example of the bugging plot by Dutchie Holland to illustrate what he and his colleagues were up against. The Gardaí had been forced to carry out 'sweeps' for bugging devices in the offices of Garda headquarters, the Criminal Assets Bureau and Lucan Garda station. Hickey testified that part of the discussion at the Lucan meeting concerned the calibre of people the Gardaí were dealing with and in particular Gilligan and his associates. Investigations had revealed that they were ruthless people and that Gilligan had threatened to shoot anybody whom he thought was going to get in his way. The meeting's concern was that if Gilligan had knowledge of what they were trying to do he would do anything to frustrate those attempts. Therefore the consensus was to seek a search warrant for his solicitor's offices.

Andrew Smyth, who had been President of the Law Society at the time of the search, told the court that he felt a great wrong had been done to the firm. He had written to the Garda Commissioner suggesting that a public apology to the firm would be in order. He was extremely disappointed when the Commissioner did not express regret about the incident.

In his evidence Barry Galvin criticised Andrew Smyth's request. Galvin said that as President of the Law Society, Mr Smyth had asked for an apology for a media leak relating to the search for documents. If the Commissioner had been approached in a manner other than seeking to blame the Gardaí for the leak, Galvin could see no reason why an agreed statement would not have been forthcoming. Galvin said he believed "a process" was taking place in which Gardaí were trying to find out how the anonymous calls came to be made. He felt that a Law Society statement following the search ought to have been in terms that solicitors had nothing to fear from proceeds of crime investigations and that there was nothing wrong just because a search warrant was being served on them. The firm of Michael E Hanahoe and Company was well-known for acting in criminal cases and was known for its integrity.

On November 14, the High Court delivered its judgement in the case. Mr Justice Kinlen ruled that the issuing of the search warrant in the District Court had been lawful. But he awarded the company IR£100,000 (€127,000) in damages against the State, over the leak to the media. He said it had been: "A wilful act which had done the Hanahoes considerable and probably irreparable harm ...It was an outrageous interference with their privacy and their constitutional rights...". Mr Justice Kinlen said that as "a matter of probability" the leak emanated from the Gardaí.

He stated: "This court must mark its strong disapproval of this conduct and try and make some amends to the applicants for the damage done. I hope that this judgement will clarify public perception of the wrong that was done to these eminent solicitors."

The Gardaí involved in the case continued to stress their belief that it was not one of their people who had leaked the information. However senior officers were happy that the search warrant had been upheld. If the court had quashed the warrant it could have had long-term damaging implications for the future of the Criminal Assets Bureau.

* * * *

John Gilligan continued to dominate the headlines over the next decade. In 2001, the Special Criminal Court convicted

Gilligan on drug trafficking charges and jailed him for 28 years. But he was acquitted of the murder of Veronica Guerin. The nasty godfather had used his favourite weapon to escape conviction. Two vital witnesses, Martin Baltus and Gilligan's former girlfriend, Carol Rooney, refused to testify at his trial. The life of Baltus' daughter was threatened by members of Gilligan's gang in Holland – if Baltus gave evidence she would be murdered. The evidence of Rooney and Baltus would have provided essential corroboration that would, most likely, have resulted in Gilligan's conviction for murder.

The godfather's sentence was subsequently reduced to 20 years on appeal. He continued to fight his conviction but in November 2005 he lost his final appeal in the Supreme Court. In its judgement, the highest court in the land, suggested that there had in fact been enough evidence to convict Gilligan of the murder in 2001. In other words the Supreme Court would not have overturned a murder conviction against Gilligan based on the evidence presented before it in the appeal.

John Gilligan also kept the Criminal Assets Bureau busy as he fought them every inch of the process. In February 2006, the High Court dismissed another attempt by Gilligan to stop the CAB confiscating his property. The President of the High Court, Mr Justice Joseph Finnegan, dismissed a claim by Gilligan and his wife Geraldine that the Proceeds of Crime Act did not apply to their property and that sections of the Act were repugnant to the Constitution. As the tenth anniversary of the Bureau approached in June 2006, John Gilligan's attempts to stop the CAB in the courts were nearing the final stages. The Criminal Assets Bureau was confident that they would soon be selling off Gilligan's properties.

Meanwhile the Untouchables had not given up their quest to uncover the rest of Gilligan's drug fortune. Drug trafficker Liam Judge was suspected of laundering a huge portion of Gilligan's millions, buying a large portfolio of property and businesses in Alicante in Spain. Judge, who had also worked for the Penguin, George Mitchell, and the Gardaí as a secret informant, died suddenly from a heart attack in December 2003. Judge, who was from Allenwood in County Kildare, had been living with Treacy Gilligan in Spain. His death caused the mob boss a major headache as all the properties were legally in Judge's name. In 2004 Garda intelligence sources confirmed that they believed Gilligan was again operating a drug trafficking business from his jail cell. As part of ongoing operations, the Garda National Drug Unit had busted several members of Gilligan's gang in Spain and Dublin and seized cocaine with street values running into millions of euro. The CAB also suspected that the drug money is still being laundered in Spain by Gilligan's associates.

At the time of writing, the officers of the Criminal Assets Bureau were spending a lot of time in Spain. John Gilligan's name will feature in their files for a long time to come.

Six

The Monk and his Mob

The queue of people waiting to sign the Book of Condolences filled the lobby of the busy newspaper building. The line stretched out the front doors and for some distance down Middle Abbey Street. The public had turned out in large numbers to convey their disgust at Veronica Guerin's murder. Signatures and flowers expressed their sense of anger and sadness. The leaders of Church and State, the captains of industry and various celebrities had joined them. The signatories came from every walk of life. Even the country's most illusive criminal mastermind came to scribble his name.

The lightly built, well-dressed man didn't get a second glance as he stood quietly amidst the throng. He was an anonymous face in the crowd, just another person who had come to register his outrage and disgust. The two detectives who were watching him did not stand out much either. A lot of cops had also come to sign their names. They shuffled up behind Gerry Hutch, alias the Monk, as he took his turn to sign the book in the HQ of Independent Newspapers. When he had signed, the officers quickly wrote their names and hurried through the door after him. The Monk had condemned the journalist's murder as a senseless crime. He had predicted that it would make life difficult for the ordinary decent criminal, like himself. But he had no idea of just how much difficulty he was going to experience as a result. In a cruel twist of fate the murder was about to change his world forever.

Within days of its establishment in August 1996, the Bureau commenced a top-secret investigation into the Monk's gang. It was codenamed Operation Alpha. At the time the Bureau used the Greek alphabet to denote each operation in order of priority. Despite the investigations into John Gilligan, the Monk was officially given first place. Operation Alpha would last longer than any other investigation ever undertaken by the CAB.

Two years later, on June 12, 1998, a *Sunday World* photographer caught the publicity-shy godfather, as he left a gleaming Dublin office block with his accountant and solicitor. Also in the frame were Detective Superintendent Felix McKenna and Detective Inspector John McDermott from the Criminal Assets Bureau. Armed officers kept watch from discreet vantage points in the side streets – just in case there were any misunderstandings between the gangster and his tormentors. Hutch was fighting a huge tax bill and had been attending a hearing before the Revenue Appeals Commissioner. The bill for IR£2 million (€2.5 million) had been calculated on his earnings from the largest cash robberies in the history of the State. The Monk and his associates stole over IR£4 million (€5million) in two of those heists. It was inevitable that his name, and the names of his fellow gangsters, were going to feature high on the first hit list drawn up by the Untouchables.

In a ten year period – between 1996 and 2006 – Operation Alpha had uncovered an incredibly complex web of money laundering, involving a fortune that ran into tens of millions of euro. The investigation operated like ripples on a pond. Hutch and his armed robbery gang were at the centre point. And as the ongoing inquiry spread out, other individuals, including several businessmen and professionals, were also exposed and their names were added to the hit list.

By spring 2006, Operation Alpha had still not reached the outer ripples of this enormous conspiracy. By the early summer a hard core of twenty people, including Hutch and his gangland pals, had either paid, or were in the process of paying, tax assessments worth in excess of a staggering €40 million. The Criminal Assets Bureau had made the Monk's heists pay – for the public exchequer.

* * * *

Gerard Hutch was born in Dublin's bleak north inner-city in April 1963. He was the sixth child in a family of eight, born to 'Masher' and Julia Hutch. Masher Hutch worked as a labourer in the Dublin docks, unloading coal from ships. Like the rest of their neighbours and friends the Hutchs were forced to grow up in poverty. The family lived in Corporation Buildings, a rundown tenement where the children had to sleep in one room and a communal toilet served the whole block of flats. When Hutch was eight they moved to nearby Summerhill.

In the same year, 1971, Hutch received his first conviction when he appeared in the Children's Court, charged with larceny. Growing up in such a deprived area, which society had effectively ignored, with poor levels of education, living conditions and employment, crime was a way of life. It was the only way that people felt they could get on. There was no respect for the law in this criminogenic environment. By the late 1970s, Hutch and his peers hung out in a gang of tough young teenage tearaways who terrorised the city centre. They were nicknamed the Bugsy Malones, after the famous children's gangster spoof movie in which the bad guys were armed with machine guns that fired cream cakes. The Bugsys, however, preferred to use bullets instead of cream cakes. The youngsters would rob banks by racing inside, jumping over the counter and ordering the tellers to load the cash into bags at gunpoint. They were often in and out of a bank or post office in minutes, before vanishing into the maze of inner-city streets that were their natural habitat. They were also involved in highly dangerous joy riding, racing stolen cars and jousting with the police during chases. One of their favourite stunts was to spend the proceeds of robberies on foreign holidays and then send postcards, addressed to individual officers, to the local Garda stations at Store Street and Fitzgibbon Street.

The gang attracted considerable media attention as a result

of their exploits. On one occasion RTÉ radio did a news item on the gang during which 16-year-old Gerry Hutch was interviewed. It was the only candid interview he ever gave, either to the media or to the cops in numerous Garda interview rooms.

The cheeky youngster bragged: "I can't give up robbin'. If I see money in a car I'm takin' it. I just can't leave it there. If I see a handbag on a seat I'll smash the window and be away before anyone knows what's goin' on. I don't go near people walking along the street...they don't have any money on them. They're not worth robbin'.".

When he was asked what he wanted to be when he grew up he giggled: "I'd like to be serving behind the bank... just fill up the bags and jump over the counter."

In a later newspaper interview with Veronica Guerin in 1996, Hutch made no secret of his criminal origins: "We were kids then, doing jump-overs [jumping over bank counters to steal cash], shoplifting, robberies, burglaries, anything that was going we did it. That was normal for any inner-city kid then."

Gerry Hutch notched up over thirty convictions for burglary, assault, larceny, car theft, joy riding and malicious damage in the twelve years following his first appearance in the Children's Court. He was jailed eleven times and served his sentences in the notorious St Lawrences Industrial School in Finglas, Saint Patrick's Institution for Young Offenders and later Mountjoy Prison. While inside, he taught himself to read and write, firstly by reading comics and then books.

From childhood the gangster harboured a deep affection for his own people and the neighbourhood where he grew up. From his late teens the hoodlum stood out from the rest of his peers as different and much cleverer. The quiet, intense young man didn't drink and assiduously avoided the heroin scourge that devastated his neighbourhood in the early 1980s. Several of his old friends from the Bugsy Malones became addicts and at least four of them died as a result. Several of his cousins, the Dixons, also perished, as did members of his wife's family.

As a result Hutch despised the hard drug culture and the criminals who prospered from it.

The Monk was also a dedicated family man. Hutch was careful with his money and looked after his girlfriend, Patricia Fowler, when she fell pregnant with their first child, a daughter, in December 1981. The couple soon married and would have five children together. Unlike many of his associates, the marriage remained solid through the years. In the same month that he became a dad, the eighteen-year-old Hutch paid IR£10,000 (€12,500) for a home for his new family on Buckingham Street, in the heart of his old neighbourhood. The Monk believed in giving his kids all the opportunities he didn't have while growing up – with a little help from the proceeds of his various heists.

In 1981 Hutch was almost caught after an armed hold up. A gang of armed and masked men, carrying machine guns and pistols, hit the AIB branch in Mary Street in the city centre. As they left the bank they were rumbled by a passing Garda patrol. Shots were exchanged as the mobsters made a run for it in a clapped out old van they had stolen earlier. Hutch and his mates were later arrested and questioned about the attempt but there was insufficient evidence to sustain a charge against them. The Monk's associates and the Gardaí who knew him best, all claim that Hutch swore he'd never get involved in another badly planned 'stroke' again.

A year later, in November 1982, his friend Eamon Byrne, a fellow member of the Bugsy Malones, died after being shot in the back of the neck by Gardaí during a botched raid on a ship in Dublin docks. The Gardaí claimed the shooting was an accident. Hutch and his friends later took part in protests against the Gardaí as part of the Prisoners Rights Organisation. They were also suspected of involvement in the violent crime mob called the Prisoner's Revenge Group, who targeted prison officers in a campaign of intimidation.

In December 1983 he was jailed for two years for malicious damage. He was released in May 1985. It was to be his last recorded conviction and Hutch promised himself that he would never do time again.

When he came out of prison Hutch moved into the big league of organised crime. He soon earned a reputation as a clever criminal mastermind who carefully planned robberies, down to the last detail. But he was also regarded as a potentially dangerous enemy. One former associate recalled: "Gerard was a very cold fish and very calculating. He didn't go looking for trouble and minded his own business but if you fucked with him you were walking on thin ice."

The Monk stood out from many of the other young criminals because he was shrewd with money and learned from the older villains on the block. His favourite role models were two of Dublin's most feared criminal brothers, Eamon and Matt Kelly.

As a youngster Hutch ran 'errands' and worked for the Kellys, who were also from the north inner-city. Eamon Kelly, who was also listed as a memeber of the Official IRA, was a professional armed robber with a fearsome reputation for violence. He was later jailed for 15 years for his part in a cocaine-smuggling operation. Matt, his older brother who was born in 1944, however was not connected to the drug trade. He was the brain behind other criminal enterprises. Unlike his sibling, Matt had only incurred a handful of criminal convictions involving larceny, burglary and assault.

The brothers had owned a large carpet business, Kellys Carpetdrome, on the North Circular Road. Garda intelligence at the time believed that the business was used for the purpose of laundering money but nothing could be done about it. In 1981 the carpet company had been wound up by the High Court and a liquidator was appointed on behalf of the Revenue Commissioners, over unpaid taxes. In a controversial landmark case, the liquidator issued proceedings against the brothers to have them held personally responsible for huge debts.

The long-running case had hit the headlines in 1983 after several people involved were threatened and intimidated by the Kellys and their associates. On the first morning of the hearing, the home of the counsel leading the case for the liquidator had been targeted in an arson attack. The State's entire legal team – revenue officials, witnesses and the judge himself, Mr Justice Declan Costello – were given armed police protection for the duration of the case. Kelly's former accountant, Brendan McGoldrick, who had agreed to testify in the case, told the court that he had been threatened with murder if he opened his mouth. He said Matt Kelly and an underworld associate, Mickey Deighan, had made the threats. As a result the two hoods had been jailed for contempt of court. The accountant, who had admitted falsifying company documentation on behalf of Kelly, was forced to live under armed police protection for several years, such was the gangster's reputation.

The court later held that the business of the company was carried on from October 1976 to February 1980 with "intent to defraud creditors" and for "other fraudulent purposes". The court also ruled that both brothers were "knowingly parties" to carrying the business on in a dodgy manner. Both men were held liable for all debts, including a IR£1.8 million (€2.3 million) tax bill and Matt Kelly was made a bankrupt, meaning that he was barred from setting up any business or company until he had paid his debts. Under Irish Bankruptcy Law he was obliged to disclose all of the assets he acquired to the Official Assignee in Bankruptcy – the legal official who deals with bankruptcy cases. But despite his problems the former carpet king secretly became an extremely wealthy property developer. And he would teach Hutch everything he knew about laundering money. It wouldn't be long before the Monk would have plenty to invest.

* * * *

At 5.30 pm on January 26, 1987 the three-man crew of a Securicor van made their last pick up, IR£125,000 (€159,000), at the Bank of Ireland at Marino Mart, Fairview in north Dublin. During the day they had collected a few hundred pounds less than IR£1.5 million (€1.9 million) which they were transporting to Securicor's main cash holding centre. As the front seat observer, Brian Holden, was getting back into the van outside the bank a red BMW pulled up behind it and three armed and masked men jumped out. One of the raiders, armed with a handgun, pointed it into his face. "Get out or I'll blow your fucking head off," he shouted. A second raider armed with a rifle joined the first and they both pulled the guard from the van and threw him to the ground. The security officer was kicked and warned to stay down or have his head "blown off". At the same time a third raider appeared at the opposite door and pointed a gun at the head of the driver, Thomas Kennedy. He was ordered to hand over the keys and get out.

The Monk and one of his accomplices jumped in behind the wheel of the van and they drove off. The other two robbers got into the BMW and followed. Up the road they stopped and pushed out a third security officer, Simon Foley, who they had discovered in the vault, in the back of the van. The gang drove the van a short distance into the grounds of Colaiste Mhuire, off Griffith Avenue. They stopped on waste ground behind the college complex, near Saint Vincent's GAA club where they unloaded the loot. The robbers abandoned the car and the van and took off in a second car. Twenty minutes later Gardaí located the abandoned vehicles. Both the cash and the Monk's mob had vanished.

Later that night Hutch and his crew met in a safe house to count the cash. They had expected to get between IR£25,000 (€32,000) and IR£100,000 (€127,000). It took them the whole night to count the money. When they had finished the robbers were, according to former associates, absolutely stunned. The large stack of money sitting in the middle of the floor came to IR£1,357,106 (€1,723,000). They had just pulled off the largest cash robbery in the history of organised crime in Ireland. The Monk and his mates had elevated themselves to the hierarchy of serious crime.

Hours after the heist, Garda intelligence nominated a

number of possible suspects for the audacious crime. The General, as a matter of course, was high on the list and so too were the villains associated with John Gilligan. But cops based in the north inner-city mentioned the activities of a small group of new hoods on the block.

Matt Kelly advised the Monk to take charge of disposing of the money. The plan was to simply lodge it in a number of financial institutions across the border in Newry, County Down. Hutch approached two men to move the cash. Francis Joseph Sheridan and Lonan Patrick Hickey were perfect for the job. They weren't known to the police and had no criminal records. Thirty-one-year-old Sheridan was a timber salesman who lived with his wife and three children in Swords, County Dublin. An ex-soldier, he had been introduced to Gerry Hutch by another older criminal figure, Niall Mulvihill.

Hickey was the same age as Sheridan and lived at Church Avenue in Drumcondra. Well-educated and fluent in French and Spanish he once had a promising career. At the age of seventeen he had worked as a translator for a Mexican TV company. He moved to live in the USA and got involved in the carpet business as a salesman, a job he continued when he returned to Ireland. But Hickey hit hard times when his business went bust and he broke his back in a car crash leaving him mildly disabled. Shortly after that he became unemployed. He was in serious financial difficulties when Hutch offered him a chance to earn IR£2,000 (€2,500) in cash.

Four days after the robbery Sheridan met Hutch in the car park of the Halfway House pub on the Navan Road in Dublin. The Monk handed over IR£320,000 (€406,500) in cash. Sheridan was told he would be given instructions over the next two weeks about delivering quantities of the cash to Hickey.

On February 3, Hutch instructed Sheridan to deliver IR£30,000 (€38,000) to Hickey at Church Avenue in Drumcondra. Following the hand over Hickey drove to the Ulster Bank in Newry, where he tried to buy a sterling bank draft, made payable to the Abbey National Building Society.

The bank advised Hickey to go directly to the building society himself and open an account there. The building society, however, would not accept the IR£30,000 (€38,000) as an opening balance until he changed it into sterling. Hickey opened an account in his own name with Stg£26,697 (€39,000).

The following day, February 5, Hickey met Hutch in the Cat and Cage pub in Drumcondra and explained the trouble he'd had lodging the stolen money. The Monk had also travelled to Newry the same day and opened an account with the Anglia Building Society at Marcus Square in the town. The account was in Hutch's name and gave his address, Number 25, Buckingham Street. He had opened the account with a lodgement of Stg£1,372 (€2,007).

The following day, Hickey returned to Newry with IR£40,000 (€51,000). His first call was to the Abbey National Building Society where he withdrew the Stg£26,000 (€38,000) he had lodged two days earlier. It was in a sterling bank draft made out to Gerry Hutch. Hickey then went to the Anglia Building Society and lodged the IR£40,000 (€51,000) into Hutch's account. That evening he gave the bank draft to the Monk.

Four days later Hickey collected another IR£40,000 (€51,000) from Sheridan. In Newry he converted it into sterling and lodged it to Gerry Hutch's building society account. The balance in the Monk's name now stood at Stg£75,279 (€110,000).

In the meantime, however, the investigation team in Raheny Garda Station and the Serious Crime Squad had been tipped off that Sheridan was moving large amounts of cash from the Marino Mart heist. The following morning Hutch called Sheridan and told him they were stepping up the laundering process. This time he instructed the bagman to bring IR£80,000 (€101,500) in cash to Hickey. At 8.25 am the undercover team tailed Sheridan in his Volkswagen Van to Church Avenue. When Sheridan arrived in Church Avenue, Hickey was waiting in his car. Sheridan handed him a large bag. Two minutes later the detectives swooped on Hickey as he drove towards Newry. He tried to drive away but was blocked by an unmarked squad car. Five minutes later another team arrested Sheridan on Gracepark Road in Drumcondra.

Later, during questioning, Sheridan admitted that the cash was from the Marino Mart job. He showed the officers the rest of the money which he had hidden in the attic of his home. In a search the detectives found two large bags containing a total of IR£129,361 (€164,000). At the same time Hickey's home was also being searched in Drumcondra. Detectives found two building society books, one in Hickey's name, the other one in Hutch's. Later Sheridan and Hickey both admitted to Gardaí that they had been working for Gerry Hutch. The two men subsequently pleaded guilty and were each sentenced to 21 months in prison. They were the only people ever charged in connection with the heist. In the Circuit Criminal Court defence counsel for the pair claimed "dangerous and ruthless men" had used Sheridan and Hickey. Hutch was referred to as 'Mr X' and he was described as being particularly dangerous.

At the same time the Gardaí contacted Securicor who then obtained an order in the Belfast High Court freezing the Monk's account. The sterling bank draft that Hickey had given Hutch was also cancelled. For a while it appeared that things were not looking good for the Monk. A file was subsequently forwarded to the Director of Public Prosecutions recommending that Hutch be charged with handling the proceeds from the heist. In the end, however, it was decided not to proceed with the case because the bagmen were not prepared to give evidence against him in court.

Despite his near miss Hutch was determined not to give up on his 'hard-earned' cash. He promptly defended the Securicor injunction in the Belfast High Court seeking its return. The company made an appeal under the Police Property Act claiming that the money was their property. The Monk actually attended some of the hearings in Belfast. In the absence of money laundering legislation he was quite literally untouchable by the law, to the utter frustration of the Gardaí. Hutch claimed in court that Hickey had been acting as his agent when he lodged the money to the account in his name in the Anglia Building Society. He didn't offer a credible explanation about the origins of the cash.

On July 30, 1992 the Right Honourable Lord Justice Murray ruled that the money in Hutch's account was in all probabilities the proceeds of the Marino Mart heist and ordered its return to Securicor. Hutch, however, was not giving up and appealed the case to the Appeal Court of Northern Ireland.

The Lord Chief Justice upheld the High Court decision on November 22, 1992. The cheeky Monk then appealed the case, this time to the House of Lords in London.

On February 23, 1994 the Lord's Appeal Committee unanimously refused the Monk leave to appeal the case and ordered that the criminal mastermind pay all costs in the various actions. After that the Monk threatened to bring the case to the European Court but he later dropped the appeal. The extraordinary events surrounding the huge robbery illustrated what life was like in the criminal underworld in the days before the CAB. The case was often cited in following years, during discussions about the need for adequate money laundering legislation across Europe. Following the introduction of such laws, by the end of 1994, a criminal who tried a similar scam would face criminal prosecution. A similar stunt today would be regarded as an act of lunacy.

* * * *

The Monk and his gang earned a formidable reputation as a result of the Marino Mart job. In the underworld he was celebrated and respected. From the Gardaí's perspective, at the time, it meant he moved up a few places on their list of most wanted gangsters. By the end of 1987, the Gardaí had compiled a report detailing the activities of major organised crime gangs in the country. The top three crime bosses in the city and country were listed as Martin Cahill, John Gilligan and Gerry Hutch. In the meantime the Monk's gang continued robbing, but not always with the same level of success.

Thomas O'Driscoll, one of the Monk's closest friends had been suspected of taking part in the Marino Mart heist. Twenty-three-year-old O'Driscoll was also a heroin addict and had served time for armed robbery in the past. Another member of the mob and a close associate of Hutch was Geoffrey Ennis. Originally from the North Strand, Ennis was a suspect in most of the gang's large-scale robberies. Both he and O'Driscoll had been in and out of detention centres and prison at the same time as Hutch.

On September 1, 1987 O'Driscoll, Geoffrey Ennis and a third robber from Crumlin hit the North Cumberland Street Labour Exchange where they collected their weekly unemployment assistance. Shortly after 10 am O'Driscoll and the Crumlin hood burst into the building. Ennis was waiting outside in the getaway car. Armed with a sawn-off shotgun, O'Driscoll covered his partner, who smashed the glass partition at Hatch 33 with a sledgehammer. But the robbery went terribly wrong when they were challenged by an armed Garda who was on duty inside the exchange.

Detective Garda Dominick Hutchin pulled his .38 revolver and ordered the hoods to drop their weapons. The two robbers opened fire on the detective, hitting him in the face and body. The injured detective fired all six rounds in his revolver at O'Driscoll, hitting him five times. The robber fell back into a sitting position still pointing the handgun at Hutchin, who retreated back inside the staff area to reload his gun and raise the alarm.

The Crumlin gangster pulled O'Driscoll to the waiting getaway car being driven by Geoffrey Ennis. O'Driscoll had been critically injured in the shooting. After a short distance he was pushed out of the getaway car and left on the side of the road, in the hope that he would receive medical aid. He died minutes later.

Gardaí later arrested thirty-seven-year-old Crumlin criminal Martin Leonard in connection with the robbery.

Geoffrey Ennis went into hiding and a third man Laurence Alford, who had loaned Ennis a car for the heist, was the only member of the gang charged. The IR£25,000 (€32,000) taken in the raid was never recovered. O'Driscoll's death had a profound affect on the Monk who was not involved in the botched robbery. A friend later told *Magill* magazine how the godfather reacted to the loss of his pal. "The only time I ever saw Gerard cry was at Thomas O'Driscoll's funeral. He was inconsolable, the tears were streaming out of him."

Geoffrey Ennis and the Monk were also suspected of masterminding a daring robbery from an Allied Irish Bank cash holding centre in Waterford. A number of months earlier the Gardaí in the area had mounted a surveillance operation after an amateur radio enthusiast taped the gangster's voice as he sent messages to an accomplice on a two-way radio. The gangster was clearly staking-out the cash centre and noting the movements of security personnel and Gardaí at the building.

But after months of inactivity the surveillance operation was called off. When the gang were sure the heat had died down they made their move. A team of armed and masked men breached a weak spot in the centre's tight security and made off with an estimated IR£2 million (€2.5 million) in cash. No one was ever charged with the job and none of the money was recovered.

* * * *

Apart from the money recovered in Dublin and Newry after the Marino Mart heist the remaining IR£1 million (€1.3 million) was never traced. On the ground, however, Garda intelligence sources were reporting that Matt Kelly and Gerry Hutch had become involved in a number of major property deals in Central Dublin. Detectives had a good idea that the two men were laundering the cash through property deals that on the surface appeared legitimate. It wasn't until Operation Alpha was launched several years later that the truth was finally uncovered. Analysis of the huge volumes of financial and legal documentation, uplifted by the Untouchables during scores of searches, gave a clear picture of how the money was laundered through the system.

A key player was Kildare man Paddy Shanahan, who had a promising career as a successful businessman until he decided to get involved in serious crime for the fun of it. He was a very unlikely villain. Born in 1946 into a respectable family, he was well-educated and studied in university. Later he worked in various jobs and set up a number of businesses. But he had a natural talent for armed robbery. He worked with the Dunnes while they were still holding up banks and with the General. Later he went to England and began specialising in the theft of antiques. For his trouble he got a five-year prison sentence. When he returned to Ireland he went to the General with a plan to rob the priceless Beit paintings. Cahill liked the idea and in 1986 pulled off the second largest art heist in the world, without Shanahan's assistance. Fed up dealing with double-crossing villains, Shanahan set up a building company and began buying properties around Dublin in the years before the Celtic Tiger. In 1987 he went into business with Matt Kelly and Gerry Hutch.

Within a few months of the Marino Mart job, Paddy Shanahan agreed to buy a large property portfolio on Talbot Street and Foley Street in the north inner-city. The robber-turned-builder purchased the property from an old acquaintance of his, property developer Jim Mansfield. The pair had met in the early 1980s when they were both involved in a successful business venture involving machinery, vehicles and scrap that had been abandoned following the Falklands War in 1982. Mansfield had bought up the war materials and later auctioned them off in the UK for a large profit. The sharp businessman used the profits to speculate on the property market. Mansfield went on to build a huge hotel and property empire which was worth hundreds of millions of euro by 2006. According to documentation later unearthed by Fachtna Murphy's officers, Shanahan appeared to act as a front man in the purchase of the Talbot and Foley Street properties, on behalf of Hutch. In one search the Bureau found an un-executed deed and correspondence for the property in Hutch's name. The Untouchables discovered that Shanahan had really purchased the properties for Hutch and Matt Kelly.

In October 1987, Shanahan's construction company, Manito Enterprises, began refurbishment work at Buckingham Buildings in the heart of Hutch's old neighbourhood. The disused tenement complex was to be turned into modern apartments. The second stage of the development was the erection of a new block of apartments on a vacant site next door. Buckingham Village, as it was renamed, contained 100 apartments in total. They were largely rented by the recipients of Eastern Health Board rental support and later on by foreign immigrants and asylum seekers.

The development was the first to qualify for the tax incentives designed to encourage growth in the inner-city areas. As part of the CAB investigations it was discovered that Shanahan had also been laundering money through his construction business for a number of other major gangland figures. But the majority of the money invested in the project could later be traced back to the Monk and his mentor. Operation Alpha would also uncover a number of other investors, including George 'The Penguin' Mitchell, who either directly or indirectly had strong links with organised crime. Buckingham Village, they discovered, was built on the proceeds of drug trafficking and armed robbery. In hindsight it is ironic that the criminal fraternity were behind the first major investments in the depressed inner-city before the construction boom began in the mid-1990s. In the meantime Hutch continued to invest in the property market.

In August 1989, Hutch paid IR£20,000 (€25,000) for two more houses on Buckingham Street which were next door to the one he already owned. He converted the houses into rented accommodation for the Eastern Health Board. In 1993 he purchased another property on the street. When the Criminal Assets Bureau came knocking on his door the clever crook claimed the Department of Justice had actually given the money to him! The Department paid him IR£25,000 (€32,000) in compensation for two personal injuries claims while he was an inmate in Mountjoy Prison. With a wide grin on his face he could also prove the origins of another IR£8,000 (€10,000) he had received. The money was compensation for a "whiplash" incurred when a Securicor van shunted into the back of his car!

In the same year he decided to go legitimate with his landlord business and availed of the controversial tax amnesty. Under the terms of the amnesty, which was designed to give tax dodgers a clean slate and bring them into the tax net, Hutch did not have to disclose how he made his money in the first place. He claimed that he had earned just over IR£30,000 (€38,000) renting out his properties between 1991 and 1994. He paid a total of IR£9,000 (€11,500) in back tax, after signing a declaration that his statement was true and accurate. Marino Mart was not mentioned.

Although the north inner-city was his spiritual home, the Monk decided to move his family to more upmarket Clontarf. And while it was geographically only two miles to the north it was a world away from his old neighbourhood. The crime lord paid IR£100,000 (€127,000), IR£70,000 (€89,000) of which was in the form of a mortgage, for a comfortable four-bedroom house in a quiet cul de sac in the leafy coastal suburb. By that time his fifth child had just been born and he wanted his kids to have all the things he did not have. He enrolled all his children in private fee-paying schools on the south side of the city. It wouldn't be long before he needed a fresh injection of cash.

In 1993 Shanahan began construction of a shop and apartment complex called Drury Hall in Stephen Street, on the south side of the River Liffey. Again Hutch and Kelly could be identified as secret financial backers. Four years later, the Untouchables traced the payment of two sterling bank drafts worth Stg£130,000 (€190,000). They were lodged into a company owned by Shanahan. The Bureau discovered that the money had been withdrawn from an account held in the name of Hutch's wife, Patricia Fowler, in the First Trust Bank at Queen's Square in Belfast. The lodgements had been made on October 28 and November 3, 1993, as work commenced on the project.

In August 1994, Shanahan's old friend Martin Cahill was shot dead. After that the builder appeared to be extremely stressed and on edge according to his friends. Then two months later, on October 14, a lone gunman emerged from the shadows as Shanahan walked into his gym in Crumlin, south Dublin. The assassin shot the former gangster once in the face at point-blank range. The killer calmly walked out to the nearby roadway and jogged off, disappearing into the busy traffic and the gathering gloom of an autumn dusk. It was the last thing either Hutch or Kelly needed at that point in time. Gardaí still suspect that Shanahan was murdered by one of the underworld associates whose money he had been laundering through the construction business. Detectives who investigated the gangland murder said they were confident that they knew the identity of the killer and the criminal who organised it. They later sent a file to the Director of Public Prosecutions, recommending that he be charged with murder. However the DPP decided there was insufficient evidence with which to proceed and the case was dropped.

It was later discovered that Hutch in particular was extremely angry over the callous execution. Apart from the prospect of losing a lot of money as a result of the murder, Shanahan had also been a friend. It was a volatile period in gangland, after the murder of two major gangland figures in such a short space of time. It was reported that the godfather confronted the man suspected of organising the murder but within weeks the Monk had other matters to occupy his active mind. He and his gang were plotting another historic heist.

* * * *

In January 1995 five armed and masked men took off with

IR£2.8 million (€3.6 million) from the Brinks Allied security company's cash holding depot in North Dublin. It was a meticulously executed robbery that had taken months of planning. The Brinks Allied depot was housed in a specially converted factory in Clonshaugh Industrial Estate in Coolock on the northern edge of Dublin. At the time it was surrounded by undeveloped land and to the west the M1 Motorway was under construction.

Planning for the job could be traced back to October 1994. Two days after the Shanahan murder a businessman, who was working for Hutch and Geoffrey Ennis, had rented a disused shed at Oldtown in North County Dublin to store the vehicles which would be used on the job.

Garda intelligence later reported that the so-called Brinks team included long-standing associates of Hutch, Gerry Lee and Willy Scully who were both originally from Coolock. Paul Boyle and Noel Murphy from East Wall were also on board. The gang had carried out surveillance on Brinks Allied cash vans, as they made collections around the city and transported them back to the depot. Gardaí also suspected that the gang were helped by a member of staff, working for the large security company.

In November 1994, there had been a major alert when Gardaí spotted a member of the gang watching a security van at the North Side Shopping Centre in Coolock. The Monk and his associates were placed under secret surveillance. At the time it was suspected that the gang were planning a repeat performance of the Marino Mart job, by hitting a cash van in transit. Surveillance teams, backed up by the Emergency Response Unit (ERU) and the Serious Crime Squad, had watched the suspects for almost two months. But just before Christmas the operation was scaled down because it seemed that the gangsters had abandoned their plans. But the surveillance teams were wrong.

On the night of December 1, 1994, the gang had organised the theft of two Mitsubishi Pajero jeeps from a garage compound in Limerick, despite the Garda attention. The jeeps were hidden in the rented shed in north Dublin. Ten days later two more jeeps had been stolen for the heist. It was more than a coincidence that one of them belonged to Paddy Shanahan. He had been driving the Pajero on the night of his murder, three months earlier. A second stolen jeep belonged to the world-renowned musician Phil Coulter. On December 8, an associate of the gang, John Good, who owned a motor bike and jet ski company in central Dublin, had ordered four sets of false number plates from a motor parts company. The plates had been collected the next day. Gardaí were later told that Good had been asked to order the plates by Paul Boyle.

On January 17, 1995 another urgent Garda circular had been issued to all stations and units warning that Hutch and his gang were planning a major-armed robbery. The document named Gerry Hutch and eleven other suspected members of the gang, including Lee, Ennis, Boyle and Scully. The document stated: "Information to hand suggests that a number of prominent criminals are planning a major armed robbery. The likely target is money in transit by a security company."

At 6.25 pm on the evening of January 24, a security van with call sign Yankee 29 returned to Clonshaugh Industrial Estate. It had collected almost IR£3 million (€3.8 million) in used notes from various AIB branches in the south-east. The security van drove through the front gate of the Brinks Allied complex and around to the rear of the building for unloading. The police and troops who had been escorting the van during the day turned and drove away, once it was safely inside the complex. Two other vans and their escorts had arrived earlier and entered the complex. The gang knew that Yankee 29 was to be the last van back to the depot that evening. Eyewitnesses later recalled seeing a flare being fired into the air as the escort left the area.

The plan was to strike at the rear of the building, just as the last cash van was returning. The raiders would approach through the fields, from a roadway that had been blocked off due to ongoing motorway works. The area provided perfect cover for the gangsters. It was unlit and there was no traffic.

In the days before the robbery a section of perimeter fence between the fields at the back of the depot had been removed. A ditch had been breached to allow the gang to drive through to a second field immediately behind the Brinks Allied premises.

At 5.30 pm five men were spotted driving in a jeep up Turnapin Lane towards the fields. They drove through the hole in the fence and joined a second jeep that had already driven into the field. The gang then drove up to the perimeter fence at the rear of a warehouse adjoining the Brinks Allied depot. Outside a ditch bordered the fence, six feet deep. The clever crooks had bridged the dyke the previous weekend, using railway sleepers and sheets of fibreboard. The top portion of the makeshift bridge had even been painted green to camouflage it. Strips of timber had been fastened to the top sheets to improve the jeeps' grip when they were driving across.

The perimeter fence at the warehouse had also been loosened in the preparation work and took only seconds to remove. The two jeeps drove across the bridge and through the fence into the warehouse yard. Now all that separated them from the cash-loading bay was a simple steel fence. Again there was evidence of the meticulous planning involved. The gang had already weakened the dividing fence by cutting the support bars some time earlier.

As Yankee 29 drove into the loading bay, the roller shutter doors were being lowered. The first jeep drove at speed through the weakened fence between the warehouse and the Brinks Allied depot. It then rammed the shutter door, pushing it inwards and up, leaving a gap large enough on either side for the raiders to get in. The shutter door was hit with such force that it also shunted the security van forward.

Three armed gang members ran in under the door and threatened the startled staff who were unloading the cash into the depot's vaults. The raiders, one of whom was carrying an AK-47 assault rifle, had fired a number of shots into the air to subdue the staff. They then began grabbing the cash bags and carrying them to the second jeep which had reversed up to the dividing fence between the warehouse and the cash depot.

The gang were finished in less than ten minutes. They jumped into the jeep and, in darkness, drove out through the hole in the warehouse fence, across the makeshift bridge and down through the adjoining field. A reflective road sign, from the motorway construction site, had been left at the breach at the ditch bordering the second field to indicate the position of the hole.

The Monk, his gang and the largest haul of cash ever stolen in the Irish Republic then vanished.

The success of the Brinks' gang had exposed glaring weaknesses in the security at the depot. The perimeter fences were not alarmed and the security shutter to the bay was not strong enough to resist ramming. When detectives studied the security video footage they found them to be of such poor quality that they could not even make out descriptions of the raiders. Later that night Geoffrey Ennis was arrested under Section 30 of the Offences Against the State Act near his home on the North Strand. A search of his car revealed a number of traffic cones and wet and muddy overalls and boots. He was held for 48 hours and released without charge. He had refused to open his mouth. Within days most of the gang, including Hutch, brought their families on a luxury holiday to Florida. The heat of the sun was a welcome alternative from the sort of heat they were attracting back in Ireland.

Inevitably the Brinks Allied job created a new criminal celebrity – one who could replace the General. The media revealed that the suspected mastermind was a faceless character, nicknamed the Monk. It was the first time the public became familiar with the name and overnight Gerry Hutch was a household name. Within hours Garda intelligence had quickly nominated the gang responsible for the robbery. Hutch, Scully, Lee, Boyle and Murphy were arrested the following September. In a strange coincidence the gangsters were lifted on the same day John Gilligan attacked Veronica Guerin at his home. None of the gang was ever charged in connection with the spectacular crime and the money was never located.

A year later the *Sunday World* ran an exclusive front-page picture of the Monk and other members of the Brinks gang when they attended Gerry Lee's funeral. A lone gunman had shot Lee twice in the chest as he was celebrating his 31st birthday on March 9, 1996 in a house in Coolock. He had died instantly from his wounds. At first it was thought that Lee had been hit because of his involvement in the drug trade. He was suspected of investing his share of the heist in ecstasy. But detectives later discovered that a woman had ordered the murder.

As a result of the major exposé and speculation after Lee's death, Hutch agreed to do an interview with Veronica Guerin at her home. He was anxious to let it be known that he was not involved in the drug trade, even though the *Sunday World* had not suggested that he was. Although he flatly denied any involvement in the Brinks job he was quoted as saying: "The Brinks was a brilliant job. The best of luck to whoever done it."

Guerin asked Hutch where he got his money. "I don't think it's your business where I get me money from. The guards know where I got it and they know it's legal," he replied.

Hutch also explained his insistence on loyalty among friends and associates which had kept him on the right side of a prison fence. "My philosophy in life is simple enough. No betrayal. That means you don't talk about others, you don't grass and you never let people down."

Hutch had taken a major step in coming out from the shadows to talk to the reporter. It was ironic that the same reporter's murder would have such dramatic consequences in the life of the country's most successful thief, less than three months later.

* * * *

The Monk might have been adamant that it was no one's business where he got his money, but nobody had the courtesy to pass the message onto the Criminal Assets Bureau. The Untouchables now knew that they would soon have the power to go and find that out for themselves. They wouldn't even have to disturb the gangsters – just yet! Nor would they be scared off by threats and intimidation. The Brinks Allied investigators could find no forensics and no witnesses to help them catch the robbers. But there were plenty of forensics of a different kind available for the Untouchables to pursue. The purpose of the Bureau was to make criminals pay, even if they had not been convicted. As a result, the CAB's main success was punishing crime lords who would otherwise have escaped the net. Operation Alpha was about to give some of the hardest men in the criminal world something to fear.

In the first meetings between Fachtna Murphy, Barry Galvin and Felix McKenna, the Monk was foremost in their minds. Recalled one insider: "When we went after Gilligan we had effectively taken over Operation Pineapple which had begun with another unit. We were also working in conjunction with the Lucan Investigation. But Hutch and his gang were always going to be top of the Bureau's list and his name was one of the first mentioned at our initial meetings. He was the target of our first full-scale Bureau investigation. That is why we called it Operation Alpha. Everyone wanted to get stuck into them but no one dreamt just how far out the ripples on this particular pond would extend. As we examined the affairs of each gang member we uncovered other names and began probing them. Further searches and production orders led us to more assets and hidden accounts. Over the ten years I would say we conducted at least 100 searches alone as part of our enquiries."

Operation Alpha was launched in August 1996 and centred on Gerry Hutch, Geoffrey Ennis and the rest of the immediate gang. The four agencies accessed every piece of information they had on the gang members. Of particular interest were the files on Hutch's attempts to repatriate the money seized by the Belfast High Court in 1987 and his tax amnesty application in 1993. Properties and bank accounts were identified in the Republic and financial institutions were served with production orders. The offices of several solicitors, accountants and auctioneers were also raided and searched.

A week after losing their tax case against Geraldine Gilligan in February 1997, the CAB searched nine homes belonging to the Monk and his mob and seized hundreds of documents. Each target also received a letter informing him that the Criminal Assets Bureau had become his new Inspector of Taxes. It was the first time that the gang realised they were being scrutinised. As the investigation progressed, the Untouchables followed various money trails from the Republic, to Northern Ireland, the UK, the Isle of Man, Jersey and Portugal. They uncovered an extraordinary web of money laundering, involving several individuals including a major international underworld figure, who was originally from County Clare. As part of the complex web the Untouchables unearthed hidden accounts held in the name of one of the criminal's lady friends. Between December 1994 and 1998 they discovered that over Stg£1.1 million (€1.6 million) had passed through an account held in the National Westminster Bank in the Isle of Man. The money was later redistributed in one hundred and eleven separate transactions to companies and banks in the United States, Isle of Man, the UK, Ireland and Northern Ireland. Other transactions were made to a hotel and apartment complex owned by the Clare godfather on Portugal's Algarve. The Bureau also discovered that Hutch had deposited IR£386,000 (€490,000) on February 23, 1994 to another account at the Halifax International Bank in Jersey. The account was again in his wife's name. The Gardaí later confirmed that they suspected this money came directly from the Marino Mart heist. From studying records it could be seen that all the accounts became particularly "active" after the establishment of the CAB.

One incident during the investigation illustrated the efforts to which the Bureau went to expose the money trail. They received intelligence that Hutch had been seen, about a year earlier, in the offices of an international courier company in

Dublin Airport. Officers from the Bureau spent days searching the office until they found a receipt for a package he had sent to a post office box address in Jersey. When the officers went to the address they discovered it was next door to a bank. Later they discovered that Hutch had sent copies of his driving licence and passport to open an account with the bank.

In the meantime the Bureau's revenue officers assessed Hutch for tax, based on the proceeds of the Marino Mart robbery. On Friday, June 13, a registered letter arrived at the Monk's home in Clontarf. Hutch claimed that he learned of his CAB tax demand when he read it in the *Evening Herald*. When he got home he discovered a registered letter had arrived for him four days earlier. "I thought tax demands were supposed to be private," he told a reporter. For the tax year 1986/87 he was assessed as owing IR£393,658 (€499,500). The bill would continue to rise, as interest and further tax assessments were made. Eventually the total bill topped over IR£2 million (€2.5 million).

Hutch's initial reaction was to think about packing up his family and leaving the country, like so many other villains had done after the establishment of the Bureau. But instead, the gangster decided to stay put and face the music. He later told friends that if he had run then people would think that he was a drug baron. The effect of the CAB's attentions inevitably meant that he became a hot news story. One of the side effects of the Bureau's activities was that it exposed unknown criminals. The media could now safely photograph and identify the various criminal targets for the first time, based on the CAB's actions against them. Before that, in the absence of a criminal conviction, a known hood could sue the media. In fact the Monk did just that during the early 1990s and settled with the *Sunday Tribune* for a small sum of cash. But now that the Bureau could go into the civil courts and openly accuse organised crime bosses, hitting them for huge tax bills in the process, it was difficult to silence the media. The very fact that someone was the target of the Criminal Assets Bureau meant that there had to be a criminal dimension to the target.

Otherwise how could an individual who claimed to be unemployed pay the Bureau a million euro?

Gerry Hutch immediately began the process of appealing the tax demand to the Revenue Appeals Commissioner. His accountant, John McGrattan, was almost as colourful as the Monk himself and would feature as an adviser to other individuals identified in many of the Operation Alpha investigations, including Matt Kelly. He later admitted to the Untouchables that he had been involved in several suspect property transactions. His enthusiasm for the legal profession had landed him in hot water with the Gardaí and the Law Society.

Over a twenty-year period John McGrattan had been found guilty of misrepresenting himself as a solicitor three times. An ill-fated legal partnership set up in 1978 had come to an untimely end a year later when he was convicted in Dunshaughlin District Court on four counts of misrepresenting himself as a solicitor. In 1983 he was brought before the Circuit Criminal Court, on charges of embezzling funds and forgery relating to the same partnership but was found not guilty by a jury. During the hearing his former partner in the business revealed that McGrattan had claimed he won second place in Ireland in the Incorporated Law Society exams. In 1991 the Law Society obtained a High Court injunction restraining him from ever acting as a solicitor when they discovered that he was still doing so from an office in Dublin. McGrattan's wife, Gabrielle Wolfe, who was a properly qualified solicitor, was legal adviser to Hutch and Kelly throughout the appeals and courts process. But Hutch's appeals would prove to be unsuccessful.

On February 22, 1999 the Appeal Commissioners officially turned down his appeal and confirmed that he owed IR£2,031,551 (€2,579,500). Hutch appealed against the demand to the Circuit Court and the High Court. In June Mr Justice Fred Morris also upheld the CAB demand.

Negotiations began, behind-the-scenes, between the Untouchables and the criminal's representatives. Barry Galvin and Felix McKenna normally attended such meetings on behalf of Fachtna Murphy, on whose approval the outcome depended. Within a year or so of being in operation the men running the Criminal Assets Bureau had realised that they would ultimately have to negotiate with targets. It had soon become apparent that if the Bureau wanted to completely clean out their targets, the process would take many more years. As a result a modus operandi evolved, in which the CAB obtained the highest realistic settlement figure. Once a target became "tax compliant", then he or she was subject to rigorous revenue scrutiny in the future. If a target had lied about assets and cash in negotiations, the Bureau reserved the right to go after that person a second time. Barry Galvin had a particularly robust approach to such negotiations. Once a figure had been agreed the target had to pay up by a set date. If the criminal did not do so then Galvin "re-assessed" the figure, increasing it in the process. As one former insider remarked years later, "Once Galvin did that it fairly focused minds. It drove them [targets] mad".

On March 23, 2000, Gerry Hutch officially became tax compliant when he agreed to pay IR£1,200,000 (€1,524,000) in "satisfaction of all taxes due by him". One of the reasons the Monk was anxious to settle was that his wife, in whose name some of the offshore accounts were held, was about to be arrested and charged with money laundering offences. Hutch himself had also been threatened with the possibility of criminal proceedings, based on tax and money laundering laws. During one angry exchange with the detectives attached to the Bureau, Hutch indicated that he "might have to take action" if they pushed him too hard. At the time it was interpreted that he might have to organise another major robbery to pay them.

But in the end he opted for the more legitimate route. As part of the deal he sold off two of the houses he had bought in Buckingham Street. In an earlier High Court hearing Hutch's counsel had challenged the CAB's right to seize the deeds to the two properties. The Monk claimed that he had bought the properties with compensation money paid by the State. In a clever legal argument, Richard Humphries BL for Hutch, claimed that it seemed bizarre that the State should pay for its own negligence and that a State agency should then seize the deeds of those properties bought with compensation money, claiming they were the proceeds of crime. In any event Hutch sold the houses for less than IR£700,000 (€889,000) and handed over a bank draft to the Untouchables. But there was still over IR£500,000 million (€635,000 million) outstanding, so the Monk did something that he could never have even dreamt of in a past life. He walked into the Bank of Ireland on Talbot Street with a haversack full of over IR£500,000 (€635,000) in cash. Throughout his career he had specialised in doing the exact opposite. Hutch's negotiators had reached a bizarre agreement with the Untouchables. He would make a cash lodgement to an account which he would open in his own name. He would then withdraw the money and hand it over to two officers.

Felix McKenna ordered a major security operation on the day the Monk had arranged to hand over the cash. Detective Inspector John McDermott and other armed officers went to the bank branch to inform the rather nervous managers of what was going to happen. There was a real fear at the bank that Hutch might organise an armed robbery to get the cash back after he lodged it. As part of the operation members of the Emergency Response Unit and CAB officers were deployed in the streets around the bank. A number of ERU snipers were even positioned on the rooftops of nearby buildings. A security van was also on standby to transport the cash immediately to the bank's main cash-holding centre. Hutch had collected the cash from a number of known criminal associates and walked through the streets of his old neighbourhood to make his first ever legal lodgement. The Gardaí also wanted to ensure that he was not 'mugged' on his way.

While the Monk was fighting his corner, so too were many of his associates and family members. Between them Paul

Boyle, Geoffrey Ennis and William Scully eventually paid over IR£610,000 (€775,000) in individual settlements by 2002. The Monk's drug trafficking brother Derek paid €120,000. Another brother Eddie had a bank account seized, containing over €156,891. John Good the man who had ordered the false registration plates used during the Brinks Allied heist agreed to pay €350,000 in January 2002. As a result of the CAB's investigation of Good they also hit one of his business associates for another €150,000.

The owner of a taxi firm who was suspected of being a front man for Gerry Hutch also came under the spotlight. By 2006 he was assessed as owing over one million euro. Two other associates of Hutch, who were closely connected to drug trafficking, also came into the realms of Operation Alpha. The men had extensive connections to organised crime gangs in Europe and the UK. The pair, who had never been convicted for drug offences, had moved into property development, in conjunction with the Penguin and an English crime gang. One of the men, originally from Clontarf, had a large property portfolio in County Kerry. The two men readily agreed to pay up one million euro in taxes, between them.

* * * *

Matt Kelly soon found himself a full target of CAB as they began to delve into the secret finances of his protégé. One Bureau insider revealed: "It was obvious from the beginning that Kelly had been closely linked with Hutch. We uncovered the various property deals between them and Shanahan. We discovered that he had become a very wealthy property developer." Kelly had used a network of people and fictitious names to front his ownership of an Irish property portfolio valued at approximately IR£4 million (€5 million). It was also revealed that he was the beneficial owner of three nursing homes in Lincoln and Gainsborough in the UK.

Det. Chief Supt. Murphy's detectives had also uncovered secret bank accounts held by Matt Kelly under the name Peter

Kelly. They had traced the lodgement of IR£419,000 (€532,000) from a total of IR£659,000 (€837,000) that they believed was paid to Kelly for Buckingham Village. This money was lodged in the name of Peter Kelly, with an address in Buckingham Village and was held at the Ulster Bank in Blackrock, in south county Dublin. The detectives positively identified their target from the bank's CCTV security footage. Between October 1992 and February 1993 a total of IR£385,250 (€489,000) had been lodged to the account before it was closed.

It was also discovered that Matt Kelly had used a number of solicitors and a financial consultant to carry out various financial transactions. One of those transactions exemplifies the complex route through which the cash was moved around. In March 1997 a solicitor obtained a loan from Anglo Irish bank to buy a property for IR£250,000 (€317,000) on Dublin's North Circular Road. The idea was that the loan would be repaid by supposed 'rent' from the property. The property, which was owned by one of Kelly's front companies, was actually valued at IR£650,000 (€825,000). The solicitor paid only IR£220,000 (€279,000) of the purchase price to a financial consultant who had offices on the south side of the city. The financial consultant in turn lodged the money to his bank account at Ulster Bank in Ballsbridge. Another IR£20,000 (€25,500) was paid directly to one of Matt Kelly's front companies and the final IR£10,000 (€12,500) was split into individual lodgements.

Five days later the financial consultant returned to the bank. On May 1, 1997, he withdrew the cash in the form of a draft made payable to one Peter Kelly. The following day the same Peter Kelly, alias Matt Kelly, opened a new account in the Ulster Bank in Blackrock by lodging the IR£220,000 (€279,000). He then lodged a further IR£10,000 (€12,500). Three weeks later Kelly closed the account when he ordered three separate bank drafts of IR£75,000 (€95,000), each in the name Peter Kelly, amounting to a total of IR£225,000 (€286,000). He then negotiated the drafts, cashing them at bank branches in Phibsboro. The money eventually trickled through to a number of businessmen associated with the former carpet salesman. The Criminal Assets Bureau managed to seize one draft for IR£92,000 (€117,000) that had come from Kelly's original lodgements. The money was then paid over to the Official Assignee in Bankruptcy. In the meantime the Bureau assessed Kelly as owing IR£2,950,000 (€3,746,000) in unpaid taxes, between 1985 and 1996.

Like his friend Hutch, Kelly was determined to fight the CAB all the way. The case continued in the courts for three years. In sworn affidavits Kelly had denied that he made his money from criminal activity and claimed that he had been ready to pay off all his debts and come out of bankruptcy. Barry Galvin, however, accused the crime lord of simply stalling for time. Behind-the-scenes there had been intense negotiations between Galvin and Kelly's representatives. As Kelly continued to prevaricate, Galvin added to the growing bill which eventually reached €3.6 million. In February 2000, the High Court granted CAB a partial decree against Kelly for payment of €662,000. In the meantime the two sides reached agreement. In July 2001, Kelly's lawyers said he had agreed to hand over the €3.6 million due. But his bill did not end there. Together with his tax bill and capital gains taxes, Matt Kelly paid €7.1 million. In order to pay up he was forced to sell off part of his property portfolio but like Hutch he was not left penniless. One of the properties he sold fetched €11 million. After that he was officially declared to be no longer bankrupt. From the CAB's point of view Operation Alpha was making the crime lords hurt.

During their trawl of Matt Kelly's myriad business dealings the CAB had uncovered links to Charlie Duffy, a well-known scrap dealer and motor parts dealer who operated from premises at Smithfield in central Dublin. Born in 1942, Duffy had made a fortune in his business which specialised in motor vehicle breaking and a scrap yard in the old markets area of the north inner-city. Duffy had a number of previous convictions for serious assault and road traffic offences but was not involved in drugs or armed robbery. In September 1997 the Bureau officers working on the Kelly case had discovered a connection between Duffy and Kelly. The investigators found that Duffy had effectively laundered IR£250,000 (€317,500) for the former carpet king.

The Untouchables traced two bank drafts worth IR£21,000 (€27,000) and IR£23,000 (€29,000), which originated from Kelly, through a complex trail involving a solicitor and an accountant. One of the drafts was lodged to Duffy's account and the other, which was made out in the name of Peter Kelly, was lodged to a second account Duffy owned. The investigators had then discovered that Duffy transferred over IR£800,000 (€1,016,000) to Barclays Bank in Jersey after they sought assistance from the Jersey Police and Customs Joint Financial Crimes Unit. In total the CAB believed that Duffy had handled up to IR£250,000 (€317,500) on behalf of Kelly. The scrap metal dealer had now become a target of the Untouchables.

When officers travelled to Jersey, as part of their mission to trace the destination of the Monk's loot, they encountered what Felix McKenna liked to refer to as "the pot of gold at the end of the rainbow". One of Duffy's hidden accounts held over Stg£10 million (€14.6 million). Back in Dublin they had begun investigating Duffy under the taxation laws and sought orders to freeze various accounts. Like previous cases the Bureau were expecting a long drawn out battle. But the scrap dealer took them completely by surprise. After some negotiations with the CAB, Duffy closed down the Jersey account and handed it over on December 13, 2000. When it was converted into euro the total payment came to a staggering €17,142,526. It was one of the largest single settlements achieved by the Bureau, in its first ten years in action.

Duffy has always maintained that he had no knowledge of any connection with either Gerry Hutch or Matt Kelly and that he dealt with them unknowingly through a third party.

As the investigation continued, the Bureau also uncovered links between Matt Kelly and former IRA terrorist Thomas

McFeely. The connection was made when the Bureau began investigating alleged links between the Monk, Matt Kelly and an inner-city hotel. It was discovered that Kelly and McFeely had been business partners in various dodgy deals. Born in Dungiven, County Derry in 1948, McFeely was first convicted for terror related offences in 1973 when he was jailed for 18 months in the Special Criminal Court in Dublin. In February 1977 a Belfast court jailed McFeely for 26 years on two counts of attempted murder, robbery, possession of a stolen rifle and possession of bomb making equipment. While inside he took part in the hunger strikes staged by Republican prisoners to obtain political status.

Shortly after his release in 1990, McFeely had arrived in Dublin where he started working as a sub-contractor. He became involved with various criminal figures, including Matt Kelly. He was suspected of involvement in fraud and extortion including so called "C2 Fraud". This is a highly lucrative racket and widely used by the IRA and its political wing Sinn Féin to fund their activities. The criminals use false C2 tax certificates to fraudulently obtain tax repayments for non-existent building works. In Ireland the crime is estimated to cost the Revenue tens of millions of euro each year. Through the years McFeely built up a multi-million-euro property empire. The Untouchables discovered that he had never made a personal income tax return and whatever tax his companies had paid was seriously in arrears. Despite this, in 2001 the former terror boss paid over €5 million for a mansion in Ailesbury Road, Ballsbridge, Ireland's most exclusive neighbourhood. As investigations continued the CAB also established links between McFeely and the former deputy president of Sinn Féin, Phil Flynn. In 2006, Flynn was acting as a mediator in the proposed sale by McFeely of a multi-million euro property at the Square shopping centre in Tallaght, Dublin.

A former trade unionist and Government-appointed negotiator Flynn was also a member of the board of several major companies including the Bank of Scotland. In 2005

Flynn became a target of the Bureau as a result of their investigations into the laundering of over €30 million stolen by the IRA from the Northern Bank in Belfast in December 2004. McFeely initially tried to fight the CAB but in the end he agreed to pay the Criminal Assets Bureau over €9 million to regularise his affairs in June 2006.

* * * *

Meanwhile Operation Alpha continued to make the Monk's pals pay dearly. Carlos Portalanza from Equador had arrived in Ireland in 1984 at the age of 25. He had four convictions for larceny and owned a number of properties in the city centre including an electrical appliance shop. Intelligence received by the Gardaí suggested that the businesses were in fact really owned by Gerry Hutch. Portalanza agreed to pay over $400,000.

Noel Duggan was Hutch's closest friend for many years and was the largest cigarette smuggler in the country. As a result he more than earned the nickname 'Mr Kingsize'. The former butcher-turned-criminal operated a thriving cash and carry business with his business partner Christy Dunne, on Queen Street, around the corner from Smithfield. The large complex also included a furniture business and a block of apartments. For many years he had featured high in the files of the Serious Crime Squad where he was described as an organised crime boss. A local Garda said at the time: "You name it and Kingsize will sell it, at the right price from cigarettes to toilet rolls."

Born in 1958 and originally from Cabra in north-west Dublin, Duggan began his career as a butcher. But crime was a much more lucrative profession and he received several convictions for receiving stolen goods, forgery and burglary. In the early days of his business Duggan dealt with the major villains Gilligan and George Mitchell, who both specialised in warehouse robberies before moving into drugs. His business grew so large that the retailers' representative group,

RGDATA, complained to the Government that their members were losing huge amounts of profit because Kingsize and Dunne were undercutting them. Many jobs, they argued, were at risk because of the smuggling operation.

In December 1996, a joint Garda and Customs investigation, codenamed Operation Nicotine, was launched into his operation and millions of smuggled cigarettes were seized in the process. The investigation, however, was taken over by the Criminal Assets Bureau and in October 2000 Dunne and Duggan were both assessed as owing a total of €6 million in unpaid taxes.

In December 2002, Kingsize handed over the keys of his Queen Street property in person to Felix McKenna and Barry Galvin, who then put the property up for auction. In 1999 McKenna had been promoted to the rank of Chief Bureau Officer, after Fachtna Murphy was given a well-earned promotion to the rank of Assistant Commissioner. Taking possession of Duggan's premises was also one of Galvin's last duties as the Bureau's legal officer. In 2003 the pioneering Elliot Ness style legal eagle retired from the Untouchables and returned to private practice in Cork. He was replaced by lawyer Richard Barrett, from the staff of the Attorney General's office.

After negotiations with the Bureau the two smugglers agreed to pay over €2 million to the exchequer. The night after he handed over the keys the colourful gangster told this writer: "They [CAB] have taken everything and now I haven't even got the price of a packet of smokes! It nearly fucking killed me handing over those keys. I'm on my second bottle of brandy already. I was in those premises for over seven years and I have spent most of my life in that area, wheeling and dealing. Maybe if all those thieves over in the Dáil paid up like me then we would have a decent health service."

As a result of the Kingsize investigation the Untouchables were led to two Cork brothers who were involved in the furniture business. The brothers were also close friends and associates of both the Monk and Duggan and both men attended the wedding of one of the brothers. The Untouchables raised a large tax assessment on the Corkmen based on the belief that they had been involved in money laundering and aided Mr Kingsize's smuggling rackets. As an indirect result of their friendship with the Dublin villains, the brothers agreed to settle for €750,000. Another player on the periphery of the Hutch circle of hoodlums also agreed to pay €360,000.

By the summer of 2006 the income generated by Operation Alpha had reached over €40 million. However there was no sign that it had yet reached its outer limits. As a result of the operation, several other businessmen and professionals who had involvement with Operation Alpha targets were referred to the mainstream tax inspectors and assessed for taxes involving a few million euro. A lot of people had been forced to pay up because the Monk went out to rob!

* * * *

Hutch, meanwhile, had decided to set up his first legitimate business – driving a taxi. But that wouldn't happen without a fight either. While his High Court appeal against the CAB tax demands was pending, Hutch applied to the Carriage office for a licence to drive a public service vehicle (PSV). Superintendent Liam Collins, however, refused the application on the grounds that the Monk was under investigation by the Bureau. When Hutch appealed the decision to the High Court, the Garda officer said that he was aware of "public disquiet" over Hutch being a "notorious member of the criminal community". The Monk was refused the licence.

Following his settlement with the Untouchables, however, Hutch returned to the District Court to appeal the decision of the Carriage Office. Inspector Philip Ryan, who had been involved in Operation Alpha informed the court that the Monk was "now fully tax compliant" and he had no other outstanding tax liabilities. In response to a question from Hutch's solicitor Ryan said that he would not be nervous travelling as a passenger in the gangster's cab. Based on the evidence presented, the Judge ruled that Hutch could apply for a PSV licence which he subsequently obtained, much to the annoyance of the many Gardaí who had investigated his serious crimes. As he was leaving court Hutch was asked about his involvement in organised crime. "I haven't been involved in crime. I had a bit of a tax problem, like several other people – its all over," he replied with a smile, before walking briskly away.

One of the consequences of all the publicity about the Monk was that Hutch became Ireland's first celebrity gangster. Unlike Martin Cahill he has regularly been photographed and written about in the newspapers, although he still refuses to do any interviews. In 2005 he hit the headlines when he went into the limo business and bought a stretched Hummer limo. He posed for pictures beside the monstrous white machine, complete with a wide grin and a chauffeur's hat. Since then he has hardly been able to keep up with the demand for his services. The so-called law abiding community simply love the novelty of being driven to parties in luxury, by the country's most successful armed robber. In his old neighbourhood he remained a local hero of sorts, especially through his work with the local boxing club, Corinthians, which he helped to set up for local kids in 1998. The Monk, who is a friend of former world heavy-weight boxing champion Mike Tyson, can regularly be found in the club, helping out with the day-to-day running of the place. Inevitably the club attracted media attention because of its infamous founder. But the Monk and his mates turned it into a good news story for the area and the once notorious armed robber was pictured posing with the kids in the ring. He told reporters that it was a way of keeping the kids off the streets and away from the drug pushers. Local people will tell anyone who will listen that Gerry Hutch is helping keep the kids out of crime. In 2006 the once publicity-shy mobster won another unexpected accolade when he was voted one of Ireland's 100 sexiest men by a glossy magazine.

* * * *

The Criminal Assets Bureau investigation was a major success and when most of the criminals who were targeted recovered from the pain of paying over so much cash they discovered that they were still fairly well off. In the words of that famous TV wide boy and hustler Del Boy Trotter, "everyone's a winner."

Seven

The Foreign Villains

Several major international drug traffickers fell in love with Ireland in the years before the establishment of the Criminal Assets Bureau. But it was not just the breathtaking scenery, friendly pub culture or romantic history that inspired this great affection. Nor was it the fishing or sight-seeing they came for. The gangsters were drawn to the peace of our countryside because it was good for business. The big drug trafficking cartels particularly liked the hundreds of deserted inlets and coves along the craggy south-west coast. It was from this coastline that they transported huge quantities of drugs onwards into the UK and European markets.

In the 1980s, southern Ireland was a sleepy place on the farthest edge of the European Union where coastal patrols by Navy, Customs or Gardaí were practically non-existent. The godfathers had discovered one of the safest drug smuggling routes in Western Europe. Several international hoods decided to buy luxurious homes here and used them as bases from which to launder money and run their operations abroad – at a safe distance from the reach of police forces in their own countries. Ireland had become a drug smuggler's paradise.

An example of how important Ireland had become in terms of the international trade can be seen by an analysis of drug seizures by the Gardaí, Navy and Customs in the seven-year period between 1988 and 1995. During that time they seized eight cannabis shipments, with a combined street value of IR£200 million (€254 million). Using the traditional, and generally conservative, international law enforcement criterion that one in ten drug shipments are intercepted, the real value of the drug smuggling operations along the coast at that time could have been as high as a staggering IR£2 billion (€2.5 billion). Six of the seizures were made along the Cork and Kerry coastline while the remaining two seizures were on the Galway coast. Most of the seizures were the result of co-operation between Gardaí, Customs and their international counterparts, in tracking the shipments from around the world. Others were stumbled upon quite by accident. But everyone involved agreed that the seizures were only the tip of the iceberg. In most of the operations Irish criminals had teamed up with fellow crooks from countries such as Canada, the UK, Holland and Spain. These were the first indications that crime in Ireland was no longer confined to national borders.

In 1992, Barry Galvin was the first professional involved in the area of law enforcement to expose the fact that Ireland had become a vital transit point for drug trafficking and a bolt hole from justice for crime lords. As soon as the CAB came into existence, Galvin and Fachtna Murphy began compiling a target list of known foreign gangsters who had come to live in the Emerald Isle. The Untouchables soon sent a message to organised crime around the world – Ireland would no longer be a safe place to hide their money. Their targets included three individuals who were among the UK's richest godfathers – Scottish mob boss Thomas McGraw, Englishman David Huck and Mickey Green, the London villain known across the world as 'the Scarlet Pimpernel'.

In their pursuit of the ill-gotten gains of organised crime from 1996 onwards, the CAB became the owner of a diverse portfolio of seized assets. Apart from hard cash, the Bureau took apartments, warehouses, houses, plots of land, a farm, an island and pubs from Irish and the ex-patriot criminal community. They also seized cars, motorbikes, vans, trucks, trailers, household furniture and industrial equipment. They even took possession of prize racehorses and ponies. But one of their oddest acquisitions was a sea-going tugboat owned by a Dutch and Canadian drug trafficking consortium. *The Aegir* had been on route to pick up a huge drug shipment destined for Canada when the harsh Atlantic weather forced it to shelter off the Irish coast. But the drug syndicate got a lot more than shelter and a friendly Irish welcome. The CAB were about to seriously upset a IR£30 million (€38 million) drug deal.

On the night of February 10, 1997 Gardaí and Customs officers joined the crew of the Naval Ship the *L.E. Eithne* just off the Galway coast at Rosaveal. A short time later the officers and armed naval personnel boarded *The Aegir* in Killeany Bay, just north of the Aran Islands, where it had been sheltering with engine trouble as a result of the severe weather. Detective Sergeant Sean O'Grady officially detained the vessel and its nine-man crew under the Misuse of Drugs Acts and later it was towed to Galway Harbour for a thorough search.

Five days earlier the 44 metre tug boat had been boarded by customs officers in Killala Bay, just off the north Mayo coast where it had been at anchor for a number of days. Again the ship's engines had been damaged by water during ongoing storms. The officers had searched the boat but found nothing illegal, although they were suspicious about the vessel's true mission. *The Aegir* was essentially a port tug and totally unsuitable for the high seas. It was also fully loaded, with enough fuel and supplies to allow it to remain at sea for months. The Dutch captain, Rene Koerts, told the officers that he had left Rotterdam on January 23 and first headed for St Petersburg in Russia. However, after three days at sea, he claimed he had received instructions to change direction and sail for Belfast and then onwards to the Azores in the Atlantic. During their three-hour inspection the Customs officers had also taken details of the passports of the crew on board.

When they had returned to shore, they did an intelligence check on some of the people aboard the tug and their suspicions were justified. For a start, according to their colleagues in Rotterdam, there was only supposed to be a crew of six on board. The most interesting character on board, and of whom there was no official record, was thirty-eight-year-old Canadian criminal Normand Drapeau who had been a long-time suspected international drug trafficker. According to Canadian police intelligence, Drapeau was a central player in a plot to import over seven tonnes of cannabis that had been seized by them in September 1995. Canadian police had also linked him with several other drug trafficking operations, including the importation of cocaine and heroin.

But the mention of his name also sparked alarm bells at the Garda National Drug Unit (GNDU). Drapeau had been a member of the international cartel involved in the attempt to import over IR£150 million (€190 million) worth of cannabis into Ireland in November 1995. Undercover Gardaí from the GNDU had secretly offloaded that shipment from a mother ship, *The Master Star*. The Penguin, George Mitchell, had been in charge of the Irish end of the operation. Gardaí had spotted Drapeau at a meeting in Cork with Mitchell's sidekick, John Noonan, a drug dealer from Finglas in north-west Dublin, several weeks before the drugs were due to be landed here. The daring undercover operation had come unstuck when gang members became suspicious and decided not to intercept the shipment which was being transported to Dublin in an articulated truck, driven by an undercover cop. The Gardaí were left with no choice but to 'find' the huge shipment at Urlingford, County Kilkenny. Forensic tests on the wrappings on the seized hashish shipments in Canada and Ireland were later found to have come from the same batch. When *The Aegir* ran into engine trouble Drapeau was still under active investigation by the Canadian authorities in an operation codenamed Hearth.

Another crewmember was Dutch national GJH Van Genderen who had been jailed for nine years in 1990 for importing cannabis into the UK. It was time for the authorities to have a second look at *The Aegir*.

The Irish Navy was immediately alerted and the *L.E. Eithne* had begun another search off the west coast to locate the boat which had meanwhile pulled out of Killala Bay. Unfortunately for the drug syndicate *The Aegir* had developed further mechanical troubles as a result of the storms and had been forced to seek shelter in Galway Bay. Officers later discovered that Rene Koerts had contacted his boss in the operation, Dutch national Albert Wilhalm Rave who had purchased the rusty tugboat and recruited the crew on behalf of the Canadian/Dutch gang. Rave, had instructed his captain to remain off the Irish coast and arranged to fly to Ireland with spare parts for the engines. But in the meantime the vessel had popped up on the *Eithne's* powerful radar.

Koerts, Drapeau, Van Genderen and another Canadian national, fifty-year-old Jean La Forest were arrested by the Gardaí and taken to Mill Street station for questioning. *The Aegir* was towed into Galway where it was placed under armed guard. Detectives also seized $20,700 dollars (€16,200) in cash that was found in the ship's safe. In the meantime specialist naval personnel, including engineers, mappers and divers began a minute examination of the boat, in conjunction with the Customs National Drugs Unit. Naval officers found a hand held Global Positioning System (GPS) unit on board which showed that it had been activated outside Montreal in Canada on February 3, 1997. The navy also discovered that the ship's log had been falsified. According to the log, around the time *The Aegir* had limped into Killala Bay it was attending a mysterious rendezvous over 300 miles off the north-west coast!

The Gardaí knew that they had stumbled onto a major drug trafficking operation but there were no drugs. Armed with the new provisions of the Criminal Justice (Drugs) Act, one of the new pieces of legislation introduced after the murder of Veronica Guerin, the Gardaí had the power to detain their suspects for questioning for up to seven days. Before the Act's existence they could only hold suspects for a maximum of 12 hours. The officers in Mill Street also contacted Fachtna Murphy in the Criminal Assets Bureau for advice on what they could do. Murphy told his colleagues that if they could ascertain a criminal connection he could be in the High Court within 24 hours to seek an injunction seizing the ship as the proceeds of crime.

As the investigation progressed the skipper of *The Aegir*

gave the CAB what they needed. On the morning of February 18, Rene Koerts gave Superintendent Anthony Finnerty the true purpose of *The Aegir's* mission – to collect a consignment of 30,000 kilos of cannabis from a mother ship near the Cape Verde Islands, off the African coast on March 10 and to deliver the load to Canada. The mother ship was sailing from Pakistan. A number of machine guns and bazookas were also to be loaded aboard *The Aegir* at this stage, for use against the Navy or coast guard if an attempt was made to board the vessel along its route.

Koerts told the Gardaí that Rave had purchased the ship and hired him with the understanding that this was to be a drug trafficking operation. Drapeau, Genderen who acted as the first mate and La Forest had been smuggled on board *The Aegir* before it left Rotterdam. Koerts told the Gardaí why they had decided to sail around Ireland: "Our reason for going around the west coast of Ireland was that it was quiet and we did not want to attract any attention, so much for that heh?"

In the meantime Rave had arrived in Galway and presented himself at the Garda station as the ship's agent and asked to speak with the skipper. But instead the underworld Mr Fixit was arrested and questioned. He later made a detailed statement in which he admitted the ship had been purchased for the purpose of drug trafficking. A check with Dutch police also showed that Rave had three previous convictions, including one for possession of firearms. In his statement Rave admitted that he was in the process of procuring other ships for drug trafficking gangs. He had personally loaded twenty-five special waterproof bags to hold the drugs and had stocked *The Aegir* with enough food and supplies to sustain the crew for three and a half months at sea. From their knowledge of the law neither Koerts nor Rave believed that they had anything to worry about when making their admissions – after all no drugs were aboard. They reckoned that they would have to be released and allowed to sail off into the sunset.

But before the ink had dried on the two statements Fachtna Murphy was preparing a High Court application in the form of a sworn Affidavit seeking the seizure of *The Aegir* under the Proceeds of Crime Act. With the admissions of Koerts and Rave and the criminal background of some of the people on board, the CAB had clear evidence that the ship had been bought with the proceeds of crime, for the commission of crime.

On the morning of February 20 the Untouchables made their application. The High Court in Dublin appointed Galvin, an accomplished yachtsman himself, as the Receiver of the boat with permission to sell it as the proceeds of crime. The court also granted a seizure order for the cash found in the ship's safe. That evening, officers from the Bureau drove to Galway to serve documents on Koerts informing him that the vessel had been seized by the State.

Part of the cash seized was used to pay for the flights of the various crew members who were immediately deported. On April 10, the CAB sold *The Aegir* at auction for over €54,000. When added to the cash seized, *The Aegir's* engine problems had cost the mob €67,000. But the true costs were much higher. The syndicate had missed the collection of their drug shipment which on the streets had a value of over IR£30 million (€38 million). The episode also provided the Canadian authorities with invaluable intelligence and some of the main players were subsequently caught and jailed for other drug offences in that country.

The Untouchables had shown other law enforcement agencies the effectiveness of the new CAB legislation. Four months later an Irishman called the offices of the Criminal Assets Bureau claiming to represent a Galway-based company with interests in *The Aegir*. He wanted information to find out exactly what had happened to the drug boat. When detectives did a background check on the mystery man they discovered he was also a suspected international drug trafficker. He and his colleagues were anxious to know just why they had lost their precious ship. The Untouchables decided not to bother calling him back. The case was closed.

* * * *

Around the same time that the Bureau was preparing to sell *The Aegir,* the Untouchables also obtained a High Court freezing order on properties owned by flamboyant English villain David Francis Huck. This was the man who most epitomised how international drug traffickers had fallen in love with Ireland. In a special investigation by the BBC in 2004, Huck was placed at number seven in the top ten wealthiest organised crime bosses in the United Kingdom, with an estimated personal wealth of Stg£30 million (€43 million). Twelve years previously Barry Galvin had referred directly to Huck when he described the lavish lifestyle of the international criminals using Ireland as their base of operations.

Huck, who was born in Ayrshire, Scotland, in March 1946, had been in the international drug trafficking business for twenty years by the time he arrived in Ireland in 1990. Although he had featured in intelligence reports as a major facilitator by Spanish, American, UK and Dutch police and customs, Huck had never actually been caught. In fact prior to arriving in Ireland he had never even been arrested for questioning. Even though the charming Englishman had been involved in organising shipments of cocaine from Colombia and cannabis from Morocco and Pakistan. Before that he had been living on the sun-drenched Spanish island of Ibiza with his estranged wife. However when the Spanish police began keeping a closer eye on him he decided to make the move to Ireland.

Huck decided to make the west of Ireland his new base of operations. He bought a 17th century thatched cottage and a bungalow next door on five acres of land on the shores of Lough Derg at Ogonnolloe, County Clare. His portfolio of properties also included a house in Dublin, a prized Morgan sports car and a high-powered speedboat he berthed on the lakeside at the bottom of his garden. He also owned two imposing homes in Ibiza and a restaurant on the Algarve in Portugal. At the same time as his move to Ireland, Huck paid IR£250,000 (€317,500) for a 65-foot long Ketch called *The*

Brime. Using this yacht and other vessels, Huck was suspected of smuggling an estimated IR£150 million (€190.5 million) worth of cannabis through Ireland alone while he was living here. In Canada and the US, drug enforcement agencies suspected that Huck was also behind a IR£30 million (€38 million) drug shipment which had been seized in Maine.

Between drug deals Huck devoted every day to the pursuit of pleasure. He was the quintessential playboy who threw money around like confetti. His passions included beautiful women, fine foods, vintage wines and hand-rolled cigars. A female acquaintance once described him in an interview with the *Sunday World* newspaper: "You could not help being bowled over by David. He dazzled everyone who came in contact with him. The ladies found him irresistible. He could turn sluggish company into a major party. He was a warm and engaging fellow who could make people feel at ease within seconds of meeting him. But he had a dark and very mean side."

In March 1992, Huck celebrated his 46th birthday by throwing a lavish party, taking over a wing in one of the country's most exclusive hotels, Dromoland Castle, in County Clare. Huck's guests flew in from around the world for the party and he paid all their expenses. One of the guests later recalled of the event: "You couldn't put your hand in your pocket. It was champagne, gourmet meals, vintage ports and expensive cognac all the time."

A year after he set up his new home in Clare, Huck's brother, Will, his wife Suzanne and their child moved from the US to live in the bungalow beside his cottage. Will, a talented engineer and designer, had dreams of running a successful wheelchair manufacturing business. David Huck promised to finance the project. The brothers rented a factory unit in the nearby village of Tuamgeaney and employed two local men but the venture foundered after a short time.

Huck often bragged to his associates around the world that he had found the perfect location from which to organise his drug trafficking operation. His neighbours thought he was just another very wealthy and rather eccentric English businessman. Apart from the likes of Barry Galvin and Tony Hickey, who was in charge of national drug investigations in Garda HQ, no one knew Huck's real source of income. In 1993, Huck told one of his associates that he was totally confidant that there was "absolutely no risk of being caught" smuggling drugs through Ireland's deserted south-west coastline. But he was proved wrong only a few months later.

In July 1993, Huck organised the importation of two tonnes of hashish with a street value of IR£20 million (€25 million). The drugs were to be collected off the coast of Morocco by a four-man crew using his yacht *The Brime*. Despite his bragging the operation was not to go as planned.

From the time of his arrival in Ireland Tony Hickey and his officers had been keeping a discreet eye on Huck. They had also begun sharing intelligence with their counterparts in Europe, particularly Scotland Yard. Hickey had arranged a conference to specifically discuss Huck in Madrid in Spain. The purpose was to exchange information on his activities between the Spanish, Danish, Dutch and UK law enforcement agencies.

Around July 8, 1993 Gardaí in Kerry were tipped off by fishermen that the crew of *The Brime* were acting suspiciously some distance off the Skelligs. The drug smuggling run had been dogged by a series of mishaps since Huck had dispatched *The Brime* from Holland three weeks earlier. The yacht had been forced to shelter, due to bad weather and failed to make its first rendezvous with the mother ship carrying the drugs. By the time they had arrived in Irish waters the crew were running out of food. At the same time Huck, his Dublin girlfriend Marie Kennedy, Will and Suzanne Huck were spotted in the area acting suspiciously. They were identified and arrested on July 9 and brought to Cahirciveen Garda Station for questioning. At the same time Gardaí found a mobile phone in a hired car being used by Huck. Another car was located at Cork Airport. Hickey's people suspected that a shipment was about to be landed. But they didn't know where or when.

By this stage, the crew of *The Brime* were on the brink of mutiny. They were frantically trying to contact Huck but with little success. They had been calling Huck's mobile phone every half-hour. There was no contact either on a radio system Huck had specially fitted in the boat for contact with the shore. In the meantime the law proved to be on Huck's side. He could only be held for a maximum period of twelve hours before being released.

On July 10, Huck and the three others were released and within hours he had packed his bags and left the country for Spain. At the same time the Gardaí had re-charged the mobile phone they found in the hire car and were waiting for it to ring. The Navy had also been put on alert that a possible drug shipment was to be landed somewhere in the area. When the increasingly frantic crew of *The Brime* rang the mobile a short time later Inspector Jim Fitzgerald pretended to be Huck's brother, Will. Dublin man Gerry Fitzgerald, who had been living in Amsterdam, had been hired by Huck because he had an Irish accent. Huck thought that the Dubliner's accent would not arouse suspicion if it was overheard on the radio airwaves off the coast. Inspector Fitzgerald, working closely with the Navy, lured *The Brime* into a trap, just off Fenit, north of Kerry, where Gardaí and naval personnel intercepted the yacht. Gerry Fitzgerald, Dutchman Egbertus Von Onzen, Belgian Frank Loopmans and Englishman Wayne Bland were all subsequently jailed for ten years each. But Huck had completely slipped the net.

After the crew members were convicted *The Brime* was the first property to be confiscated by the State under the 1994 Criminal Justice Act. The Act provided for the seizure of property used in the commission of a crime in the event that a conviction was obtained. *The Brime* was assigned to the Navy for a time and later sold by the State for IR£58,400 (€74,000). In the meantime the Huck escapade was used to illustrate the need for legislative reforms in the area of detention periods.

If Huck could have been held for longer than twelve hours he would certainly have been charged with drug trafficking and jailed. An international arrest warrant was applied for by the Gardaí but Huck had vanished.

Two years after his lucky escape Huck ordered his brother Will to quit his home in County Clare. The heartless hoodlum ordered his brother, wife and young child out of the house through a firm of lawyers in Dublin. At the time Will, who died some years later from a heart condition, told the *Sunday World*: "I would have thought he has caused me, my wife and our son enough suffering without now trying to make us homeless. David has ruined our lives. I deeply regret ever having being associated with him. I had no contact with him after he suddenly departed this country. If I was to meet with him again I would have certain strong words to say to him, but they are unprintable."

At the time the Gardaí kept a close eye on developments in case the drug trafficker tried to slip back into Ireland. In the meantime the international mobster sold off most of his property interests in Ireland and there was nothing anyone could do about it.

Huck eventually re-emerged in October 1996 when the UK Customs and Navy arrested him as he skippered another expensive yacht, *The Fat Morgan,* with a shipment of cannabis worth Stg£12 million (€17.5 million). *The Fat Morgan* was intercepted off the Cornish coast in treacherous waters. In September 1997, Huck was jailed for fourteen years.

In the meantime the CAB raised a tax assessment on the philandering gangster for almost IR£450,000 (€571,000) which they claimed he owed in unpaid taxes and interest for the years 1992 and 1993. The Untouchables seized his last remaining property on the shores of Lough Derg and put it up for auction. During the investigation it was discovered that planning permission for the lands at Ogonnolloe had been obtained by Huck in "suspicious circumstances". Officers suspected that the crime lord had used intimidation to get the permission. By the time it came up for sale the planning permission had dropped off because no construction had taken place for seven years. It was highly unlikely therefore that it would be given again. As a result the value of the property had dropped considerably. The Untouchables, however, played a clever hand at the auction in April 2002. They had been hoping the property would fetch €95,000, but the highest bid was €80,000. They took a gamble and withdrew it from the market, sparking off a bidding war, which resulted in the site finally selling for €150,000.

* * * *

While David Huck was making himself comfortable in his adopted home in County Clare so too was another major international player – Dutch godfather Jan Hendrik Ijpelaar. Only an hour's drive down the road, near Sneem on the Ring of Kerry, Ijpelaar had purchased magnificent Clashnacree House, a 19th century six-bedroom mansion standing on 20 acres of land, overlooking the Atlantic Ocean. Clashnacree also boasted an adjoining gate lodge, stables, swimming pool and tennis court. The estate even included a private island which was officially designated Island 69.

Born in April 1947, Ijpelaar was the leader of what Dutch police described as a major international organised crime gang specialising in the sale of ecstasy, hashish, cocaine and heroin. According to Dutch police intelligence sources, the gang controlled the flow of the drugs, both to and from Holland, as well as a large distribution network in the country.

In 1991, the Dutchman officially purchased Clashnacree House for IR£300,000 (€381,000) cash with a fake mortgage registered with a British Virgin Island Company. The godfather went to great lengths to disguise his ownership of the estate and put it in the name of his mistress. Ijpelaar spent a fortune lavishly refurbishing and decorating Clashnacree House – the fit out even included gold taps in all the bathrooms and jacuzzis. At the time Ijpelaar planned to use Kerry as the new hub of his international business interests. It was more than a coincidence that it was situated so close to the Atlantic Ocean, complete with its own island.

Unfortunately for the gangster he didn't get an opportunity to fully enjoy his luxurious Irish bolthole. In April 1992, Dutch police arrested Ijpelaar and six associates in what at the time was described as one of the biggest anti-crime operations ever in Holland. In the dramatic swoops, involving 120 specialist police officers, an ecstasy factory was discovered and 200 kilos of the drug, worth a conservative IR£5 million (€6.3 million), were seized. Several firearms, high performance cars, cannabis and a large amount of cash were also seized in the operation. In October of the same year, Ijpelaar was convicted of being the leader of an organised crime gang and also on three counts of dealing in narcotics. When compared to other countries, the Rotterdam District Court gave the godfather a typically lenient sentence for such serious criminal activity – six years.

During his trial, reference had been made to property in Ireland that Ijpelaar had bought with the proceeds of his criminal activity. At the time of his arrest the Garda Drug Squad, who had been aware of his presence in Ireland, raided Clashnacree House but nothing of an evidential value was unearthed. During the search the officers were stunned by the mansions extravagantly decorated interior.

In the meantime the drug lord had started his six year sentence. In the end he spent just four years in jail and in 1997 he visited his Irish property briefly but left again. Since 1992 it had become run down and was in bad repair.

By that time the Criminal Assets Bureau had also begun an investigation into Ijpelaar's background. They carried out a number of searches of a solicitor's office where they seized the files relating to the sale of Clashnacree House. They found clear evidence of how the gangster had bought the property with cash and had purposely tried to conceal his ownership. Their enquiries also found that the mortgage company, Howard Financial Services, had been struck off the companies' register since the purchase. The Bureau uncovered further evidence that the drug trafficker had secretly purchased a further ten-acre parcel of land near Clashnacree House.

In August 2000, the CAB obtained a High Court order seizing Ijpelaar's estate. The court appointed Barry Galvin as the Receiver of the estate, with the power to put it on the market for sale. By this stage Ijpelaar was back in business and again featuring high on the 'most wanted list' of the Dutch police. There was surprise among the CAB officers when he appeared in the High Court in Dublin on September 13 to fight their attempts to sell off his dream home. He claimed that he had bought the property with money earned honestly in the early 1990s and claimed that he could produce income tax documents to back up his claim.

Ijpelaar said he did not have legal counsel representing him because he could not afford to pay for them. Despite his protests Barry Galvin was given the go ahead to sell the property and it was advertised for auction for Wednesday October 25, 2000. In the meantime the Dutch godfather had other troubles to occupy his mind. The Gardaí had tipped off their colleagues in Holland that their number one target had re-emerged to fight their court applications. The Dutch had been trying to find Ijpelaar for several months and could now place him under surveillance.

On October 11, he was arrested by police in Rotterdam. In his possession they found 3,000 litres of precursor chemicals capable of making 50 million ecstasy tablets. The chemicals could have been used to make a staggering IR£500 million (€635 million) worth of ecstasy tablets. The gangster, who had just told the High Court in Dublin that he was broke, had failed to mention that he was coming into money – a lot of money. The ecstasy haul was one of the largest ever seized in Europe.

Two weeks later, Clashnacree House was sold for IR£1 million (€1.25 million) by the CAB. Later Chief Superintendent Felix McKenna told reporters that he was very happy with the sale. He had had no intention of selling for a penny less than a million.

But Ijpelaar hadn't left Ireland for good. In 2004 detectives attached to the National Bureau of Criminal Investigation (NBCI) uncovered direct links between the Dutch godfather and a cartel of Irish drug traffickers who were targeted in an undercover operation, codenamed Bingo. One of the central players in the gang, Alan Campbell, who was in his mid-forties and had an address in Castlepollard, County Westmeath, had been arrested in Holland with 150,000 ecstasy tablets in the mid-1990s. Garda intelligence discovered that Ijpealaar had paid Campbell around €30,000 for his assistance during the Dutchman's later dealings with the Bureau. Between April 2003 and June 2004, as part of Operation Bingo, the NBCI seized three shipments of cocaine and hashish worth €24 million.

Today Ijpelaar is still classified as a major player in international drug trafficking.

* * * *

In February 1996, the Paradise Bar opened in the centre of Donegal Town amid much excitement and fanfare. The new pub's owners, John and Mary Hughes, a friendly middle-aged couple from Glasgow, had flown in *Coronation Street* stars, Shaun Wilson and Peter Armitage, who played characters Martin Platt and Billy Webster, and were guests of honour for the big night. Also in attendance was Glasgow Celtic's IR£2 million ($2.5 million) star player Phil O'Donnell. The opening had been the talk of the entire county and business had been good from the start.

The pub continued to flourish but exactly two years later, the Paradise Bar was back in the headlines and was again the talk of the county. Only this time the whole operation had been exposed as being at the centre of a complex CAB investigation into money laundering by an international drug trafficking gang based in Scotland. The Untouchables were about to move into the pub business.

In February 1998, John and Mary Hughes, neither of

whom had criminal records, were arrested and questioned for 36 hours by officers from the Bureau. The Untouchables wanted to talk to the couple about their links with one of Glasgow's most ruthless godfathers, Thomas McGraw. McGraw was known in the Scottish media as the Mr McBig of organised crime in Scotland. The Hughes were also quizzed about their associations with McGraw's sidekick, Charlie 'Chicken' Glacken. The arrests resulted from a request for assistance from Strathclyde police and HM Customs who had been conducting a major investigation into McGraw and his mob since the summer of 1996, codenamed Operation Glendullan. This was the first such call for the Criminal Assets Bureau's assistance in a money laundering investigation involving criminals in another country. Soon the CAB would be receiving dozens of similar requests from other police forces investigating organised crime around the world. Within a very short period in operation the Untouchables had achieved an impressive international reputation.

McGraw, who was born in 1957, controlled the drug trade in Glasgow. In 1995 he was described as the city's new godfather at the trial of three of his associates, armed robbers Gordon McLeod, Thomas Bagan and James Scougal, who were facing armed robbery charges. During the hearing, the officer leading the police investigation, Detective Inspector Derek Ingram, told how Mr McBig had put a contract out on his life in 1988 because he had arrested one of McGraw's associates. Mr McBig was suspected of involvement in protection rackets, the supply of firearms to other criminals and armed robbery.

Also known as "The Licencee", McGraw, who had several convictions for serious crime, had taken over the reins of power in Glasgow's extremely violent underworld from dead gang boss Arthur Thompson. Since then he had built up a multi-million pound drug empire, specialising in the sale of cannabis, ecstasy and cocaine. Through his associates he bought a number of taxi companies which were used to launder drug money. He also owned several pubs and clubs in the city. Police believed that McGraw bought a number of cab companies by making their owners offers they couldn't refuse! If they didn't take his offer he threatened to have them severely beaten or shot.

One of the most important players in Mr McBig's organisation was Charlie Glacken, a convicted drug trafficker from the Springboig area of Glasgow. Glacken, who was born in 1962, was considered to be a particularly violent criminal with convictions for assault and indecent assault. He specialised in organising the purchase and transportation of the gang's drug shipments between Spain and Scotland. In 1989 he was jailed for three years, for smuggling hashish for McGraw. In September 1992, the "unemployed roofer" was again caught with 5,000 ecstasy tablets. He was also subsequently arrested in 1994 on an armed robbery charge. Glacken went on the run shortly after that and was believed to be in hiding in southern Spain.

An illustration of how important Glacken was to Mr McBig was the offer McGraw made to the UK Customs shortly after his sidekick first went on the run. McGraw suggested that if the charges were dropped against Glacken he could help them recover 100 kilos of drugs, 25 firearms and a rocket launcher. The offer was turned down.

Glacken, however, didn't need a deal. In January 1997 the Canadian authorities arrested him when he tried to enter the country on a false passport. Glacken was returned to Scotland to face trial but was released from custody the following November when the drugs and robbery charges were dropped. Immediately after that he fled to Spain.

Meanwhile Operation Glendullan had established that during the period between 1994 and 1997 McGraw's gang imported around 2,000 kilos of cannabis from Spain, with a total street value of Stg£18 million (€26 million). The actual cost of buying the drugs was IR£2.4 million (€3 million) when purchased in Spain at the wholesale price of IR£1,200 (€1,500) per kilo. McGraw's net profit when he sold it on for IR£2,000 (€2,500) per kilo was around IR£1.6 million (€2 million).

In April 1997, as part of the ongoing police investigation, Spanish police caught three of McGraw's associates as they prepared 470 kilos for transportation to Scotland. The gang used the cover of a specially-converted Mercedes coach which was ostensibly used to transport school kids and youth groups from under-privileged areas of Glasgow for holidays in Marbella. In September 1997, police and Customs stopped the bus on a return journey to the UK and found 90 kilos of hashish hidden inside. It had travelled from Benidorm in Spain, overland through France and by ferry to the UK. As a result of the follow-up investigation McGraw and nine other associates were arrested and charged with drug trafficking and money laundering offences on December 1, 1997.

It was during the follow-up enquiry that the Scottish authorities uncovered the Irish link to the huge criminal operation. While following the money trail they discovered that Mary Hughes had paid IR£45,000 (€57,000) to David Deans, one of Thomas McGraw's money launderers, in the months immediately preceding the September shipment. Deans had also been charged with money laundering offences on December 1, 1997. Mary Hughes had earlier withdrawn the cash from her own bank account with the Allied Irish Bank branch in Donegal town and transferred it to an account she held with the same bank in Glasgow.

Within days of Mr McBig's arrest the Scottish police contacted the Criminal Assets Bureau and arranged a conference to discuss the investigation. As a result the Untouchables and their colleagues in the Money Laundering Investigation Unit obtained court orders under the Cirminal Justice Act 1994 to access bank accounts belonging to the Hughes in Donegal. They discovered that while Glacken was on the run in 1996 he had visited the Hughes on several occasions. John Hughes had personally introduced Glacken at the bank in Donegal where he opened an account and lodged IR£200,000 (€250,000) between May and December 1996. The Bureau also discovered that Thomas McGraw had also visited Donegal with Glacken and the pair had discussed buying property in the area. On December 18 the High Court granted the Bureau an order freezing Glacken's Irish accounts.

It was also discovered that the Hughes had opened an account at the same branch of the AIB in Donegal in January 1996, with a lodgement of IR£135,000 (€171,500) that they used to buy the Paradise pub.

In the beginning of February 1998, the Untouchables arrested John and Mary Hughes for questioning under money laundering legislation. During their interviews the Glasgow couple made some astonishing admissions. The real owner of the bar was Thomas McGraw. He had given them the money in Glasgow with which to buy the premises, in a bid to hide his drug money.

Armed with overwhelming proof of criminality and money laundering, the Criminal Assets Bureau became the owner of a pub. And a month later, on March 29, the Untouchables sold the bar for IR£215,000 (€273,000) at auction. Meanwhile back in Scotland the McGraw gang had effectively been broken up. The Mr McBig of organised crime was acquitted in July 1998 after being held in custody for seven months. Three of his associates, however, were convicted and jailed for sentences ranging between six and ten years. Four others were also released from custody after the court ruled they had no case to answer.

As soon as he was released, McGraw left Glasgow fearing that he was about to be murdered by underworld rivals.

* * * *

In November 1998, the Criminal Assets Bureau sold a second pub belonging to another major international drug trafficker. This time Barry Galvin had been authorised to sell Cahir Bar on Main Street, Corofin in County Clare for €200,000. The agreed price was possibly a drop in the ocean when calculated against the drug smuggling rackets organised by Englishman Henry James Dumas. The Londoner had been operating an elaborate cocaine-trafficking route between South America and the UK until January 1998. His operation came to an abrupt end when HM Customs seized Stg£20 million (€29 million) worth of the drug which was being smuggled in the specially adapted wheels of a Land Rover jeep.

Although Dumas managed to slip the net, ten members of his organisation were arrested and charged with money laundering and drug trafficking. A follow-up enquiry uncovered information that the racket had been in operation for two years before it was finally rumbled. During that time Dumas and his associates had changed Stg£4 million (€5.8 million) into various currencies at a Thomas Cook Bureau de Change in London.

When the Criminal Assets Bureau was asked to help with the investigation they tracked down two bank drafts for a total of Stg£250,000 (€365,000). They were used by Dumas to buy eight properties in County Clare. The Untouchables were also in a position to prove a direct link between the cash Dumas had exchanged in London and the purchase of the properties in County Clare, including the pub in Corofin. Within months of the Stg20 million (€29 million) cocaine seizure, Dumas had managed to sell off his properties in Ireland with the exception of the pub. He had also managed to slip out of the country by the time the UK authorities issued a warrant for his arrest. But he wasn't disappearing without some pain. The Untouchables obtained a court order to seize the pub just weeks before Dumas also sold it off. On Thursday November 26 the Bureau stepped in and sold the premises, finishing the sale which had been negotiated on Dumas' behalf.

Henry Dumas never turned up to fight the sale or to try to reclaim the cash. Another international drug trafficker had just learned that Ireland was no longer the welcoming place the underworld had thought it to be.

****

Michael John Paul Green made the other ex-patriot gangsters who came to live in Ireland look like mere paupers. Suitably nicknamed the Scarlet Pimpernel of international organised crime, Mickey Green was one of the biggest drug traffickers in the world. With a personal fortune estimated to be worth in the region of Stg£100 million (€145 million), in the hierarchy of organised crime, Green truly was a king. Born in Edgeware, North London on June 23, 1941, the Pimpernel had risen up through the ranks of serious crime, rubbing shoulders with some of London's most infamous godfathers, to become one of the richest gangsters in Europe.

He earned the sobriquet the Pimpernel because, even though he was one of Europe's most hunted criminals, he had evaded capture for over two decades. At various stages in his colourful career Green had been wanted in Holland, France, Spain, Belgium and Britain, in connection with drug trafficking and gold smuggling rackets worth hundreds of millions of English pounds. He was on the target list of every customs and police force in Europe, the US Drug Enforcement Agency and the FBI. The Pimpernel had done business with the US Mafia and the most infamous Colombian drug cartels. But in the end the Criminal Assets Bureau was the only law enforcement agency in the world to cause Mickey Green any real heartache.

The Pimpernel's close shaves with capture, in several different countries, are the stuff of gangland legend. It was after one of those dramatic near misses that he decided to come to live in Ireland, the only place where he felt he would be left alone. In 1993 Green had been arrested in the US on foot of arrest warrants from Holland and France. But as a result of incompetence, corruption and sheer good luck, he had successfully fought off both extradition attempts. In December of that year he was released from prison and deported to Ireland because he held an Irish passport. Green's legendary luck had held again.

As he boarded the flight to Dublin on December 17, Green was a happy man. He had beaten the DEA, the Dutch, French and British authorities. The legend of the Pimpernel had become the hot topic of conversation in both law enforcement and criminal circles across the world. Green decided that he had had enough of tangling with the law and that Ireland would be his new home.

In August 1994, Green paid IR£243,000 (€208,500) for Maple Falls, a magnificent mansion newly built on four acres near the village of Kilcock in County Meath. At the same time he bought a new three-bedroom penthouse apartment for IR£135,000 (€171,000) in Dublin's upmarket Customs House Docks development. One of his bagmen had arranged the transfer of the money, through a network of false companies, and he paid for the properties in cash. Green had instantly fallen in love with Maple Falls. He went on to run his huge drug empire from the estate, organising deals and entertaining some of Europe's biggest criminal godfathers.

Maple Falls, a single-storey house, was a handy twenty-minute journey from Dublin. It had three receptions rooms; five bedrooms, four bathrooms and a gym complete with a full size sauna. The house also had an indoor heated swimming pool and a snooker room. Green spent a fortune on décor, with antique furniture and hand-woven, custom-made carpets. Both the Dublin penthouse and Maple Falls also had the most advanced sound systems that money could buy.

The multi-millionaire drug lord spared no expense on the grounds either, with a stable and paddock, a floodlit tennis court and a large pond, situated in the middle of a beautifully manicured garden. Green spent thousands of pounds stocking the pond with exotic Japanese Ki Carp fish that were valued at up to IR£500 (€635) each. Next door to the pond was a fully equipped bar and conservatory for entertaining his many criminal guests. Associates would later recall how Green would literally spend hours on his own gazing into the pond as he planned his various business deals and scams.

But in the months before the murder of Veronica Guerin the Pimpernel's cosy lifestyle was coming under threat. Driving his Bentley at high speed while drunk in the early hours of the morning, Green had been involved in a horrific car crash during which he killed a taxi driver. As a result of the inquest into the smash the *Sunday World* newspaper had exposed Green for the first time to the rest of the world. The godfather decided to leave Ireland for a number of months until everything died down. When he came back to live at Maple Falls the new Criminal Assets Bureau was getting a lot of media attention but Green felt he had very little to worry about – he was wrong.

Events soon took a dramatic twist when Green's most trusted bagman and business organiser, Michael Michael, was arrested by HM Customs when they busted a huge cocaine and hashish smuggling operation, worth almost Stg£12 million (€17.5 million). Michael who had already been recruited as an informant by a corrupt Scotland Yard detective decided to become a supergrass in return for saving his own skin. His evidence was so powerful that he became known in London gangland circles as the "super-supergrass". Michael Michael had enough dirt to help put the Pimpernel behind bars for a long time. In an eleven-month period, up to the time of his arrest in April 1998, Michael had personally supervised Mickey Green's hashish smuggling operation which had turned over a staggering Stg£28 million (€41 million) in cash. But Michael's arrest, and the resulting trials were to be kept secret until the end of 2001. Within weeks of his arrest, however, the Pimpernel realised something was wrong when his bagman didn't reappear. It was then that Green decided to leave Ireland again – only this time it was for good.

By that stage the Pimpernel had already been a secret target of the Untouchables for almost a year. During that time the Bureau had established that both Maple Falls and the penthouse in Dublin had been bought with the proceeds of crime.

Following Michael Michael's arrest the Head of the CAB, Felix McKenna attended a number of secret meetings with the HM Customs officers heading the Michael investigation, which was codenamed Operation Draft. The Irish end of the international investigation was codenamed Operation Damask. Michael had already divulged how he had helped use Green's drug money to buy the Irish properties. His evidence gave the Untouchables a strong case with which to move against the Pimpernel.

On July 6, 1998 the HM Customs investigation team invited the Bureau to attend a secret conference in London. The officer directly in charge of the CAB enquiry, Detective Sergeant Paul O'Brien, and a Bureau legal officer attended the conference during which it was decided that Green's Irish properties should be seized. An international hunt had been ordered to try and locate Mickey Green who had literally vanished.

The CAB raided four premises in Dublin and Kildare on July 30, including Green's two properties and the home of his driver and assistant, Paul Boulton. The searches were to prove crucial to the international search for Green. The Bureau discovered that Boulton was secretly in direct contact with the Pimpernel. It was only a matter of time before they would smoke out the slippery godfather.

In December 1999, the Criminal Assets Bureau was ready to make its move. Armed with affidavits from HM Customs and the information gleaned from Michael Michael, the Bureau obtained a High Court order freezing the two properties in Dublin and Kildare. At the same time the Michael Michael cases were proceeding behind closed doors and maximum security at Woolwich Crown Court in London. The Crown Prosecution Service had issued warrants for the arrest of Mickey Green on charges of drug trafficking and money laundering, but no one could yet locate him.

In a secret memo sent to HM Customs Felix McKenna said his officers were confident that within days of seizing the elusive gangster's properties they would get a fix on his whereabouts. The CAB strategy paid off. Green was extremely agitated when he heard that his beloved Maple Falls was to be taken from him and he decided to fight the seizure tooth and nail – and that was his mistake.

Early in January Det. Sgt. O'Brien and his team discovered that Green was living under a false identity in the

Barcelona area of Spain. Later he pinpointed the Pimpernel to the Ritz Hotel and informed HM Customs.

In the first week of February 2000, Mickey Green was arrested by Spanish police and remanded in custody to a prison in Madrid.

At last, it appeared that finally the Pimpernel's number was up. But from his jail cell Green began fighting the Customs extradition case and the CAB case in Dublin. For the next 16 months Green fought his legal battle from his Spanish cell. In the end the Pimpernel's extraordinary luck held out when the London courts ruled that they could not rely on Michael Michael's uncorroborated testimony. Some of Green's closest associates, whose counsel had mounted the successful challenge against Michael's evidence, also had the charges against them dropped. The Crown Prosecution Service dropped the charges against the Pimpernel and he was released from prison.

In the end, in Green's entire criminal career, it was the Criminal Assets Bureau who caused him the most aggravation. It was their intelligence work that had led to him being held in a Spanish jail for over a year. And then in 2002 they sold off his two properties in Dublin and Kildare for a figure in excess of €1.6 million. Associates who know Green best say that he bears a "dreadful grudge" against the Bureau for effectively cutting his ties with Ireland. The loss of his beloved Maple Falls, they say, has been one of the worst blows he ever suffered at the hands of the law enforcement community.

* * * *

The Criminal Assets Bureau's success in denying international criminals the ability to enjoy their wealth in Ireland was dealt a potentially serious blow when they began pursuing another notorious London criminal – Geoffrey Donovan. In one of the single most significant setbacks since the CAB's establishment, the Supreme Court ruled that the Proceeds of Crime Act, under which the Untouchables operated, did not apply to the proceeds of crime committed outside the State.

In May 2004 the five-judge panel overturned a High Court order granting the Bureau permission to sell off the luxury home of drug trafficker Donovan who had been an ideal target.

Born in 1939 in Lambeth, South London, Donovan had been a lifelong criminal figure. He progressed from petty crime to armed robbery and then large scale drug trafficking. His long string of criminal convictions included malicious wounding and armed robbery. In 1983, he was amongst an organised crime group which was responsible for a complete overhaul of the British jury system after he and a number of associates were convicted of "nobbling" a jury, by offering them large bribes to return not guilty verdicts. Donovan, who was already serving a six-year sentence for robbery and handling stolen goods, was jailed along with seven other south London villains. They had offered Stg£1,000 (€1,500) bribes to jurors hearing a case against a gangland pal, John Goodwin, who was being tried for a Stg£1.25 million (€1.8 million) burglary. At the time an Old Bailey judge described Donovan's activities as a "growing menace against the criminal court system". Donovan was jailed for four years for his part in the bribery scandal.

Following his release from prison he joined the rest of his gangland partners and got involved in the much more lucrative drug business. Scotland Yard would later describe Donovan as "a very significant middle man" who co-ordinated the distribution of all types of category A drugs between international dealers and the street. He was closely associated with a London-based Turkish heroin dealer who had been high on Scotland Yard's most wanted list for years but who had managed to evade conviction. Meanwhile Donovan lived the high life, indulging his love of expensive watches. At one time he owned two Rolex and Cartier watches worth over Stg£14,000 (€20,500).

Donovan found his little piece of heaven in 1989 when he decided to settle in Ireland. He paid €128,000 in cash for a beautiful home, The Pines at Tinode, Manor Kilbride near Blessington in County Wicklow. He built a large shed at the rear of his new bolthole where he reared greyhounds. He also continued to control his criminal empire from Wicklow. But a Scotland Yard undercover operation was to interrupt his idyllic country lifestyle. In March 1992, cops in the UK arrested him with more than Stg£300,000 (€438,000) worth of hashish, cocaine and ecstasy powder, as well as a .38 revolver and ammunition. He was jailed for a total of nine years in December 1992.

On his conviction the gangster was served with a confiscation order for more than Stg£140,000 (€204,000) which he refused to pay. As a result the tight-fisted criminal was given an additional three years behind bars, which he was ordered to serve on top of his existing sentence. In 1998 Donovan was moved to an open prison but he absconded and returned to Wicklow.

For the following two years he kept his head down and avoided the attentions of the Gardaí. Scotland Yard believe that he continued to organise his drug business with the Turkish heroin dealer during that time. And as time went by Donovan grew more confidant that he had beaten the cops. He began commuting back and forth to the UK by car. In 1999, however, the Criminal Assets Bureau was tipped off about Donovan's presence in Ireland in an anonymous letter.

While that discreet inquiry was progressing, however, Donovan was re-arrested in July 2000 as he passed through Holyhead ferry port in Wales. He was returned to prison to complete his sentence.

A month after his return to jail in August officers from the CAB visited him at Altcourse Prison near Liverpool. They served documents notifying him that they intended to seize his home.

When he was released from prison on April 4, 2001 Donovan returned to Ireland to contest the Bureau's High Court application to sell the house, which was then valued at IR£500,000 (€635,000). During the six day hearing in May 2001, Felix McKenna described Donovan as a career criminal who was involved in major distribution of drugs in the UK.

Officers from Scotland Yard's Financial Unit also gave evidence of his long criminal record.

In his own testimony Donovan claimed that, in between jail sentences, he earned money from a men's clothing business and from buying, selling and racing greyhounds. He claimed that he had bought the house on the proceeds of his success breeding and racing greyhounds. His legal team also argued that even if the house had been bought with drug money he had already served his time – the additional three years – for not paying up on the confiscation order served on him at the time of his original conviction. The Bureau's legal team, however, argued that under the Irish Proceeds of Crime Act this did not matter – the house was bought with dirty money and therefore was liable to be seized. Mr Justice Joseph Finnegan did not accept Donovan's arguments and granted the confiscation order to the CAB. At the time the gangster told this writer: "There are very serious issues here of human rights and constitutional rights. It is all very unfair."

But Donovan appealed the decision to the Supreme Court. Among his grounds of appeal was that the Proceeds of Crime Act did not apply to the proceeds of crimes committed outside the State.

In a decision which had clear implications for the work of the CAB, the five-judge court upheld Donovan's action on the grounds that the 1996 Act clearly had effect only within the boundaries of the State. The court ruled that it was clear the purpose of the legislation was to freeze, and ultimately confiscate, property acquired with or representing the proceeds of crime committed in the State. Donovan was allowed to keep his Wicklow home.

The ruling had other implications for assets sold by the Bureau and held under the seven year provision contained in the Proceeds of Crime Act before being transferred to the Department of Finance. Yan Ijpelaar, for example, demanded the return of the proceeds of the sale of his Kerry properties, as did Mickey Green. Ijpelaar paid Alan Campbell €30,000 because he had tipped him off in Holland about the Donovan judgement. However, as a result of tough negotiations with Felix McKenna and his staff, both men agreed to give the State over half of the monies now technically owed to them. After the Supreme Court decision the Government moved quickly to close the loophole exposed and amended the Proceeds of Crime Act in 2005. Since then the Act caters for the seizure of assets derived from criminal activity outside the jurisdiction.

By the summer of 2006 the Untouchables had targeted at least twenty foreign drug traffickers, armed robbers and fraudsters, and seized a large quantity of assets and cash.

Eight

Patriots and Smugglers

The Border between the Irish Republic and Northern Ireland has acted as a symbol for the political and terrorist conflict since the Anglo-Irish Treaty of 1922 provided for the partition of the country. Its existence contributed to the bloody Civil War in the Republic and abolishing it was at the heart of the terrorist war that lasted for almost three decades, from the late 1970s until the cease-fire in 1996. This invisible meandering line has been a central symbol in the policies formulated by the Provisional IRA and its political wing Sinn Féin. Republicans have fought and spilled much blood in their quest for its replacement and the achievement of a united Ireland. The Border and all the problems it represents has also been high on the agendas of successive Irish Governments and all the northern political parties. Since the beginning of the Peace Process the Border has continued to dominate the political landscape. Democratic debate and negotiation may now have replaced the bomb and the bullet in negotiations but there is another hidden dimension to this divisive boundary.

The lands that straddle the Border have long been dubbed Bandit Country – and for good reason. The term was first used to describe the impenetrable stronghold of Republican terrorism in South Armagh. And the Border lived up to its reputation in other ways as well. As a result of the Troubles, the Border was firmly established as the epicentre of a vast underworld economy, sustained mainly through smuggling. Republican activists, criminals, corrupt farmers and businessmen have been the main beneficiaries of a myriad of rackets, including the smuggling of alcohol, cigarettes, livestock and oil. Many republicans and their various partners-in-crime have also controlled the distribution of illegal growth promoters such as Angel Dust. VAT fraud provides another cornerstone of this black economy. Bandit Country even has its own underground banking system to keep the industry ticking over. Today the Border rackets generate so much criminal wealth that they come a close second to the narcotics trade. Confidential figures compiled in 2002 by HM Customs calculated that the UK Exchequer was losing up to Stg£20 million (€29 million) per month as a result of oil smuggling alone – a racket which was, and still is, controlled by Sinn Féin/IRA godfather Thomas 'Slab' Murphy.

In the process Bandit country has turned many so-called freedom fighters and their travelling companions into multi-millionaires. This vast organised crime empire has also contributed significantly to the funding of the Sinn Féin political party which, ostensibly, wants to eradicate the lucrative cash cow that is the Border. Cynics say that the Republicans will suffer the most financially in the event that they ever achieve their goal of a united Ireland.

The Criminal Assets Bureau first exposed the true extent of this extremely well-organised criminal machine. By the summer of 2006 the CAB, working in conjunction with its newly established counterpart in the North, the Assets Recovery Agency (ARA), was at an advanced stage of an eight year investigation into Bandit Country's millionaires. It uncovered an extremely complex web of financial intrigue, involving a diverse group of individuals from hard line Republicans, to farmers and businessmen. Operation Ballybough was just one of the investigations involved and serves as an example of what was going on.

In early 1998 the Bureau had received an intelligence report that two IRA members were attempting to sell investment properties. They wanted to get rid of the premises before they came to the notice of the Untouchables. Between them John Bernard McNally and Philip Anthony Fox owned 30 properties, most of which were on Dublin's north side. All the properties had been rented out, mainly to the recipients of

Social Welfare payments. The main player in the conspiracy was McNally, who was born in South Armagh in 1953 but later moved to live in Navan, County Meath. McNally had been a hard line Republican all his life and his brother was shot dead by British soldiers during an IRA attack. He had spent time in prison for explosives' offences, larceny and escaping from lawful custody.

Further investigations would later reveal that McNally, who used four different aliases for various bank accounts, was also involved in the Peace Process negotiations on behalf of Sinn Féin/IRA. Certain Republicans have consistently tried to use their involvement in the peace process in a bid to wriggle their way out of trouble with either the CAB or the ARA. For several years, while supposedly taking part in the "struggle for freedom" McNally had turned a crust through his involvement in the distribution of Angel Dust and smuggling rackets. The IRA man was also suspected of being involved in a VAT carousel fraud, involving the sale of plastic silage wrap and baling twine to farms along the border. (Put simply carousel fraud involves claiming back VAT, which was never actually paid, from the taxman on goods which are sold through a series of bogus companies between two countries. In some cases the bogus goods are exported between two countries over and over again, hence the name carousel.)

His partner-in-crime, Philip Anthony Fox, was born in 1947 and was from Bailieboro, County Cavan. He had also served time for possession of firearms and explosives. Like John McNally, Fox used no less than six aliases but he was considered to be a smaller shareholder in the 'business'.

The CAB investigation had soon begun to unravel a complex money laundering operation, involving millions of euro being moved through up to twenty bank accounts. Operation Ballybough also identified the names of 25 individuals who were involved at various levels of the rackets. The money trail would eventually lead the CAB to Texas and the Isle of Man.

The Untouchables were particularly interested in two bank

accounts held at AIB in Carrickmacross, County Monaghan, which were both in false names. It was later established that these names were aliases used by McNally and Fox. IR£7.5 million (€9.5 million) had moved through the two accounts over a three year period. But the account was closed, like so many others, as soon as it was known that a Criminal Assets Bureau was going to be set up in 1996. Further intelligence revealed that several individuals from Bandit Country had also moved substantial amounts of money out of the country to places such as the Bahamas, the Isle of Man and Jersey. Two bank drafts withdrawn when the Carrickmacross accounts were closed, led the Untouchables to the Laredo National Bank in Laredo, Texas.

In Texas the account was operated by three Irish individuals, two of whom were suspected of being front men for McNally and a number of other racketeers. The Irishmen were part of a business project involving the purchase and fattening of cattle in what are known as 'feed lots'. These are huge cattle sheds, which house several hundred and sometimes thousands of cattle, who are fattened on a diet of maize, corn and other foodstuffs. In the USA, growth-promoting hormones are legal and widely used. One of the front men in the new venture was identified as South Armagh smuggler Gerard Mackle, who was well known to law enforcement agencies in Ireland and the UK. The second member of the cartel, who was from County Cavan, was also suspected of involvement in distributing Angel Dust and smuggling livestock. The third investor in the Texas project was Eamon Galavan the owner of a successful animal feed manufacturing company, Galavan Supplements Ltd., in Enniscorthy, County Wexford.

Of the three shareholders Galavan was the odd-man-out. He had no involvement with smuggling and got to know the Border men through selling them foodstuffs. When McNally's associates invited him to get involved in the proposed project in Texas he jumped at the chance because he had already looked at the feed lot fattening method. His involvement in the company would add credibility to the venture. Each of the three men invested IR£300,000 (€380,000). Eventually, however, after two years, Galavan decided to opt out of the partnership when he became unhappy with the way the operation was being run. By the time the CAB traced him in the system his former partners had bought out the Wexford businessman.

Unfortunately for Galavan, the money he earned from the Texas venture went back to an account in the Isle of Man. When the CAB took a closer look at his financial affairs they discovered that he had been secreting millions out of the country to avoid paying tax in Ireland. He was arrested in October 2000 and questioned about his involvement with McNally's associates. Despite the fact that he had no criminal involvement with the smugglers he suddenly found himself facing potential criminal proceedings under the tax laws. He agreed to settle his affairs with the CAB and within days of his arrest promptly paid a hefty IR£4 million (€5 million).

News of the settlement had leaked to the media and his case was reported by RTÉ news and followed up by a number of daily newspapers. In the reports Galavan was linked to the distribution of Angel Dust and money laundering. In a statement at the time he claimed the story was a "total falsification of the true position". He said: "I am innocent. It was during an investigation that they happened on me and discovered that I owed money to the tax people. We agreed to pay and get on with our business. We couldn't believe it when details of the agreement appeared in the media. I am innocent. I am a victim. I have been damaged. My name appeared on a joint account in an American bank and it is only for that reason that I came to the attention of the CAB."

Another individual identified by Operation Ballybough was farmer and businessman from County Cavan. Although they couldn't prove it, the Bureau suspected that the farmer had also been a secret investor in the Texas project. He was also investigated by the Department of Agriculture. As part of their probes into the distribution of illegal growth promoters, department officials had searched his property on a number of occasions throughout the 1990s. By the time the Untouchables got to him, however, the farmer had moved to live in Australasia. He had built up a huge farming empire and had become one of the country's richest businessmen. One of his farms was stocked with up to 5,000 cattle.

Back in Ireland, the Bureau had discovered that he had availed of the controversial tax amnesty in 1993. They also untangled a complex web of bank accounts that led from the north-east of the country to the West and north-west. The money trail then led to the Channel Islands, the USA and New Zealand. The farmer, who potentially faced criminal charges, was served with large tax assessments based on his income between the years 1983 and 1997. Four months before Galavan's arrest in 2000, the farmer agreed to pay a sum in excess of IR£4 million (€5 million). It was understood that he agreed to pay because he still held a large property portfolio in Ireland. The farmer had already made €12 million from the sale of a small portion of a 200-acre estate he had purchased near Navan, twelve years earlier. The land had been re-zoned for development and jumped in value.

Another long-standing associate of McNally was a South Armagh farmer. He was suspected of being one of the first Border Bandits to get substantially involved in the illegal importation and sale of animal growth hormones. He had been investigated on several occasions by the Department of Agriculture and the Anti-Racketeering Unit in the mid-90s. By that time he had also featured in Operation Ballybough and become a full target. It was discovered that almost IR£4 million (€5 million) had gone through bank accounts which he had placed in false names, over a five-year period up to 1999. He was subsequently forced to pay a large tax demand.

In the meantime the original targets of the investigation, McNally and Fox, were also served with tax assessments and they later agreed to settle their affairs. McNally, who is still under investigation for smuggling rackets, paid IR£350,000 (€444,000), while Fox paid up IR£150,000 (€190,500).

By the time Operation Ballybough was completed, the

CAB had recovered over IR£10 million (€12.7 million) through actions brought under Revenue and Proceeds of Crime Acts. In the big picture, however, Ballybough was just one of several such operations, many of which are still ongoing investigations.

* * * *

With so much money being generated by the Border rackets it created an inevitable problem – how to launder the proceeds of the various crimes. In order to get around the difficulties, a number of illegal banks were established along the Border to facilitate this secret, thriving economy. Kieran Byrne and his father James Byrne Senior ran a family business that owned two Bureau de Change outlets on either side of the Border. In 1998, the Money Laundering Investigation Unit (MLIU), received a suspicious transaction report concerning the Byrne's secret Border Bank at Dromad, which is literally a few yards inside the border from South Armagh. Over the next year, the MLIU carried out a secret investigation into the operation of the underworld bank, in conjunction with the CAB and the Northern Ireland police.

The Dromad money laundering operation had the perfect front. It was an official Bureau de Change situated on the side of one of the busiest roadways in the country and was next door to the local Garda station. Its core business was exchanging Irish punts and sterling for people crossing the border in both directions. But behind-the-scenes it was being used to launder millions for smugglers and drug traffickers alike. It is ironic that Republican smugglers and drug traffickers used the same facilities to clean their dirty money. Several well-known Republican racketeers used the 'bank' to launder millions of pounds in sterling and punts. One of its biggest customers was border smuggler Kieran Smyth, from Dundalk. His haulage company facilitated the trafficking of every kind of contraband, including drugs, guns and cigarettes for Republicans and drug dealers alike.

In the Summer of 1998 the Garda National Drug Unit uncovered a link between Byrne's Bureau de Change and a heroin dealing gang, headed by a thug called Seanie Comerford from Ballyfermot in south-west Dublin. Comerford's Dublin operation had turned over an estimated IR£5 million (€6.4 million) in less than two years. In a joint investigation between the GNDU and their colleagues in Manchester, Comerford and several of his associates were busted in swoops on both sides of the Irish Sea in October 1998. A total of 18 kilos of high quality heroin was also seized. One of Comerford's men, who was subsequently convicted of drug trafficking, was also arrested as he drove to Dromad to change Irish currency into sterling, for onward shipment to Comerford in Manchester. He later confirmed to detectives that he had personally brought around IR£600,000 (€760,000) to Kieran Byrne over a number of months, on the instructions of the Comerford gang.

In October 1999, the CAB, the MLIU and Customs finally swooped on the secret bank in Dromad in an operation codenamed Factual. At the same time, police and customs officers also raided the Byrne family premises in Newry, just north of the Border. Several other addresses were searched and six members of the Byrne family, including Kieran Byrne and his father, were arrested and questioned under the Criminal Justice (Drug Trafficking) Act 1996. During the swoop, cash, cheques and drafts worth €2 million were seized in Dromad. Detectives also found the secret ledgers for the underworld bank. It would later emerge that in the period from January 1996 to June 1999, the Byrne's had put IR£63.9 million (€81 million) through their company's legitimate bank account, Dromad Enterprises Clients Account. North of the Border their company account there had total funds of Stg£7.5 million (€10.9 million). But investigators believed that the actual figure the Bureau de Change had handled could have been as high as IR£200 million (€250 million).

Records also showed that the secret bank had 150 clients

all of whom were recorded under false names. Gardaí were able to identify a number of aliases for Kieran Smyth. They found that between January 1998 and October 1999 he had laundered IR£12 million (€15 million) through Dromad. Records also showed that the Byrnes had electronically transferred money to and from Europe, the US, Japan, South Africa, South America and Eastern Europe, for unnamed clients including, intelligence sources later revealed, several well-known members of Sinn Féin and the IRA.

The closure of the bank sent shock waves through Bandit Country. It was to the black economy what the sudden demise of the Central Bank would be for the Irish economy. But within a few days alternative arrangements were made and another two 'banks' had been set-up. As a result of the Dromad raid, several other known smugglers and traffickers were targeted by the Bureau, including Kieran Smyth. In February 2001 he was abducted from his home. His body was found four days later, dumped in a ditch near Ashbourne, County Meath. A post-mortem showed that he had been beaten, bound, blindfolded, gagged and shot twice in the head with a shotgun at close range. Intelligence sources believe that the murder was connected to the closure of the bank and also fears by certain criminal/Republican elements that Smyth might decide to spill the beans in order to save his neck.

A year later, in February 2002, Kieran Byrne was jailed for four years when he pleaded guilty to money laundering and operating an unauthorised Bureau de Change between 1998 and 1999. The court heard that while there was no evidence that Byrne himself had been actively engaged in crime, he had provided an essential service for criminals. His defence barrister Paddy McEntee SC claimed that smuggling was seen as a "way of life in the Border area" and his client had "succumbed to the blandishments of others". "Byrne," he said, "was also owed €2.5 million by some of his clients but was unlikely to receive any of it."

Byrne later agreed to pay the Criminal Assets Bureau a

total of €2,865,000. And after his release from prison he paid another sum of €328,000. His father James paid a total of €110,000 in income tax.

Despite the success of the investigation, Border banks continue to operate, although a number were also closed down. Since then the Border Bandits, especially the Republicans, have been using alternative methods for laundering their cash. Form the late 1990s major smugglers have bought up huge amounts of property in Ireland, the UK and across Europe. But Gardaí believe that the banks are still operating to keep the day-to-day criminal machine working. And as one is shut down another replaces it. As one officer involved in the investigation remarked: "This is a huge business and it will only cease when the Border disappears, and no one involved in the criminal rackets, including a lot of so-called hard line Sinn Féin and IRA people, want that to happen anytime soon."

* * * *

Just four months after the dramatic swoop on Dromad and the follow-up investigation, the Untouchables found themselves in the forefront of another agricultural crisis. It was one of the biggest crises in recent Irish history and was sparked by another smuggling racket. As a direct result of the Foot and Mouth Disease that gripped Ireland in early 2001, the Criminal Assets Bureau was deployed in the forefront of a major investigation. The Untouchables were going into the farming and livestock business.

Foot and Mouth disease, which is highly contagious and affects cattle and sheep, is one of the most devastating plagues that can hit the agricultural sector. An epidemic broke out in England and Wales in February 2001. Within weeks tens of thousands of animals were being burned in huge pyres throughout the countryside, as the authorities desperately tried to prevent any further spread of the disease which had the potential to bring the country's agricultural industry to its knees. In response, Ireland launched a major national emergency plan to turn the country into a veritable fortress. Thousands of troops and Gardaí were drafted in to seal off every roadway, lane and track on the Border, to prevent the movement of infected animals to the South. As a consequence of the unprecedented security measures, which had rarely been seen even in the worst days of the Troubles, the Border smugglers and racketeers found themselves temporarily out of work.

On February 28, the Government's fears became a reality. A case of the deadly disease was found in a flock of sheep, north of the Border at Meigh, in South Armagh. Within days, it was discovered that animals from the same infected flock had been smuggled across the Border and had turned up in the Kepak meat factory at Athleague, County Roscommon. Sporting and other major public events were cancelled throughout the country. Hill-walking was banned and mats containing disinfectant were placed at the entrance to every farm, public building and business in Ireland.

And there was good reason for the dramatic action. Foot and mouth threatened the very existence of the food industry in Ireland – an industry that was worth an estimated €11 billion a year. Despite the fact that the State eventually managed to contain the crisis with only one confirmed case of the disease, it had a huge effect on the economy. A report published by the Department of Agriculture and Food a year later in March 2002, showed that the overall bill to the Exchequer for dealing with the disease, was €107 million. The Department of Agriculture and Food spent a total of €44 million on the operation, while the Garda and Army security operation cost €50 million. A further €13 million was spent promoting tourism as a result of the crisis. In real terms the disease had cost the sector an estimated € 210 million in the first six months of 2001.

Every arm of the State was mobilised to prevent the spread of the disease – and to track down those responsible. Within a short period it was discovered that one man, a dodgy livestock dealer, called John Walsh, had been responsible for the fiasco.

Never before had one individual caused such a potentially catastrophic situation for the economy of a nation. The Gardaí, in collaboration with the police in Northern Ireland and the UK, commenced an immediate investigation to catch the smuggler. It was inevitable that the Criminal Assets Bureau was called in as part of that ongoing inquiry, to follow the money trail.

John Walsh was a typical rough and ready cattle dealer, who had a lot in common with the notorious character Bull McCabe in the movie *The Field*. Born in 1950 in Dunlavin, County Wicklow, he started out as a cattle dealer with just IR£50 (€63.5). He used to travel the country in a battered old van buying and selling suck calves. He had a history of assault and not paying his debts. He was jailed in 1985 for failure to pay fines he owed. Nevertheless he made enough money to invest in a hotel in County Kerry, earning himself the nickname 'the Kerryman' as a result. But his business foundered after a few years and he sold the hotel. He later bought a run-down Georgian residence, Longford House and 250 acres of land near Clanreen close to Birr, County Offaly. By 1999 his company, Kingdom Livestock Agents, had run up debts of IR£280,000 (€355,500).

Walsh lived in rough conditions and neglected his livestock. One visitor to Longford House once claimed he saw two of Walsh's dogs eating a rotting sheep in the kitchen. 'The Kerryman' was also accused of deliberately infecting some of his animals with BSE or Mad Cow disease in order to get grants from the Department of Agriculture. In February 2000, he was convicted for failing to bury 200 dead and rotting sheep on his land. But Walsh continued to be involved in the livestock trade and was well-known in marts and meat factories throughout the midlands and north-west. Department of Agriculture officials suspected that he was part of an organised group of corrupt cattle dealers involved in smuggling animals along the Border. One of his preferred rackets was buying large numbers of sheep in the UK and smuggling them back into Ireland. He would then sell them to Irish meat factories, who rarely asked questions about the origin of the produce. The meat was then passed off as Irish lamb to the huge French market, which was boycotting English produce at the time.

In 2001 he bought a flock of 215 lambs which he tried to transport by boat from Stranraer to Belfast. He was using a veterinary certificate issued to him the previous week for a different flock of 170. When the shipment was stopped, he took them back and bought more sheep. This time he hired a different lorry and driver and got a fresh certificate for 291 animals. He then left Britain on February 18 with 393 sheep. About 70 animals were dropped at a field near Newry, County Armagh on February 19. The rest were taken to a holding pen in Meigh, County Armagh, where their identity tags were removed.

Under cover of darkness, Walsh then smuggled ten animals across the Border, to a farm near Enfield, County Meath, and delivered another 21 sheep to Irish Country Meats in Navan, under a false name. Two other sheep died and 248, the bulk of the remainder, were taken to the Kepak factory at Athleague, County Roscommon early on February 20. Walsh was known by a member of staff who signed him in, under the name of another farmer who was a totally innocent party. Walsh also gave a false registration for the lorry by concocting a mixture of the numbers from his own lorry and jeep. He didn't want to draw attention to the Northern Ireland registration on the truck he was using to transport the animals.

Walsh was paid for the sheep with four cheques totalling IR£13,097.37 (€16,630) from Kepak in the false name he had furnished, with the full knowledge of certain staff at the factory. The smuggler took the cheques to the AIB bank in Roscommon where a startling arrangement existed. Walsh could exchange the cheques for a sterling draft without showing any identification. All he had to do was go to a particular counter and use a special number given to him at the factory. He could also obtain payment from the factories for the sheep plus a VAT rebate of between 4.2 per cent and 4.5 per cent by using the name of a 'flat rate' farmer, a legitimate farmer who was not registered for VAT.

But the secret world of the smuggler was about to be exposed. The sheep he had smuggled were infected with Foot and Mouth disease. Two days after he shipped the flock to Northern Ireland the disease manifested itself in the UK. Nine days after Walsh arrived in South Armagh, February 28, his sheep were the first to be detected with the deadly plague in the North. It was the first outbreak of the disease on the island of Ireland.

A few days later the rest of the flock had been traced to the Kepak plant. Walsh had become Ireland's new Public Enemy Number One. When more of the infected sheep turned up in County Louth it sparked a major emergency. As soon as he heard the news, Walsh fled to England.

The National Bureau of Criminal Investigation (NBCI) begun an immediate investigation to track down Walsh and locate every one of the sheep he had smuggled into the country. Within a week the detectives had traced every sheep in the infected flock. The NBCI then began a criminal investigation of Walsh under legislation relating to illegal movement of livestock. As that operation continued Felix McKenna ordered a CAB investigation into the smuggler's finances. Under CAB legislation, the Bureau could seek settlement of outstanding tax in cases where suspected criminal activity, which included smuggling, had taken place. Revenue officers attached to the Bureau found that Walsh had made several years of tax returns in which he claimed he had made no income. Over the next ten days, however, the Untouchable uncovered different stories when they raided the offices of his accountants. Officers also visited 20 marts and meat factories and studied records of sales to Walsh. As a result the Bureau raised a tax assessment of over IR£286,000 (€363,000) for ten years between 1990 and 2000. With interest and penalties, the sheep smuggler owed over IR£650,000 (€825,000). But the problem was locating Walsh to inform him of the situation.

Detective Sergeant Paul O'Brien and Detective Garda Philip Galvin flew to England to try and find the elusive smuggler. When they went to an address in Carlisle they found that he had left and the flat was up for rent. The officers called the letting agents and managed to get a mobile phone number for Walsh. When they rang him he told them he was living in Finchley, North London. The detectives hired a car and drove south immediately. They were amazed that Walsh agreed to meet them in the Bald Head Eagle pub. In a quiet corner of the bar Ireland's most wanted man was handed an envelope with the CAB tax demand. The officers convinced Walsh to come back to Ireland and face the music. He could not be extradited for revenue offences or illegally moving animals.

Ten days later he arrived back in Dublin and attended a meeting with Det. Sgt. John McColgan by appointment at Harcourt Terrace Garda station. The officer arrested him for questioning for an offence of obtaining money under false pretences from Kepak. The following day Walsh was released from custody by the NBCI and interviewed by Garda and Revenue Bureau officers. Later he was arrested by Detective Inspector John McDermott and charged with several offences for knowingly or wilfully delivering incorrect income tax returns to the Revenue Commissioners. He was brought before the District Court and remanded in custody.

In January 2002, Walsh was jailed for three months at Dublin District Court. He had admitted four charges of illegally importing 279 sheep into the country in contravention of EU regulations between February 19 and 20, 2001. Walsh's defence counsel said he had acted out of desperation after his cattle herd was wiped out by brucellosis in 1990 and he was denied compensation because his paperwork was not in order. Judge Haughton said that the experience should have made him more alert to the dangers of disease in livestock. Instead he had "disregarded all the precautions" for "one reason only, to make money" and had used "every devise possible to cover his trail". Judge Gerard Haughton said the consequences of John Walsh's actions had "devastated" tourism and agriculture.

He stated: "The entire country is well aware as to what occurred and will be paying for it for a very considerable period of time." Detective Sergeant John Colgan of the NBCI gave evidence of what he had uncovered about Walsh's relationship with the meat factory. He said that from his investigations it seemed the factory where Walsh brought the animals did "not seem to be fussy" when it came to verifying names of clients selling them livestock.

One of the effects of the crisis, which Walsh had helped to create, was that a huge fraud racket had been exposed. The Department of Agriculture found that there had been a dramatic drop in the number of ewe premiums or grants paid out by the Government based on how many sheep were in a flock, being claimed in the Republic following the outbreak of Foot and Mouth. Within a year, the number of applications for ewe premiums fell from 4.49 million in 2001, the year before the outbreak, to 3.8 million in 2002. The Department found that the loss of 600,000 breeding ewes from the Irish national flock between the 2000 and 2002 had "puzzled" the experts.

In May 2002, Walsh got a twelve-month suspended sentence and was fined €20,000 for making incorrect tax returns. He had pleaded guilty at Dublin Circuit Criminal Court to making incorrect tax returns and to two counts of making late returns for those two tax years. Judge Elizabeth Dunne noted that Walsh had voluntarily returned to Ireland and had co-operated with Gardaí. Judge Dunne said she also had to consider that by the time the CAB sold Walsh's farm – his only remaining asset – to meet his liabilities, he would have little or nothing left.

In 2004, Longford House and lands were sold at auction for €850,000 and Walsh moved to live in Cumbria in England. But despite all the experiences of the previous two years, they did not prevent Walsh from continuing his cruelty to animals. Around the same time that the Untouchables were selling his home, Walsh was charged with animal cruelty, after he was caught taking nine puppies on a ferry to sell them in Jersey.

He had left the animals in a car, described as a sauna, for eight hours during the trip. The car windows were left open around an inch and the puppies were cramped into two carrier boxes, each designed to carry one cat. Magistrates at Weymouth Magistrates Court subsequently found him guilty of three charges of animal cruelty. In November 2003 he had also been convicted of animal cruelty in a Scottish court when he was caught smuggling puppies and kittens.

Walsh, however, remained very aggrieved at his conviction and perceived public persecution in Ireland over the Foot and Mouth crisis which almost brought the Irish economy to its knees. He has told associates that he intends to write a book about the whole livestock trade in Ireland, which he claims, is completely corrupt. Walsh maintains he was simply the fall guy for a much bigger scandal.

If it is ever published, his book should make for very interesting reading.

Nine

Rambo's Downfall

Tall, bespectacled and grey-haired, the man in the expensive full length overcoat marched purposefully down the steps leading from the Circuit Criminal Court, looking like he had just won his case. With arrogant poise and his face frozen in a scowl, he ignored the cluster of reporters and photographers shuffling backwards on the path in front of him. They snatched pictures, shouted questions and pointed microphones at the silent gent and were clumsily reversing into each other, as if to maintain a safe distance ahead of his relentless march. Pedestrians stopped on the street to watch the commotion as they recognised the distinguished-looking figure. He strode confidently, arms swinging by his sides, to the waiting prison van. Three prison guards walked beside the man, who had once been their formidable boss. As he disappeared inside the paddy wagon and was hidden by blacked out windows, the door slammed shut behind him.

The only acknowledgement of the influence and status he once held was that Raphael Patrick Burke didn't have to suffer the indignity of wearing handcuffs. Nor did he have to share his transport on the way to Mountjoy Prison with other villains. But the measure was also motivated by a grave concern for the safety of the disgraced former Justice Minister. An hour earlier Burke's notoriously arrogant facade had slipped momentarily. He was visibly shaken as Judge Desmond Hogan jailed him for six months for successively lodging false tax returns. The Judge slammed Burke for abusing his position of power and breaching the trust of the Irish people. In an ironic twist Ray Burke was charged and convicted under legislation introduced by a Fianna Fáil government, of which he was a member.

The final chapter in the corrupt story of Ray Burke had been the result of a major investigation by the Criminal Assets Bureau. The CAB had finally achieved the downfall of a once powerful politician who had considered himself beyond the law, through 30 years of corruption. The Untouchables had marked a watershed in Irish history, as Burke became the first Minister in the history of Irish politics to end up behind bars. They had proved that the CAB could pursue criminals in high office with the same enthusiasm that they would chase a bank robber or a drug dealer. It proved that there was no longer one law for the powerful and another law for the rest of society. Burke, who had made millions from three decades of political corruption, had even tried to use his influence to ensure he remained untouched by the law. While researching this book information emerged that Burke had thwarted various Garda corruption investigations into his activities – including one during his tenure as Justice Minister. In a previous era it just was not a career option for public servants, including senior Gardaí, to go after the likes of Burke. But by the time he was jailed, on January 24, 2005, the world had changed and Rambo's downfall vindicated the Bureau's tough new powers.

* * * *

Raphael Patrick Burke, who was born in Dublin in September 1943, had been involved in local and national politics since the 1960s. A year after his birth, his father, Patrick, was elected as a Fianna Fáil TD in the constituency of Dublin North. When Ray Burke finished school he joined his father's insurance brokerage in Swords and he later took over the business. By 1968 he had expanded the family business to include an auctioneers and estate agents which became very successful.

In 1967, twenty-four year old Burke was elected as a Fianna Fáil member of Dublin County Council for the Swords area. He continued to be a councillor until 1978 and was considered to be a serious mover and shaker. He spent a further two-year period as a local representative between 1985 and 1987. His involvement in politics and real estate would give him a unique opportunity to indulge his natural talents for turning a dishonest buck.

Ray Burke entered national politics in the 1973 General Election when, with his father's retirement, he was elected to take over the Dáil seat. The thirty-year-old went on to be re-elected at every subsequent general election until he was forced to resign from public life in 1997. Former political colleagues and opponents recalled that he was an extremely ambitious young politician. One former colleague who observed Burke's rise through the ranks explained: "He was obviously hungry for power and wealth and he never made a secret of that. He had a gruff, arrogant personality. He didn't care who he bullied or swept aside to get what he wanted. Burke destroyed the careers of a number of people who had dared to cross him. Those who knew him best were aware that he was corrupt. The fact that he took brown envelopes in return for planning decisions was well known in the building trade, especially in north Dublin, for many years but there was nothing that anyone could do about it. It was good for politics that the likes of him and others in Fianna Fáil like Charlie Haughey and Liam Lawlor were finally exposed. They turned this country into a banana republic."

Burke's arrogant and aggressive style quickly earned him the nickname Rambo – and a lot of enemies. He was not known as a man who easily admitted error or misjudgement. In 1978 his ambition paid off, however, when the Taoiseach Jack Lynch appointed him as a Minister of State (Junior Minister) at the Department of Industry, Commerce and Energy.

A year after his appointment, Burke backed party colleague George Colley, in the bitterly contested leadership race of 1979 that was won by Charles J Haughey. The Boss, as Haughey became known, would also be exposed as utterly corrupt many years later. In fact Haughey, who was later exposed as having accepted at least IR£10 million (€12.7

million) in back-handers during his time in high office, put
Rambo in the shade when it came to dodgy dealings.

Despite Burke's support for Haughey's opponent, he
retained his ministerial position under the new leader. Perhaps
The Boss spotted his underling's dark side. A year later he
promoted Burke to the position of Minister for Environment,
the department which had ultimate responsibility for local
authorities throughout the country. However Burke had
another temporary lapse of faith in his leader after the party
lost the November 1982 General Election. Two months later
he presented Haughey with a petition on behalf of himself
and forty members of the parliamentary party, calling for a
leadership vote. Haughey survived the vote and punished
Burke by dropping him from the opposition front bench. But
the two men soon made their peace and Haughey reinstated
him as the party's spokesman on the environment.

When Fianna Fáil returned to power in 1987, Burke was
appointed Minister for Energy and Communications. He had
run a successful electoral campaign that brought in a second
seat for the party in his north Dublin constituency. Two years
later Burke and Padraig 'Pee' Flynn encouraged The Boss to
call an early election in the hope of winning an overall majority
in the Dáil. But the election resulted in a coalition Government
formed between Fianna Fáil and the Progressive Democrats
party, led by former Fianna Fáil Minister Des O'Malley.
O'Malley had been expelled from Fianna Fáil in 1985 and
had established the PDs in protest at what he saw as a lack of
standards in the Fianna Fáil party, under Haughey's leadership.
But in politics power is the ultimate goal and O'Malley ended
up going into government with his old foe.

In the new coalition, Burke was given one of the most
sensitive and powerful positions in the State, Minister for
Justice, with authority for the administration of law and order.
He remained in that post until 1992 when Albert Reynolds,
who finally ousted Haughey as leader, fired Burke as soon he
took office. Reynolds had long been suspicious of Burke's
corrupt dealings and wanted to purge the Cabinet of his

Disgraced former Justice Minister, Ray Burke, is led away to begin a six-month prison sentence for tax offences.

International drug trafficker David Huck, who fled after his yacht *The Brime* was intercepted with IR£20 million (€25 million) worth of hashish and his idyllic lakeside 'cottage' in County Clare which was sold by the CAB at auction in April 2002.
© *Sunday World*

Dutch drug lord, Jan Ijpelaar.

Clashnacree House, County Kerry, which the CAB sold in Autumn 2000 for over a million pounds (one and a half million euro).
© *Collins Photo Agency*

Mickey Green, the Scarlet Pimpernel of international
organised crime.
© *Sunday World*

Maple Falls, near Kilcock, County Kildare, Green's luxurious
estate which was sold by the CAB in 2002.
© *Sunday World*

Scottish gangland figure Thomas
McGraw, aka Mr McBig.

John and Mary Hughes 'the owners' of the Paradise Bar in Donegal
Town which the CAB said was really owned by McGraw.
© *Donegal Democrat*

London gangster Geoffrey Donovan, who won a landmark case against the CAB, talking to the author in 2001.
© *Padraig O'Reilly*

Donovan's then house The Pines in Tinode, County Wicklow which the CAB failed to seize.
© *Padraig O'Reilly*

John Walsh, the rogue cattle-dealer who brought foot and mouth disease to Ireland.
© *Collins Photo Agency*

Longford House, Walsh's home which was sold by the CAB at auction in 2004.
© *Sunday World*

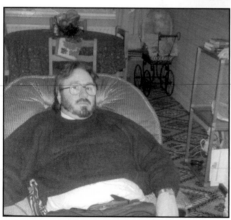

The many shapes and faces of 'Fat Boy Crim' George Mitchell, the illusive international gangster, nicknamed the Penguin.
© *Sunday World*

The Penguin's bagman, Peter Bolger, aka the Banker.
© *Padraig O'Reilly*

Michael Keating, the former Minster and Lord Mayor of Dublin, who got involved with the mob's money.
© *Photocall Ireland*

Detective Sergeant Paul O'Brien (now Detective Inspector) who led
Operation Firedamp against the Penguin and his Bagman, Bolger.
© *Padraig O'Reilly*

Cork shop-owner Alan Buckley, who also organised drug
shipments for the Penguin.
© *Sunday World*

© *Collins Photo Agency* © *Sunday World*

The Penguin's older brother, Paddy Mitchell, who was the crime lord's 'eyes and ears' in Dublin, was jailed for two years as a result of CAB investigation.

Gerard Hopkins who was jailed for an armed robbery, with George Mitchell.
© *Sunday World*

Stephen Kearney, a close associate of Mitchell, who was forced to pay a large CAB tax bill.
© *Sunday World*

An aerial shot of the General, Martin Cahill's, home at Cowper Downs which was sold by the CAB in 2005. The picture shows the garden being dug up as part of a last minute search for stolen valuables.
© *Padraig O'Reilly*

Inside the neglected and run-down house which was once the home of Ireland's most notorious gangster – the General.
© *Padraig O'Reilly*

corrosive influence. In hindsight it was a most fortuitous move. The Government had just begun the process of tackling corruption and the proceeds of crime, with new legislation, including the mandatory reporting by financial institutions of any suspicious transactions. This was the legislation that would ultimately be used by the CAB to prosecute Raphael Burke.

* * * *

Investigations instigated by the Tribunal of Inquiry into Certain Planning Matters and Payments, and later by the CAB, uncovered evidence that Burke had been involved in corruption from when he first became a politician. In return for large cash payments he had consistently used his influence to push through corrupt planning permission for various developments.

As early as June 1974, Burke, who had only been in the Dáil for a year, was linked to corruption in articles published in the *Sunday Independent* and *Hibernia* magazine. Under the initial headline "Conflict of Interest" journalist Joe McAnthony wrote two front-page stories, which for the first time attempted to lift the lid on the murky relationship between politics and planning in Dublin. McAnthony produced an extract from the accounts of the construction company owned by Mayomen Tom Brennan and Joe McGowan. The extract showed that a fee of IR£15,000 (€19,000) had been paid to Burke under the heading "planning". The fledgling Garda Fraud Squad ordered a major investigation and it continued for several months. The central focus of the probe was the close relationship between Burke and the two developers and whether they had ever paid him bribes.

Burke had been using his position as a member of Dublin County Council to secure the rezoning of lands, owned by Brennan and McGowan, for residential development in the Swords area. At the same time Burke had worked as an estate agent for the pair, selling the houses they built on the same lands and across the greater Dublin area. Brennan and

McGowan had made a practice of acquiring options on agricultural land in north Dublin that was never intended for development. Then they moved to have it rezoned with the backing of the County Councillors, often against the advice of the Council's own planners.

In the Joe McAnthony story it was revealed that around the time of the IR£15,000 (€19,000) payment Burke had seconded a motion to rezone Brennan and McGowan land at Mountgorry, east of Swords.

Another aspect of the Garda investigation was to find out how Burke had acquired his substantial family home, Briargate, on the Malahide Road in Swords. The house, on an acre of land, was designed and built for Burke by a Brennan and McGowan company, Oak Park Developments in 1973, a year after he married his wife Anne.

Detectives interviewed Burke, Brennan, McGowan and their lawyers, in a bid to get to the truth. Burke was interviewed on twenty occasions. However, while the officers clearly felt they had uncovered major corruption in the planning process, there was no legislation or indeed the will to do anything about it. They had been given a tissue of lies by Burke and his cronies including, it would be learned many years later, false bank statements concocted by corrupt bankers on behalf of the three men. In those days there were no laws enabling the Gardaí to search for evidence by accessing bank records. And accusing a powerful man of telling lies was just not an option.

It was only with the introduction of the 1994 Criminal Justice Act that Gardaí finally had the powers to examine the financial affairs of suspects. It would take another two years, and the murder of Veronica Guerin, before the cops could examine the tax affairs of individuals suspected of criminal activity. At the time, the 1974 investigation had fizzled out with no charges of wrong-doing being preferred against anyone. The only person who suffered professionally as a result of the episode was the journalist who had simply been doing his job, Joe McAnthony. After the investigation Burke and his powerful cronies used all their influence to effectively end the career of the country's first investigative reporter. Some years later, with his career in tatters, McAnthony and his family were forced to leave Ireland and start a new life in Canada.

With the cops out of the way and the media effectively silenced, Burke settled back to business as usual and the corruption continued unabated. On his last day in the job as Environment Minister he packed An Bord Pleanala – the agency that hears all planning appeals in the country – with cronies and associates. The new Executive included one of his constituency advisers and an architect who worked for Brennan and McGowan. The same man coincidentally designed Burke's home, Briargate. Shortly before they were replaced on the Board, one of the men signed his name to the permission sanctioning a large office development by a company owned by Brennan and McGowan.

In 1989 Burke was unusually appointed Minister for Justice and Minister for Communications. Part of his Communications' remit was the introduction of legislation allowing for the establishment of independent radio and TV stations. Here he found another means of using his power to make handy cash. He took a bribe from Oliver Barry, a successful concert promoter and part owner of the country's first national independent station, Century Radio. In return Burke made life very easy for the fledgling station. He issued a ministerial order forcing RTÉ to provide broadcasting facilities to the new venture.

Around the same time, Burke again found himself the subject of further allegations of corruption in the planning process and the means by which he came to own his home. But by the time the Gardaí came to interview Burke he had been appointed their boss. The CAB would later discover that, on a daily basis, Burke had secretly monitored the investigation set up to enquire into his affairs. It was unsurprising that the investigation failed to uncover any wrong-doing and that certain Garda officers found themselves being promoted.

It would also be discovered years later that Burke was determined to hang on to his illicit gains by making false tax returns and salting cash away in offshore accounts. But the whispered allegations could not be written about in the media for fear of Burke taking defamation proceedings against them.

Later that year, Labour party TD Pat Rabbitte read the contents of two pages from the book *Saving the City* by *Irish Times* Environment correspondent Frank McDonald into the record of the Dáil. The book dealt with the planning process in Dublin and highlighted the bad decisions, which were being made and which would ultimately destroy the city's architectural landscape. In the pages Rabbitte read out, McDonald had focused on the close connections between Burke, Brennan and McGowan. The journalist could not go any nearer to allegations of corruption and hoped that the public would read between the lines.

* * * *

In early June 1989, just before the General Election, three men called by appointment to Briargate for a meeting with Ray Burke. They were Michael Bailey, the Director of property company Bovale Developments, and Joseph Murphy Junior, of Joseph Murphy Structural Engineering (JMSE). The third man present was seventy-two-year old James Gogarty, the former Managing Director of JMSE. Since his retirement in 1982, he had remained on as Chairman of the company and was still working as a consultant for the owner, Joseph Murphy Senior. The purpose of the meeting was to pay Burke IR£80,000 (€102,000) in return for the rezoning for development purposes of 700 acres of agricultural land, owned by the Murphy group of companies, in north Dublin. The bribe was the brainchild of Bailey who had had many business dealings with Burke in the past. He had contacted the Murphys offering to secure planning permission in return for a 50 per cent interest in the land. Rezoning would multiply the value of the property many times over and everyone would make an enormous killing in the process. Bailey told the Murphys that, for the right price, Burke could use his influence with the majority Fianna Fáil representation on Dublin County Council to have the lands rezoned. Under a section in the planning laws, elected representatives could override the council's official planners in favour of particular developments. It was a loophole open to rampant corruption.

At an earlier meeting it was agreed that Bailey and the Murphys would each pay IR£40,000 (€51,000) to Burke. Gogarty was given the job of handing over the cash on behalf of JMSE. Before the meeting Gogarty famously enquired of Bailey if they would be getting a receipt for the money. Bailey curtly replied: "Will we fuck!"

In the dining room Gogarty and Bailey placed two envelopes on the table beside Burke who then threw them into a sideboard without a word. It was a practice that he had become well used to. But the events of that fateful evening would come back to haunt Ray Burke and all those he did business with. And it would be as a result of matters far beyond his control.

James Gogarty, who was an engineer, had first begun working for Joseph Murphy Senior in 1968 when he was appointed Managing Director of JMSE. The 51-year-old had worked closely with Murphy Senior, and helped to turn the company around. By Gogarty's retirement in 1982, JMSE had become a major player in the industry. A month before the meeting with Burke, Murphy Senior had agreed a generous IR£300,000 (€380,000) pension scheme for Gogarty and his wife. But within a few months the elderly consultant became concerned that the company was not going to honour the agreement. The relationship between Gogarty and Joseph Murphy Junior gradually descended to one of mutual loathing. Junior felt that Gogarty's pension package was over generous and had done everything in his power to prevent him getting it. The situation continued to deteriorate until it came to a head one night in June 1994, when a drunken Murphy Junior phoned Gogarty twice and threatened the pensioner with physical violence. From then on Gogarty conducted a campaign to punish Murphy Junior. He became obsessed with the belief that he had been wronged and that he wanted pay back – a year later James Gogarty would get his chance.

As Gogarty's bitterness and desire for revenge were festering, a mysterious advertisement appeared in all the national daily newspapers on July 3, 1995. A IR£10,000 (€12,700) reward was offered to anyone who could provide information leading to the conviction of people involved in corruption with the planning process. Newry-based solicitors, Donnelly Neary Donnelly had placed the notice on behalf of unnamed clients. It subsequently transpired that the mystery men behind the campaign were Michael Smith, the Chairman of An Taisce and barrister and Fine Gael party member Colm MacEochaidh. Soon the solicitors had received up to 50 allegations of corruption in the planning process. One of the most significant calls came from an angry old man called James Gogarty. He startled the solicitors by what he had to say. "I paid Raphael Burke an IR£80,000 (€102,000) bribe to secure re-zoning." It was this information that would ultimately lead to the establishment of the Flood Tribunal.

By the General Election in 1997, leaks of the allegations being made by Gogarty were being drip-fed to the media. Mention of Ray Burke's involvement rose from a whisper to a distinct murmur and it was getting louder. As a result, Bertie Ahern's decision to appoint Ray Burke Minister for Foreign Affairs on June 26 was greeted with astonishment. Outgoing Taoiseach, Albert Reynolds, had personally warned Ahern about the Burke rumours, when Ahern became the leader of Fianna Fáil in 1994. When the full scandal later exploded Ahern famously remarked that he "had been up every tree in north Dublin" to substantiate the rumours. He would also claim that he even checked Burke's credentials with Garda Commissioner Pat Byrne. In the absence of criminal convictions or charges the Commissioner could not confirm Reynolds' suspicions. But Burke's appointment was like a red rag to a bull for Gogarty and he began talking to journalists.

In July 1997, a newspaper article appeared which revealed

the payment, by JMSE and Bovale, to Burke in June 1989. The storm clouds were gathering.

The Minister for Foreign Affairs waited a number of weeks before responding to Gogarty's claims. On August 7, in typically acerbic fashion, Burke admitted that he had received an unsolicited "political donation" of IR£30,000 (€38,000) and not £80,000 (€102,000), but claimed he had done nothing in return for it. His attitude was "so what" and he acted as if he believed the controversy would go away.

But it didn't. On September 10, Burke made a much more detailed statement in the Dáil, as opposition calls for his resignation intensified. The speech was a masterpiece of lies and indignation. Burke described the IR£30,000 (€38,000) given to him by James Gogarty, on behalf of JMSE, as "a totally unsolicited political contribution". He added: "For any candidate or representative to have accepted a political donation with strings attached would have been unethical if not downright illegal. In the context of this contribution, there was no attempt to attach any strings or to ask for any favours."

Burke said he resented being forced to deny allegations made against him. "I have come here to defend my personal integrity, the integrity of my party, this Government and the honour of this house. I am taking the opportunity to state unequivocally that I have done nothing illegal, unethical or improper. I find myself the victim of a campaign of calumny and abuse."

He also warned: "If any further untruths are published about me, I will take all necessary steps to vindicate my good name and reputation."

Outside the Dáil Rambo was in an equally defiant mood when he famously declared that he had "drawn a line in the sand" between him and the rumours of corruption. As far as he was concerned it was to be an end to any allegations or doubts about his character. But the scandal didn't go away and the drip-feed of allegations continued.

In the meantime, the Government had decided to establish

a tribunal of enquiry into the various planning allegations being made by Gogarty and others. Time was running out for the Minister of Corruption.

On October 2, 1997, Burke, in his position as Minister for Foreign Affairs, signed the EU Treaty of Amsterdam on behalf of the Irish Government. It was to be his final act as a senior politician. Ironically, the new Treaty gave the EU enhanced powers to tackle organised crime on a pan-European front. In an article written to mark the occasion Burke declared: "Firstly, the Treaty establishes an area of freedom, security and justice. In doing so, it reaffirms the principles of liberty, democracy and respect for human rights, fundamental freedoms and the rule of law on which the Union is founded. It introduces important changes in the area of justice and home affairs designed to implement the principle of free movement of persons between member States. The aim is to ensure that citizens can benefit from free movement while crime does not."

Back at home events were rendering Rambo's position untenable. Having held out as long as possible, he was left with no option but to resign his ministry and announce his intention of withdrawing from public life. Five days after he signed the Treaty of Amsterdam, Burke made his resignation known to the Dáil.

In his final speech to the House of Parliament he continued to protest his innocence: "I want to clearly restate that I have done nothing wrong and that I look forward to fully co-operating with any investigation. Despite my inclination to face down these ongoing personal attacks, I feel that I can no longer justify this as being helpful to the Government on a personal level."

Despite the mounting evidence, Bertie Ahern defended his embattled colleague and said he deeply regretted the resignation. In what could be seen as at best, poor judgement, Ahern went on the attack, condemning a "sustained campaign of incremental intensity" against the bribe-taking politician.

In a long, hard-hitting statement that would eventually come back to haunt him, Ahern angrily declared: "In the case of Deputy Ray Burke, I see a much more sinister development, the persistent hounding of an honourable man to resign an important position on the basis of innuendo and unproven allegations. There comes a time when even the strongest shoulder bows, when even the stoutest heart falters, when even the best can resist no longer."

The Taoiseach concluded his statement: "I always found him to be a proud honourable man, loyal and true, persevering and principled, caring and committed but tough and a person who often lost friends very easily. On behalf of the Government and particularly on behalf of the Fianna Fáil Party, I thank him for his distinguished years in the service of his constituents and his country."

On November 4, 1997, The Tribunal of Inquiry into Certain Planning Matters and Payments was established by resolution of the Dáil and appointed by Instrument of the Minister for the Environment and Local Government. It would to be chaired by Mr Justice Fergus Flood and became known as the Flood Tribunal. Armed with the powers of the High Court, the Tribunal immediately began investigating the various allegations placed before it, including those against Ray Burke.

In 1998, Orders were issued to Burke ordering him to hand over documentation and the Tribunal finally started its hearings in 1999 when James Gogarty began his evidence.

Over the following years the Flood Tribunal provided acres of news copy and hours of TV reports, as the hidden world of corruption in politics and business was laid bare. It exposed people such as Fianna Fáil TD, Liam Lawlor, former Government Press Secretary Frank Dunlop – who agreed to spill the beans on all those politicians he had bribed on behalf of development companies – former City and County Manager George Redmond and a host of businessmen. There were many stormy, and sometimes humorous, exchanges but the revelations undermined public trust for elected representatives.

In relation to Burke, the Tribunal broke the inquiry into three modules. The first dealt with his relationship with Brennan and McGowan and the purchase of his home, Briargate. The second module dealt with his association with Oliver Barry and Century Radio. The final module focused on the allegations of James Gogarty.

On September 27, 2002, Mr Justice Fergus Flood presented his long-awaited second interim report relating to the investigation of Ray Burke's affairs. It was a damning denunciation of the former Minister. In the report Burke was accused of persistently lying in his evidence and deliberately hindering the work of the tribunal.

In summary, the Flood report made twenty-four findings. With regard to Burke's relationship with Brennan and McGowan it found that Ray Burke did not purchase Briargate in 1973 in a normal commercial transaction. The alleged price for the house and lands, IR£15,000 (€19,000), "did not represent the open market value of the property". The Tribunal found that Burke had been given the house to ensure that "he would act in the best interests of Oakpark Developments' Director Tom Brennan and his associates". The house amounted to a corrupt payment, although the Tribunal chairman said he had not been able to find out exactly what Burke had done in return.

In terms of offshore accounts opened by Burke in company names in the Isle of Man in 1982, and in Jersey in 1984, where one was preposterously named Caviar Ltd, the report stated that this was done to facilitate receiving corrupt payments from Tom Brennan and his associates. The Report said that Burke had lied when he claimed that the money in the accounts had been the proceeds of political fund-raising activities or political donations from Tom Brennan. They were made in order to ensure he would continue to "act in the best interests of those who had paid him when performing his public duties." Flood's report classified as corrupt, four payments totalling Stg£160,000 (€234,000), which had been made to Burke's offshore accounts by Tom Brennan, Joseph

McGowan, and other associates. Judge Flood said he was unable to discover what Burke had done for the money. But he declared that he was "satisfied on the balance of probabilities" that the disgraced politician "acted in their interests in the performance of his public duties as a member of Dublin County Council, and as a member of Dáil Eireann."

Flood found that Oliver Barry had also paid Burke a IR£35,000 (€44,500) bribe while Burke held the position of Minister for Communications. In return, Burke had issued a Ministerial Directive on March 14, 1989, obliging RTÉ to provide its facilities to Century. This was done "to advance the private interests of the promoters of Century and not to serve the public interest". It also found that Burke was responding to demands from Oliver Barry and Century Radio by proposing legislation that would have had the effect of curbing RTÉ's advertising revenue and diverting broadcasting licence fee income from RTÉ to independent broadcasters. The payment of IR£35,000 (€44,500) to Burke ensured that he was prepared to introduce legislation that would be beneficial to Century.

Justice Flood dealt with the allegations made by James Gogarty in the third module of the inquiry. The Chairman of the Tribunal was satisfied that the meeting at Burke's home in June 1989 was specifically arranged to pay bribes to Ray Burke. The Report found that Burke had lied when he claimed the meeting was arranged to receive a political donation. The Murphy executives present at the meeting had believed that the JMSE payment of IR£40,000 (€50,800), passed in a closed envelope by Gogarty to Burke, was being matched by an equal payment from Michael Bailey. The meeting took place with the prior knowledge, of all those involved, that the IR£80,000 (€102,000)was intended to pay Burke off, in order to ensure his support in achieving changes in the planning status of the Murphy's lands in North Dublin. The payment received amounted to a bribe and all those present at the meeting were aware of that.

Publication of the *Flood Report* sent shock waves through

the body politic. It had put down in black and white what a lot of people had long suspected. Burke later told reporters that he had been advised by his legal team not to comment on the Tribunal's findings. With an arrogant grin he said he looked forward to the opportunity to speak in the future.

The Taoiseach, Bertie Ahern, came under intense political pressure in the continuing fall out he said that he "felt saddened and betrayed" by Burke's involvement in planning corruption. In a bid to explain his controversial decision to make Burke Foreign Minister in 1997, Ahern said Burke had assured him on a number of occasions that there were no difficulties in his past. The leader of Ireland commented: "If I had known all I know now after five years of a tribunal, of course it [Burke's ministerial appointment] would never have arisen. Unfortunately Ray let us down, what was said at the time were not things that we knew of. And that is sad."

Flood forwarded his report to the Director of Public Prosecutions, the Garda Commissioner and the Criminal Assets Bureau for consideration of possible criminal proceedings. The findings of the Tribunal report or its hearings, however, could not be used to bring a criminal prosecution. But the Report could be used as a possible road map for the investigators to follow. For the first time it can be revealed that a dramatic development in the days following the publication of the Report, actually gave the Untouchables a breakthrough in their fledgling investigation.

On October 4, 2002, Burke contacted Ark Life Insurance and told them he wanted to immediately cash in a bond of €127,000. He had invested the money after the sale of Briargate in 2000 for over €3 million. Burke had sold the house and land to another development company who were developing a major construction project beside Briargate. The former minister had then bought a more modest family home at Griffith Downs in Drumcondra. Since the Ark Life investment had not reached its full term, Burke would only receive €87,000. In his haste to get his money out of the country the former Minister for law and order was prepared to lose

€40,000. Under the provisions of the 1994 Criminal Justice Act, however, the request was reported as a suspicious transaction to the Gardaí. The transaction bore all the hallmarks of money laundering and the CAB decided to make its move. On October 7, Burke transported his money by car on an Irish Ferries passage to Holyhead. He remained in the south of England for almost a month. It was never established what exactly he had been up to.

A top-level conference was held between the Garda Commissioner Pat Byrne, his deputy Noel Conroy, and the heads of the GBFI and CAB, Detective Chief Superintendents Austin McNally and Felix McKenna. They now had information, which had not been revealed in the Flood Tribunal, with which they could proceed with a criminal investigation.

Three days after Burke's sudden departure with his cash, the Bureau went to court to apply for warrants to search his new home and the offices of four firms of solicitors and accountants. At the same time McKenna's officers and members of the Bureau of Fraud Investigation resurrected the old Garda investigation files concerning Ray Burke. Revenue officials uplifted all his tax returns going back as far as the 1970s and orders were served on several banks for information concerning his various accounts.

Meanwhile the searches turned up other vital evidence that had not been presented to the Tribunal. In a search of Burke's home they found what Felix McKenna liked to refer to as the "smoking gun". It was evidence that the disgraced politician had availed of the Tax Amnesty on December 15, 1993, a year after Albert Reynolds had sacked him. The Waiver of Certain Tax, Interest and Penalties Act, which gave effect to the amnesty, had been introduced by Bertie Ahern and had been enthusiastically supported by the likes of Burke. Among documents seized, was a copy of the amnesty declaration Burke had submitted to the Chief Special Collector. In it the former minister had declared the sum of IR£5,085 (€6,500) as the only income on which tax had not been paid. Under the terms of the amnesty, Burke had paid tax at the rate of 15 per cent of the amount declared, IR£762.75 (€968). From an examination of Burke's financial statements, the CAB worked out that he had purposely furnished false information under the amnesty – which was a criminal offence. It was calculated that he had not declared his true income of IR£151,980 (€193,000).

The investigators were happy that Burke had also furnished false tax returns for several years, going back to the 1970s. Filing false tax returns is also a criminal offence but the Bureau had a difficulty – cases going back more than ten years could not be prosecuted.

In another twist, officers also found the Briargate conveyance file while searching more offices. During the Flood Tribunal it was claimed that it had been lost.

Further evidence that Burke had been economical with the truth in the past was the tax returns he had made after the corruption scandal broke in 1997. Their inquiries showed that, following a request from the Inspector of Taxes in December 1999, Burke's accountants had declared interest earned on a number of investment accounts held by him in the years 1983/84 and 1997/98. Burke had also outlined details of interest earned in his offshore companies. In total he had paid IR£155,140 (€197,000) in tax. Burke's sudden urge to be straight with the taxman gave the CAB circumstantial proof that he had been less than honest in his tax returns for other years.

Pursuing another angle, the CAB officers' analysis of the original Garda investigations, particularly the 1974 inquiry, clearly showed how the Gardaí's powers had been severely curtailed. They had no way of obtaining tax or banking records and there was no legislation with which to counteract this problem. But, more sinisterly, it appeared that at a very high level there did not seem to be the will to pursue Burke. In those innocent days no one was prepared to take on the likes of Raphael Burke. According to investigators, aspects of the 1974 case had been dealt with in a "ham-fisted" manner.

Further examination of the dusty old files also showed that the cops had been lied to and misled from the start.

It was also discovered that Burke had been able to use his position as Minister for Justice to protect himself. It emerged that he had had access to information about various investigations into corruption on a day-to-day basis. Although it could not be proved, it was suspected, that Burke used his influence to corrupt those investigations. There was no doubt that if he had held the sensitive job of Minister for Justice in the early 1990s, he would have ensured that the laws now being used by the CAB, would not have been as effective.

As the inquiry continued, McKenna's staff located the journalist Joe McAnthony and he flew over from Canada to be interviewed. Even though three decades had passed, the journalist who had first tried to expose the corruption still had his own files on Burke. At last McAnthony had been justified and vindicated. He was more than happy to help the Criminal Assets Bureau.

Over the next twelve months, members of the CAB interviewed Burke on three separate occasions in 2003, February 5, May 15 and November 4. The interviews attended by Det. Insp. Denis O'Leary, Det. Sgt. Tom Mathews, Det. Gda. Martin Harrington and a Bureau Revenue official took place in the offices of Burke's solicitor in Swords. During the meetings the former politician was quizzed about various payments he had received and the treatment of the payments in his different bank accounts. He was asked about the individuals he had been involved with and the purchase of his home.

Burke refused to answer any of the important questions. He repeatedly replied: "On the basis of the advice of my lawyers I decline to answer that question."

By winter 2003, the Untouchables did not need to hear any more of Ray Burke's prevarications. In November a file was forwarded to the Director of Public Prosecutions recommending a charge for making a false return under the tax amnesty. If such a charge was to be preferred, it had to be done by December 15, 2003, as this marked the expiry of ten years since the time the offence was committed. The file also recommended a number of criminal charges arising out of false tax returns to the Revenue Commissioners. Another suggested charge related to the fraudulent conversion of a cheque given as a political donation to Fianna Fáil from the Fitzwilton Group. Each year the group donated money to Fianna Fáil but, on one occasion Burke told the company to make the IR£30,000 (€38,000) out to 'cash' which he then lodged into his own personal account. When Fianna Fáil HQ contacted Burke about the payment he told the party official to "fuck off". Eventually, after consultation with party HQ, Burke handed over IR£10,000 (€12,700) but hung onto the rest. By so doing he had potentially committed fraud.

In the meantime, the Revenue officers attached to the CAB had calculated that he owed a tax bill of €2 million, which included interest and penalties. In November, two CAB officers had called to Burke's home and served him with the demand. He also received a letter confirming that the Bureau had become his new Inspector of Taxes. The pressure was mounting.

After reviewing the evidence, the DPP directed that Burke be charged under the provisions of the 1993 Tax Amnesty. On December 8, just a week short of the ten-year deadline, Raphael Burke was brought before the Dublin District Court by the Criminal Assets Bureau and formally charged.

In January 2004 the Bureau brought two further charges against Ray Burke, of making false tax returns. He was sent forward for trial to the Circuit Criminal Court and the case was adjourned to July.

* * * *

As Burke's trial approached, the disgraced former Minister decided that he would have to negotiate a deal with the CAB. If he continued to try and bluff things out by fighting the criminal charges and was found guilty, he ran a serious risk of a long prison sentence. But if he came clean, his legal advisors told him, there would be mitigating circumstances in his favour.

On July 9, 2004 the Criminal Assets Bureau and Burke's advisors agreed to settle his outstanding tax issues for a total figure of €596,987 which would include the €196,987 paid in 2000. It was agreed he would pay the balance of €400,000 on signature. Ray Burke and Felix McKenna then signed the three-page agreement.

Three days later, Burke pleaded guilty to the two charges of making false tax returns in the Circuit Criminal Court. In a plea bargain arrangement, the State agreed to drop the third charge relating to the tax amnesty. Judge Desmond Hogan adjourned sentencing to the following December. The two offences carried a maximum sentence of five years but Burke was confident that he now had a good chance of receiving a suspended prison sentence.

In the meantime he had other financial headaches to deal with. A week later Burke's lawyers applied to Judge Alan Mahon, who had replaced Fergus Flood as the Chairman of the Tribunal, to rule that the taxpayer should pick up Burke's €10.5 million legal bill for his involvement in the inquiry. Judge Mahon adjourned his decision to Monday, September 6, 2004, when he delivered another costly body blow to the disgraced former Minister, ordering him to pay his own costs. In what was described as a landmark ruling, the Judge said he was throwing out Burke's application because he had persistently lied to the Tribunal. As a result Ray Burke was now facing bankruptcy and financial ruin, as well as a stint in jail. In his ten-page ruling the Tribunal chairman was scathing in his criticism of Burke. Judge Mahon said that he had set out to deliberately mislead the Tribunal "at every turn". His failure to co-operate and give truthful evidence had cast a shadow over all the evidence relating to the issues being investigated. If he had attempted to co-operate then Mahon said he would have considered granting him a portion of his costs.

Judge Mahon added: "This is not an incidence of an individual witness being merely liberal with the truth, or occasionally giving false or tardy evidence, or withholding the less important aspects of a story in the hope of slowing the progress of the investigation; it is rather a case of a crucial witness setting out deliberately to mislead the tribunal in the hope and expectation that the inquiry would prove inconclusive or would produce erroneous findings. I have no doubt whatsoever that Mr Burke knew full well that his evidence and the information being disclosed by him and others to the tribunal was false and misleading."

There was little sympathy from the rest of the body politic for the fallen minister. In an amazing turnaround, Bertie Ahern said he welcomed the Tribunal's decision not to pay the legal costs of the man he had described as "proud, loyal, honourable and true" at the time of his resignation. The Taoiseach said it was "right and proper" that people who did not co-operate with tribunals, would not have their legal bills paid by the State.

* * * *

On December 14, 2004, Burke returned to court to hear his fate. Det. Insp. Denis O'Leary told the court that a search of Burke's home had uncovered a folder that contained information indicating he had failed to fully declare his income for over nine years. A folder marked "Building Societies" had contained a declaration that he had submitted incorrect tax statements. Burke's lawyers pleaded with Judge Hogan not to send their client to jail. They argued that he should not be treated any differently because of who he was. They also pointed out that he had become tax compliant and was in ill-health. He was suffering from anxiety and depression and was "only a Dáil pensioner".

Burke was granted a temporary reprieve when the court decided to adjourn the sentencing to January, allowing him to enjoy Christmas with his family. As a result Burke realised that he was likely to do time behind bars.

On January 24, 2005, Ray Burke was given six months in prison on the charges brought against him by the Criminal Assets Bureau. Wearing a smart navy suit and pink tie, he stood bolt upright, staring ahead with his hands behind his back during the thirty minutes it took Judge Desmond Hogan to read his judgement. Burke's gaze at a spot on the wall never wavered but he gulped hard when the judge said that a custodial sentence was the only option for a former Government Minister who had breached the public's trust. Judge Hogan commented: "Under all the circumstances, a custodial sentence is appropriate. However, I do not believe it should be a long one having regard to the mitigating factors."

The Judge took into account the fact that Burke had pleaded guilty, was tax compliant, his age and his "ill-health". "There is one fact in this case that I must take into consideration and that is that at the time of the commission of these offences the defendant was a member of the Oireachtas. He was in that capacity, a member of the Legislature. He was in fact a member of the Legislature at the time of the passing of the 1983 Finance Act under whose provisions he is now prosecuted for making an incorrect statement or furnishing incorrect information," said the Judge.

Less than an hour later, after conferring with his legal team, Burke put on a brave face as he marched to his prison transport. In the scheme of things he received a relatively short sentence – with one-third remission he would only serve four months. But for Rambo, it was the ultimate humiliation. His lifetime of corruption had left him practically penniless and his reputation was in ruins.

Later that evening, he was taken to Mountjoy for committal to prison. The former Minister for Justice, who had often strutted through the same prison gates as the boss, was photographed and finger-printed alongside drug dealers, robbers and rapists. Former Justice Minister Raphael Burke became Prisoner Number '33791'. He was then moved to Arbour Hill prison which houses mainly sex offenders and other prisoners who are under protection from the rest of the prison population.

Ray Burke was released the following May and promptly faded into obscurity. Burke's former colleagues say that he has become a virtual recluse and feels deeply aggrieved at his treatment. A threat that he would tell the "full story" of what else had been going on in corrupt political circles, had still not emerged by the summer of 2006.

The prosecution of Ray Burke was a major success for the Criminal Assets Bureau. It sent a clear message to some of the most powerful people in the State that if they were exposed they could also find themselves in the same position. But here is a word of caution. In the future there is the distinct possibility that a corrupt minister like Rambo might once again thwart a Garda investigation into his or her affairs. A number of senior Gardaí and other officials interviewed for this book, said they believe that the Garda Siochana Act of 2005 was open to serious abuse in the hands of a corrupt Government. It would be entirely plausible, that as investigations such as the CAB's inquiry into Republican controlled oil-smuggling rackets or money laundering could be compromised if power was in the wrong hands. Under the new legislation the independence of An Garda Siochana has been greatly undermined.

By the summer of 2006, the Department of Justice and its Minister was effectively in control of the national police force. Gardaí on the ground regularly joked that Michael McDowell seemed to have assumed the role of Garda Commissioner. The legislation was part of a major project to reform the Garda Siochana in the aftermath of various corruption investigations. But in the hands of a corrupt administration, the increased powers could again be used to interfere with police investigations and to protect individuals from the law.

* * * *

The Criminal Assets Bureau got an unexpected windfall as a direct result of Ray Burke's problems. A few days after the publication of the hard-hitting Flood Tribunal Report a retired 84-year-old planning officer walked into his bank in Bray, County Wicklow. Bank staff later told Gardaí that he appeared to be in somewhat of a panic. Their suspicions were further aroused when he informed them that he wanted to close down his account, containing €700,000 and that he wanted the money in cash. Michael Healy had worked for Bray Urban District Council until 1979. After that, it later emerged, he dabbled in property and worked as a consultant for a number of major developers. He was told that it would take a day for the bank to put so much money together. Under money laundering legislation, the bank immediately reported the suspicious transaction to the Money Laundering Investigation Unit, who passed it on to the Untouchables.

As Healy left the bank the following day, with the cash in a plastic bag, Detective Inspector John McDermott and other Bureau officers stopped him on the pavement. The money was seized and the shocked pensioner was told he would have to furnish an explanation as to where the money came from. At the time of the incident Mr Healy told the *Sunday World*: "The CAB is investigating my affairs but I have done nothing wrong. I have committed no crime. It may not have been the wisest thing in the world taking out so much cash." He said that he was confident of being cleared of any corruption or wrongdoing and denied it had anything to do with the Flood Report. "It had nothing to do with the Flood Report. I don't even know what the Flood Report is about," he claimed. When told that it was about the corrupt activities of Ray Burke he replied: "Ah sure that thing has been going on for years."

But the former planner could not come up with an adequate explanation to clarify the origin of his money. Within weeks he instructed his legal advisers to agree to hand over all the money to the State, even though he could have fought the CAB and withheld payment for up to two years. But the elderly man was not left penniless. CAB inquiries discovered that he had another sizeable nest egg in a different financial institution to tide him over.

The whole experience, the former planner later admitted to this writer, had been quite an eye opener: "It says a lot about my age that I didn't know that the banks have regulations to report the large movements of cash. Sure the police are investigating everyone these days. The whole bloody country has gone mad on sex and crime."

Ten

The Penguin, the Bagman and the Politician

George Mitchell's awkward waddle, as he struggled to carry his overweight body, earned him the rather unflattering nickname, the Penguin. But that was the only characteristic the one-time biscuit delivery-man had in common with the black and white Antarctic-dweller. For when it came to doing business and surviving in the big bad underworld, the illusive international drug trafficker could just as easily have been nicknamed the Fox or the Hawk. So when the Criminal Assets Bureau first cast their menacing shadow across gangland in 1996, it wasn't surprising that the Penguin was one of the first godfathers to sense the need to migrate to safer climes. And he didn't need his instincts to tell him that the Untouchables would soon be on the trail of his dirty money. When the CAB finally kicked in the door, however, the Penguin was waiting for them on the other side, ready to fight them all the way.

When the Criminal Assets Bureau began investigating the crime lord's business, the Bureau uncovered an extraordinary conspiracy of money laundering and corruption. In what became one of the most complex and labour-intensive investigations ever undertaken by the CAB, officers found themselves dealing with an extremely devious adversary. When the Criminal Assets Bureau was first established, Fachtna Murphy and Felix McKenna warned their non-Garda colleagues that the organised crime bosses would be no pushover. They predicted that the gangsters would fight them every step of the way and try to put them out of business.

Mitchell's advisers soon proved the experienced investigators point by launching a torrent of court actions, many of them vexatious, to stop the CAB investigation, at every stage of the process. Outrageous allegations and blatant lies, which were later proved to be untrue, were used in court in an attempt to intimidate individual officers and ultimately force the Untouchables into submission.

While researching this book evidence was also discovered that Mitchell and his henchmen plotted another more chilling course of action – the murder of one of the Bureau's most important officers in 1997. The Bureau knew it was playing for high stakes against a deadly foe but their confrontation with Mitchell's organisation soon descended into a full-scale war of attrition.

Former members of the Bureau would later confess that the legal fight put up by Mitchell's people made John Gilligan's myriad court challenges look like a mere skirmish. During the investigation detectives uncovered evidence of how the Penguin's bagman, suitably nicknamed the Banker, secretly recruited a former Government Minister to help in the smooth running of their money laundering operation. The Penguin also pooled his resources with several other gangland figures, including the Monk and John Gilligan, to mount a series of hugely expensive courtroom challenges that went all the way to the Supreme Court, in a bid to have the CAB rendered ineffective.

****

By the time the Criminal Assets Bureau was established, George Mitchell had been a major player in organised crime for almost twenty years. Born in 1951, he grew up on Benbulben Road in Drimnagh, South Dublin, one of the areas where thousands of Local Authority houses had been built to alleviate the inner-city slums. While the housing plan was well-intentioned, places like Drimnagh, Crumlin and Ballyfermot soon became disadvantaged black spots. High unemployment and poor educational facilities turned the areas into ghettos where crime was endemic. These areas came to be known as the home of organised crime in Ireland.

Mitchell grew up with a generation of young villains who between them ushered in an era of serious crime. Many of them, including members of extended families, such as the Dunnes, the Cunninghams, the Kavanaghs and the Cahills, became household names during their inauspicious careers. Mitchell's large underworld peer group also included the likes of John Traynor, Paddy Shanahan and John Gilligan, with whom he took part in several warehouse and factory robberies throughout the 1980s. Mitchell was also a member of the General's gang when they robbed the priceless Beit paintings. His brother Paddy, who was five years older, was also heavily involved in various criminal rackets. The brothers took part in armed robberies and also specialised in the handling and receiving of stolen goods.

In 1967, Mitchell began working as a truck driver for the Jacobs biscuit manufacturer in Tallaght, West Dublin. He continued to work there until he was sacked twenty-two years later. It was an ideal job for a gangster involved in plotting large scale warehouse heists. He used his day job to plan his nocturnal 'jobs'. During his time with Jacobs several wholesale confectioners around the country were systematically robbed. It was more than a coincidence that at the time Mitchell regularly delivered biscuits to the same premises.

Throughout his criminal career Mitchell was known as a very dangerous criminal, who had no problem resorting to violence, and even murder, to sort a problem. In the early 1980s, he was identified as one of the ringleaders of a sinister criminal group known as the Prisoners Revenge Group (PRG). They waged a campaign of terror against members of the prison service. Members of the IRA, the General and the Monk's gang were all involved in the PRG. A number of prison officers were intimidated and attacked. Cars and homes were also targeted and burned.

In January 1986, Mitchell was caught with one of his life-long associates, twenty-six-year-old Gerard Hopkins, after the armed robbery of a truck loaded with over IR£100,000 (€127,000) worth of Nilzan cattle drench from Connolly Haulage in the Bluebell Industrial Estate, Dublin. During the heist, the driver of the truck was locked in a refrigerated container and almost froze to death. The two hoods were charged with armed aggravated burglary and the false imprisonment of the driver.

During their trial in 1988, Mitchell's brother Paddy and other gang members made a number of attempts to get Hopkins and the Penguin off. They stole a briefcase belonging to a Clerk of the Circuit Criminal Court. It contained vital court documents without which the trial could not proceed. Fortunately, however, the thieves targeted the wrong Clerk and stole the court files for a totally different case. Paddy Mitchell, who had just completed a sentence for receiving stolen goods in the UK, was also caught trying to intimidate jurors in the case. Despite the best efforts of the mob, Mitchell and Hopkins were convicted and jailed for five years. The Penguin swore that he would never again be 'hands on' in a crime.

On July 10, 1989 the Jacobs Company wrote to Mitchell informing him that his employment was to officially cease, from September 15, because of his 18 month "extended absence from work".

Mitchell wrote back to the company registering his objection. It was a masterpiece of understatement.

Dear Sir,

I received your letter of the 10th of July last and have to say I was disappointed that the company could not wait until the difficulties I now find myself in are resolved. On previous occasions the company has made special allowances for personnel who found themselves with major problems. When you take into account that my absence is covered by other drivers and that I am not in receipt of any monies from the company, the least I would have expected after Twenty Two (years) service would be the leeway I need to resolve my problem.

However I will appeal the decision of the company when I have had a satisfactory outcome to my problem. In the meantime I would appreciate if you would have my P45, plus any monies due to me [given to] Mr. [Jacobs employee].

Thanking you,
Yours sincerely,
G. Mitchell.

* * * *

When the Penguin was released from prison in October 1991, gangland was in the midst of major change. Drugs had become the stock and trade of most of his gangland contemporaries and the Penguin wanted a slice of the action. It was also an easy option. The profits were much greater and the risks minimal when compared to robbing a bank or warehouse. Mitchell had hated his time in prison and, according to former associates, "went to bits" inside. The experience had taught him to be much more cautious in his business dealings.

It wasn't long before he had become a major player in international drug trafficking, forging links with gangs in Holland, Spain and the UK. In criminal terms he was a complete workaholic, with a finger in every pie. He also acted as a facilitator, organising firearms and transport for armed robberies and large scale burglaries.

Some of the most dangerous and ruthless villains in the country joined Mitchell's mob. Apart from his brother Paddy, the gang included Ballyfermot hood, Johnny Doran, who was one of his closest confidants. In 1981, Doran and another gang member, Frank Ward from Sligo, were convicted of armed robbery and the attempted murder of two Garda detectives during an armed robbery in Stillorgan. As they were being chased after the heist the five-man gang pulled over and ambushed the two detectives. The officers were seriously injured in a hail of gunfire that peppered their squad car. Other members of this nest of villains included, convicted armed robbers Johnny McGrail, Mickey Boyle and INLA member Danny Hamill, Dublin thief Stephen Kearney and Gerry Hopkins. Intelligence soon began to emerge that Mitchell was negotiating major deals with international drug gangs and importing firearms.

In October 1993, for example, Mitchell and Stephen Kearney, who was originally from Ballyfermot, travelled to Malaga on the Costa del Sol to organise a cannabis deal with an English gang. The plan was to swap a truck load of French wine for hashish which would then be driven by Kearney to the UK. In the meantime, Mitchell flew back to Dublin alone. When Kearney subsequently returned on the ferry from the UK a month later, Gardaí seized IR£60,000 (€76,000) in cash which they found hidden in the spare wheel of his car. Cops also discovered another IR£80,000 (€102,000) when they searched the car driven by a gang associate, who had also returned from the UK. The cops suspected the money was part payment for drugs. An unsuccessful claim was later made in the Dublin High Court for the return of the money, under a Police Property Application by a convicted London fraudster called Kenneth Chester Whitehead. On Appeal, the Supreme Court upheld the High Court decision that it did not believe Whitehead was the true owner of the cash. (This was one of the rare cases in which cash was held in the days before the

CAB. If someone had come forward with a more credible claim to the money it would have been given back. By 2006, the Bureau had officially laid claim to the money which was then valued at €200,000.)

In early 1994, Mitchell unwittingly allowed the cops to get about as close to him as they would ever be, when he rented a yard and large lock-up premises in the Mount Brown area of Kilmainham, Dublin. Tucked away down a lane, off the main street, it was surrounded by a high wall and steel gate. It became the Penguin's new corporate HQ for Organised Crime Inc.! It was to be one of the most industrious criminal operations ever set up and was a hive of activity. Shipments of all classes of narcotics and firearms were co-ordinated and redistributed from the yard. Armed robberies, shootings and hijacks were plotted and planned. It was used to store stolen vehicles for heists or re-sale and stolen goods and guns, which were sold and hired out to other criminals. Mitchell spent much of his time commuting between Dublin, the UK and Holland on 'business'. As the operation continued to expand Liam Judge, a haulier from Allenwood, County Kildare became one of Mitchell's transport managers, as did Denis 'Dinny' Meredith, a close friend of John Gilligan. Judge later helped to launder Gilligan's hidden fortune, when the haulier moved to live in Spain with Treacy Gilligan. At the same time he was also secretly working as an informant for the Gardaí, in a bid to protect his own end of the business. He would help the cops to get close to the Penguin.

Within months of the Penguin's move to Kilmainham, the Serious Crime Squad, under the command of Det. Chief Supt. Kevin Carty, discovered the isolated yard. Carty was a quintessential 'thief-taker', who loved the challenge of catching major criminals. He was widely respected within the police as a highly competent investigator who was afraid of no one. Carty used every resource available to him, including modern technology, to take on the bad guys.

One night, one of Carty's most resourceful sergeants, who was known by colleagues as 'Feshty', sneaked across the wall of the yard and planted eavesdropping and other surveillance devices. The cops soon found that they had stumbled onto a veritable Aladdin's cave of villains. It was obvious that the hoods felt totally secure inside the high walls of the yard and lock-up. Undercover officers listening to the wiretaps couldn't believe their ears, as every type of serious crime was openly discussed and planned. Criminals love to gossip and the secret listeners picked up a huge amount of intelligence about crimes and capers all over the city.

Over the next six months the Serious Crime Squad carefully selected the arrests they made. The Squad didn't want to arouse any suspicion among the hoodlums that their little hideout had been compromised. Carty saw this as a unique opportunity to put the Penguin out of business.

In the space of four months, the cops turned Mitchell's operation upside down and he hadn't a clue how it was happening. The cops made their first move when they 'recovered' two separate caches of sophisticated fire-power which had been smuggled into the country for Mitchell by Liam Judge. The weapons included deadly Glock automatic handguns and Heckler and Koch machine guns that had been intended as 'presents' for the Provisional IRA. Gang member Frank Ward and his nephew, David Lynch, were then captured red-handed carrying out an armed robbery in Longford – a robbery that had been planned in the yard. And a month later Mitchell's trusted side-kick, Johnny Doran, was caught with 50 kilos of hash which he had organised to pick up while in the yard. But the Penguin himself was still proving to be an illusive target.

In another incident, undercover cops tailed McGrail and other members of the gang after listening to them plan an armed post office robbery in Shankill in south County Dublin. The robbers drove from the yard to Shankill in a stolen car followed by a large force of undercover cops. Another stolen car had been dispatched to carry the firearms to the scene. At the last moment McGrail spotted a passing squad car and aborted the robbery. The Garda watchers stepped back into the shadows. But it wasn't a completely wasted day. They later arrested the criminal transporting the weapons back to the yard when he ran into a 'routine check point'.

In another incident Mitchell's henchmen planned the theft of over IR£500,000 (€635,000) from a security van. A flat bed truck was stolen and brought back to the yard where it was modified to carry a large metal girder to act as a battering ram. The girder was sharp and pointed and would smash through the security van doors. Unknown to Mitchell's men, their progress was again being closely monitored by Carty's squad. They hoped to catch the mob in the act.

On the morning of the heist, the gang headed off in the truck and a convoy of cars and drove towards Blackrock, where the ambush was due to take place. A large force of Gardaí, including the Emergency Response Unit, also followed. But the plot came unstuck when a civilian recognised the stolen truck and tried to stop it on the road. McGrail and company got out and walked away, not knowing how close they had come to a spectacular arrest and a long stretch behind bars. Following the abandoned 'job' Mitchell decided to shut down the yard, fearing that the cops could trace the modified truck back to it. The intelligence dried up for a time but the Penguin would soon be back in the picture again.

* * * *

By the mid-1990s Mitchell was one of the largest suppliers of ecstasy to the Irish market. The Penguin bought the drugs in Holland where they were made in huge underground factories. When Mitchell visited one of these plants he decided that it would be much more profitable if he cut out the middle man and set up his own manufacturing operation in Ireland. In late 1994 he began putting his plan in motion. Alan Buckley, a thirty-five-year-old antique shop owner from Kinsale, County Cork, was a key player in Mitchell's growing national organisation. The well-spoken businessman was an important member of a large Munster-based, international drug trafficking gang, who worked closely with Mitchell. Among his associates were Jeremiah "Judd" Scalan, Tommy O'Callaghan and Paddy McSweeney. Another member of the cartel was ex-priest and convicted drug trafficker, John McCarthy. 'Father Hash', as he was known, had been laicised by the Church twenty years earlier, when he ran off with a woman and decided to be a dope smuggler.

Dubbed the Munster Mafia, they had close links with Mitchell and former INLA drug trafficker and killer Tommy Savage, who was nicknamed the Zombie because of his mad streak. Linchpin, Alan Buckley, was well known to the Gardaí and Barry Galvin, who suspected that he had been involved in smuggling drugs along the isolated Cork coast-line. Intelligence sources had revealed that he took care of organising the logistics for drug shipments. It was known that Buckley had personally helped to unload a 750 kilo hashish shipment and had been involved in a IR£7 million (€8.9 million) cannabis haul, which was seized at Courtmacsherry in 1991. Local businessman Christopher 'Golly' O'Connell was arrested following the bust. Shortly before his trial a few years later, the Penguin organised to have O'Connell shot, amid fears that he intended testifying against the gang. O'Connell recovered from his injuries and kept his mouth shut. He was subsequently jailed.

Mitchell and Buckley used another former priest, who had been a senior member of the IRA, to buy a tablet-making machine in Liverpool for £1,000 (€1,270). The machine, which was then shipped into Ireland and stored for a while in County Kildare, had the capacity to make 62 ecstasy tablets a minute. That minute's production was worth £620 (€790), based on the average street price of the drug at that time. In full production the little factory had the capacity to churn out over IR£37,000 (€47,000) worth of the drug an hour, IR£300,000 (€381,000) per day or IR£2 million (€2.5 million) each week. It was a licence to print money.

Buckley approached Terence Fitzsimons, a 47-year-old Dubliner to organise the day-to-day running of the operation.

Fitzsimons then recruited Raymond Jones, a 36-year-old spray painter and panel beater from Blanchardstown, West Dublin, because of his familiarity with chemicals and the companies who supplied them. In turn Jones, using a false business name, rented a warehouse in an industrial estate in Mulhuddart, West Dublin for IR£240 (€305) per month. Buckley then gave Jones a list of the chemicals needed. But the gang would have a problem buying the necessary chemicals without arousing suspicion. Jones convinced legitimate companies that he was involved in the manufacture of a steroid for Spanish bulls. He claimed the steroid reduced the amount of pain the bull felt and enabled it to fight longer! The chemicals were ordered and stored by Jones.

The chemicals would then be moved to an isolated premises, Wentworth House in Lucan. Fitzsimons rented the house for IR£300 (€381) per month and Cooper made MDMA, the base chemical compound used in ecstasy, there. Buckley and Mitchell knew that remote premises were essential because of the extremely strong odours given off by the chemical mix. If the highly volatile chemicals were not fixed correctly, they were also liable to explode. The chemical compound was then to be transported to a farm shed at Spricklestown near Ashbourne, County Dublin. Fitzsimons rented the shed from farmer Laurence Skelly for IR£70 (€89) a week. Skelly was promised a bonus of IR£5,000 (€6,350) when the first 9,000 tablets were made.

But Mitchell and Buckley had no idea that 'thief-taker' Kevin Carty was on their case. Carty had moved from the Serious Crime Squad to set up the new Garda National Drug Unit (GNDU). He learned of the plot to establish the first E factory in Ireland as a result of the undercover investigation at the Mount Brown yard. In March, a major surveillance operation, codenamed Barbie, was launched. The GNDU and the Serious Crime Squad monitored the preparations from a discreet distance. The main objective of Operation Barbie was to catch Mitchell and Buckley red-handed in possession of the drugs. They watched as Mitchell and Buckley visited the farm on a number of occasions to review the preparations. The crime lord was anxious to get things up and running but full production would take another three months. In the meantime he had run into other difficulties.

League of Ireland soccer star Derek 'Maradona' Dunne, who lived with Mitchell's only daughter Rachel and his granddaughter, was one of the biggest heroin suppliers in the north inner-city. To thousands of kids the twenty-eight-year-old semi-professional football player, with St Patrick's Athletic, was a sporting hero. But off the field, 'Maradona' was a ruthless drug dealer who had little care for the youngsters who revered his exploits on the field. Dunne was one of a group of young heroin dealers who made fortunes poisoning their own neighbourhoods. In May 1995, he found himself on a one-way collision course with the Monk's extended family after he gave Gerry Hutch's nephew a severe beating which left him hospitalised and badly injured. Immediately after the incident Dunne's house was burned and he had to go into hiding with Rachel Mitchell and their daughter. Mitchell and Hutch had a mutual 'respect' and were well aware of each other's capabilities. The Penguin was insistent that his daughter and grandchild would not be caught up in the crossfire and let it be known that he would protect Dunne. For a few weeks gangland was braced for a war. Garda intelligence received reports that Mitchell had brought in hit men from the UK to deal with any problems. He also had a large group of loyal hoods around him who weren't afraid of the Monk. There was also a risk that other gang bosses would take sides. Eventually the stand-off subsided when it was agreed that Dunne would not return to the north inner-city. After that Mitchell and Hutch made up their differences.

Operation Barbie had moved into a critical stage when the 'Maradona' row erupted. Towards the end of June the secret factory was ready to go into production. But when Cooper suddenly decided to leave the country on the night of June 30, 1995 and headed for the ferry at Dun Laoghaire, the investigation team was forced to make their move. The chemist was angry that he had not been paid IR£7,000 (€8,890) which he claimed he was owed by Fitzsimons for work he had already done. Cooper decided to make up the shortfall by taking enough MDMA mix with him to make IR£157,000 (€199,000) worth of the drug when he got back to the UK. Carty's team arrested Copper as he boarded the ferry.

The following morning the cops moved in to shut down the rest of the operation. Det. Inspector John Fitzpatrick and a team of armed officers arrested Jones and Skelly, as they made the first batch of 9,000 tablets worth IR£90,000 (€114,000). Fitzsimons was later arrested at his home in Castleblayney, County Monaghan. Detectives searched the other premises used by the gang and recovered enough MDMA to make IR£2 million (€2.5 million) worth of the drug. Cooper's sudden decision to leave had effectively saved the Penguin from arrest and a long stretch behind bars. It had been another close shave for the godfather.

Alan Buckley was subsequently arrested and questioned but there was insufficient evidence with which to charge him. The arrested men informally identified Mitchell and Buckley but refused to testify against them in court because they were terrified for their lives. Buckley had told Fitzsimons that the gang had been secretly watching his wife and children just in case he didn't do what he was told. "He said my job was to get the chemicals for the gang and if I didn't I was going to be shot," he later told detectives. Jones and Fitzsimons were both sentenced to ten years each in June 1997, with the final seven years suspended. Skelly was given a five year suspended sentence. Cooper had been jailed for five years a year earlier. All of the men pleaded guilty. In direct reference to Mitchell, Det. Supt. Malachy Mulligan of the GNDU said that he was "quite capable of having people shot".

While the Penguin was mulling over the loss of his E factory, and a threatened gang war, he flew to London to meet a close business associate – East London crime boss, Peter Daly. In cockney speak Daly was in "a bit of boffer". His gang was in the middle of a bloody gang war with the equally ruthless Brindle family. The brutal feud, the worst London had seen since the days of the Richardsons and the Krays in the 1960s, had so far claimed the lives of seven people, three of whom had been innocent bystanders. Another ten people had also been shot and seriously injured as a result of indiscriminate gun attacks. In August 1994, the situation had dramatically escalated when the Brindle gang shot two men dead in an East London pub in a devastating case of mistaken identity. The murdered men, who had nothing to do with the underworld, looked like Paul Daly and one his henchmen.

As London teetered on the brink of all-out war, Daly decided that he wanted Tony Brindle dead – before Daly himself ended up on the mortuary slab. It was a case of kill or be killed. Brindle and his brother Patrick had already been acquitted of murdering one of Daly's key men, Ahmed 'Turkish Abbi' Abdullah. So Daly had turned to his reliable, and very dangerous Irish pal, George Mitchell who agreed to help him out. Around that time the Penguin had called a meeting in the home of one of his gang members in Dublin, to discuss the request for international assistance from a brother crook. Daly had originally suggested that the Irish hit men wipe out most of the major players in the Brindle organisation, by hitting them simultaneously in one dramatic swoop. But the wily Penguin knew that such operations were the stuff of gangster fantasies. In the end it was decided that they would start with Daly. Mickey Boyle volunteered for the job.

Forty-eight-year-old Boyle from Bray, County Wicklow, was a terrifying one-man crime wave, who had spent a large portion of the 1970s and 1980s behind bars for armed robbery and kidnappings. Since his release from prison in 1993, the well-educated gangster had resumed a terrifying campaign of stealing from wealthy business people in their homes around County Wicklow. In the two years before the Brindle contract Boyle had been the prime suspect behind at least sixteen armed robberies, abductions and extortion demands. When he wasn't terrorising the people of Wicklow and south County Dublin, he worked as one of Mitchell's enforcers. He was a reliable hit man who had already carried out a number of shootings for his boss. In June, Mitchell had contracted Boyle to murder Fran Preston in Baldoyle, North Dublin. Preston, who had no connection to serious crime, had crossed swords with one of Mitchell's young criminal protégés. The brutal murder, which had been seen as a favour, had also shown the Monk's associates what they were potentially up against. Boyle and Mitchell had been arrested and questioned about the murder but they were never charged, due to a lack of evidence.

In a strange twist to the story, Boyle had offered to pass on general information about Mitchell and his gang and to become an informant, when he was arrested a year earlier by detectives investigating the Wicklow crime spree. Although, at the time, Boyle had little to say about his own crimes, he later passed on one piece of astonishing information to his handler, Detective Superintendent Austin McNally – that he had been contracted to shoot Tony Brindle. McNally, who later became the head of the GBFI, had been involved in the various operations targeting Mitchell. At first he thought he was dealing with a 'Walter Mitty' character. Nevertheless he passed on the information to his colleagues in Scotland Yard who were very interested in what he had to say. Intelligence work carried out after the alert confirmed that Boyle's information was accurate.

And when Boyle actually turned up in London, in September 1995, a huge undercover police operation was launched. On the morning of September 20, Boyle waited outside Brindle's home in a stolen van. When Brindle emerged from his house Boyle shot him twice. As the East London godfather struggled to get back into his house, the Penguin's hit man jumped out of the van and ran after him, carrying a revolver and an automatic pistol. He raised one of the weapons and took aim, planning to finish off his victim. Unfortunately for Boyle, Scotland Yard's special weapons and tactics unit, SO 19 had also been watching and waiting. The sharp-shooters sprang from a parked van and fired a total of fourteen shots at

Boyle, hitting him five times in the elbow, chest, shoulder, heel and ear. Miraculously, both the assassin and victim survived the incident. In follow-up searches Boyle's 'quartermaster' for the job, David Roads was arrested and guns, explosives and a large quantity of ammunition were recovered. The news from London was not good for Mitchell. Boyle's arrest seriously implicated Mitchell in the East End bloodbath and it was likely that he too would end up as a target on two more lists – one belonging to Scotland Yard but the other would belong to the Brindles. It was turning out to be a bad year for Mitchell.

The continuing success of the police operations against Mitchell's mob was making him extremely paranoid. He conducted a number of internal witch hunts to find out who had been talking. But the cops soon became the victims of their own success because Mitchell was proving practically impossible to catch. He consistently maintained a safe distance between himself and the actual criminal activity he was organising. But at the same time he had also begun to feature in the Irish media.

In June 1995, the *Sunday World* ran the first story on the mobster and officially shared his nickname, the Penguin, with the rest of the country, a name that came from John Traynor. Although Mitchell wasn't named, the newspaper ran his picture with his eyes blacked out, and detailed his involvement in organised crime. The story centred on the ongoing dispute between the Penguin and the Monk's family, over the Derek Dunne episode. The Penguin became a household name over night.

The following October, Mitchell found himself back in the media spotlight. This time Gardaí purposely named George Mitchell as a major player in the drug trade in the city, when they objected to the renewal of a nightclub licence. Inspector Thomas Murphy told the District Court how Mitchell's men had threatened security staff at the Waterfront night club, bar and restaurant with guns, in order to allow his pushers to sell drugs on the premises. The officer clearly stated that Mitchell was "a noted drug pusher, known as the Penguin from west Dublin". Inspector Murphy revealed: "The purpose of the visit [of the gunmen] was to intimidate the bouncers and to allow Mitchell's lieutenants to operate with impunity on the premises. Mitchell sent in his lieutenants with firearms to remind them who was the boss."

The court case gave the media the chance to legally name Mitchell and to expose him to the public. Life was becoming decidedly difficult for the crime lord.

But rather than keeping his head down, the workaholic Penguin was as busy as ever. This time he was putting together a huge cannabis deal in conjunction with Alan Buckley, the Munster Mafia and a Canadian drug gang, led by Normand Drapeau (*See Chapter Seven*). Mitchell's cut of the deal was 15 tonnes of cannabis. It was to be collected from a mother ship, off the south coast, and then brought ashore. The huge haul, which had a street value of IR£150 million (€190 million), was to be distributed in Ireland, Northern Ireland the United Kingdom. But again Kevin Carty and his people were all over the plot. In November the GNDU, who had infiltrated the gang, collected the hashish off the coast and set-up a sting operation. Unfortunately they were then forced to stage an official drug 'seizure' at Urlingford, County Kilkenny, when their operation was compromised by leaked information. Mitchell's sidekick John Noonan, who was known as the Manager, got suspicious and didn't turn up for the collection. The Manager, a former truck driver from Finglas in north-west Dublin, was another of the Penguin's organisers. Mitchell had escaped the net yet again.

Despite the various setbacks, the Penguin had become a powerful and extremely wealthy gangster. He had so many irons in the fire, and so many different criminals working with him, that the cops could only latch onto a handful of his myriad scams. The fact that he had not been caught in any of the swoops between '94 and '95 illustrated how extremely cautious and hands-off he was in all his business dealings.

In 1996, Mitchell again teamed up with Alan Buckley

and 'Father Hash' when they negotiated a deal with the Colombian cartels. The plan was to smuggle three tonnes of high-quality cocaine from South America into Europe, through Ireland. The load had a staggering street value of IR£250 million (€318 million).

A vessel called *The Tia* was to collect the cocaine from Surinam and sail to Donegal. The drugs were to be concealed in a consignment of timber and hand-crafted furniture, destined for a legitimate company in Donegal. However, it later emerged, that the deal did not go ahead because the skipper, who was the brother of an Icelandic criminal living in Dublin, refused to take the drugs on board. He felt that they weren't properly hidden within the timber. When *The Tia* arrived back in Irish waters, the Irish Navy and GNDU were waiting for it. The ship was searched but nothing was found. The skipper was arrested, questioned and later charged with conspiracy to import drugs. The charges were subsequently dropped.

The Tia debacle had been one close shave too many for Mitchell. He reasoned that if the haul had been intercepted, then the people arrested would have had an incentive to testify against him and the rest of the cartel because they could have expected to receive a very long stretch behind bars. When Veronica Guerin was murdered in June of the same year, it was the last straw. The Penguin decided to emigrate to Amsterdam.

It has since been claimed that Mitchell came to this decision because he was afraid of the IRA. This rumour was circulated by members of Sinn Féin in order to win votes. The idea was that they would convince people that they had forced an evil drug lord out of the country. Nothing could be further from the truth. In fact Mitchell had many friends in Sinn Féin and the IRA, who he was supplying with 'funding' and firearms. Other individuals associated with the Republican movement had even been involved in some of his drug rackets, including the Provo Priest, who had bought his ecstasy making machine.

Mitchell decided to leave the country because he had had

too many close shaves over the previous year. His survival instincts told him that a world of trouble was coming as a result of the Guerin murder. He was particularly concerned by the reports of a powerful new multi-agency organisation with draconian powers to take the money away from godfathers like himself. The media had also been writing about him and his picture had been in the newspapers. On top of that, there was the matter of Mickey Boyle's trial in the Old Bailey, which was also looming. In the summer of 1996 the Penguin migrated to Amsterdam which he considered more secure. He settled in a modest house, not far from Schipol Airport.

In January 1997, during Mickey Boyle's three-month trial in the Old Bailey, Mitchell was exposed as the man who had organised the Tony Brindle hit. Boyle's colourful testimony and dramatic claims guaranteed widespread coverage in the Irish and UK media. He claimed that he had been a member of the IRA but had decided to leave the organisation because he said he preferred "less dangerous methods" of fighting the war. Boyle also admitted that he had been a Garda informant. He even claimed that he had told the Irish cops about the contract because he "hoped" that they would intervene and stop him! And he also put the boot into his old pal Mitchell who, he claimed, had coerced him into carrying out the botched attack.

Boyle told the Old Bailey: "Mitchell told me that if I sorted out the Brindles that he would be able to re-establish himself in London and that we would all be better off. I was only there because of the pressure I was under. If I wanted to kill Brindle I would have chosen a pump action shotgun because it would have been impossible to miss from that distance."

* * * *

With the ongoing investigations of John Gilligan and Gerry Hutch already well established, it was time for the Criminal Assets Bureau to turn their attentions to their next major organised crime target – George Mitchell. The Untouchables had received intelligence reports that the Penguin had removed cash from the country when the establishment of the Bureau was first announced. In early 1997, Team Three, which was led by Detective Sergeant Paul O'Brien, was assigned to pursue the Penguin's hidden loot. The secret operation was to be codenamed Firedamp. In order to compensate for a shortage of resources, six detectives from units around Dublin were temporarily seconded to Team Three to assist in Operation Firedamp. The ongoing inquiries into Hutch and Gilligan, had expanded dramatically as other individuals were exposed and added to the list of targets, which meant that the probes soaked up man-hours and stretched the Bureau to the limit.

For the first six months of 1997, Operation Firedamp remained top secret as the Untouchables compiled intelligence on Mitchell and his associates. In order to know where to look for the money they needed to build up a comprehensive database of information. In any CAB investigation the initial period is considered to be highly volatile and absolute secrecy is vital. Any hint that a probe is underway can result in money vanishing overnight. Searches of suspects' homes and the offices of their solicitors and accountants are always left to the final phase of an inquiry, as this is usually the first time that a target learns he or she is under investigation. A former officer explained: "Once an individual gets a whisper that we are on the case then money vanishes over night. If we move too early then there is a risk that accounts which we haven't identified can be cleared out immediately. It really is a game of cat-and-mouse."

As the investigation progressed, O'Brien's team identified a number of potential informants linked to Mitchell and his associates. Soon the information provided by informants, combined with intelligence already available to the Gardaí, built up a fuller picture of the Penguin's finances. They also identified the most important person in Mitchell's organisation – his trusted bagman, fraudster Peter Edward Bolger who was known as the Banker.

Originally from Crumlin in south Dublin, Bolger was a typical conman – confident and suave with the air of a successful businessman. Married to a secondary school teacher, the Banker was very conscious of his image. He liked to wear expensive suits and even a wig to keep up appearances. By the time his name came to light he was a central player in criminal rackets in Dublin. But he had not always been involved in crime. In 1981, at the age of 27, he had bought a pub on Old County Road in Crumlin. But in the mid-1980s the business had gone bust and Bolger was left practically penniless. It was around this time that he had met George Mitchell and discovered a whole new way of making money. During the late 1980s, before he was jailed for the Nilzan heist, the Penguin owned a second hand car company, GM Motors. It operated from premises in Crumlin that were once owned by Michael Egan. Egan, from County Offaly, was jailed in 1988 for allowing the General's gang to use the same premises to hide and sort through the IR£2 million (€2.5 million) worth of gold and jewels they had just stolen from the O'Connor's Jewellers factory. At his trial, fifty-three-year-old Egan was described as a man "with a propensity for associating with evil men" and he was jailed for seven years. Egan had been recruited into the Cahill gang by professional conmen Sean 'Fixer' Fitzgerald and John 'Coach' Traynor. They were also associates of George Mitchell and Peter Bolger.

Bolger's name was soon featuring in a number of Garda and UK police investigations in connection with major fraud rackets. In 1986 he was part of a collection of conmen involved in the infamous Great Norwegian Fish Scandal. The main players in the scam were John Traynor and former Roscommon county footballer and drug trafficker, James 'Danger' Byrne. The Icelandic criminal, who would skipper *The Tia* for Mitchell ten years later, was also involved. Byrne came up with the idea of pretending to purchase dried fish in Norway and shipping them to Nigeria. The complex scam involved a promissory note for IR£3.6 million (€4.6 million) which was drawn down by Byrne at the Norwegian Tromso Spare Bank, after being endorsed by a friendly bank official at the Northern Bank in Carrick-on-Shannon, County Leitrim. The scam was discovered after the IR£3.6 million (€4.6 million) had already been paid out but two other promissory notes, valued at over IR£12 million (€15 million), were stopped – just before the gang cashed them. The fraud made international headlines and, despite legal actions, none of the money was recovered. It taught Bolger a few tricks for the future.

Bolger next surfaced in London, where he began working as a 'financial consultant'. On September 15, 1989 he and a number of other suspected fraudsters were arrested and questioned by City of London Police following an attempt to pull off a Stg£20 million (€29 million) fraud involving Bills of Exchange. One of the people arrested with Bolger was Mitchell's associate, the Icelandic criminal but he was subsequently released without charge.

In 1990, Bolger went into business with another 'financial consultant', Edward Phelan from Garristown in north County Dublin. Between them the partners set up two companies, Corporate Finance International and Corporate Finances Investment. Ostensibly the business involved raising bank loans for clients based on the market value of their property and using the money for investment purposes. It was called 'securitising' and the two conmen were paid a commission from the sums raised by the client. However the pair soon came to the attention of the Serious Fraud Office when they forged a client's signature on a document. They had also been caught up in a Stg£156,000 (€227,000) advance fee fraud with client's money. Bolger and Phelan were subsequently charged with fourteen counts of forgery and fraudulent trading.

On March 13, 1995 they went on trial at London's Southwark Crown Court. Throughout the trial, Bolger was out on bail and was permitted to fly home to Dublin at the weekends. The wily conman could see that things were not going his way. On April 3 he returned to Dublin and stayed there. He didn't return to London for the rest of the trial. He later claimed he was suffering from a "strangulated hernia" and had been advised by doctors to stay at home. The High Court in Dublin subsequently found that there was no evidence to back up this claim.

On April 7, Bolger was convicted in his absence on one sample count of fraudulent trading and two of forgery. The other charges were taken into account. The partners-in-crime were each sentenced to three years in prison and disqualified from acting as directors of any company in the UK, for a period of five years. Phelan served his time and was released from custody 18 months later, when he returned to Ireland. In the meantime the UK authorities issued extradition proceedings to have Bolger returned to London to serve his sentence.

In September 1996, an application for Bolger's extradition failed on a legal technicality in the Dublin District Court. The fourteen warrants issued by the UK authorities contained an incorrect address for the fugitive. The Metropolitan Police were given the option of re-issuing the warrants.

As the Criminal Assets Bureau investigation into George Mitchell continued, officers discovered a connection between Peter Bolger and former Government Minister Michael Keating. Informants told the detectives that Keating, who had once been a member of Fine Gael, was a business associate of the conman and involved in laundering Mitchell's money. Over the following months the 'pillar of society' would be exposed as a consummate liar and a willing participant in the activities of organised crime. Keating would later claim to officers from the CAB that he first met Bolger in the early 1990s, when he was a member of Dublin County Council, representing the Tallaght area. Keating also knew Edward Phelan who, he claimed, reintroduced him to Bolger some time later in London. Keating told a bizarre tale of how he and another business associate were ripped off by Bolger, to the tune of Stg£50,000 (€73,000). The deal involved raising the money to buy a piece of art known as the Gaugin Coffin Box, which was valued at Stg£1 million (€1.45 million). Keating claimed that Bolger had told him that he had entered into negotiations with the owner of the art. But in order for the deal to go ahead they had to show the owner an available sum of Stg£50,000 (€73,000), to prove that they could fund the purchase. Bolger promised to then put up an additional Stg£25,000 (€36,000) each, from him and Phelan. It was a classic advance fee fraud sting. Keating claimed he never saw the money again and the deal fell through. What made the story rather unbelievable was that the smooth-talking politician continued to be one of Peter Bolger's business associates.

This was the first time that the CAB had uncovered direct links between a so-called 'pillar of society' and organised crime. The Untouchables discovered that Keating was a lot closer to the underworld than he wanted people to know. Despite his trenchant public denials in the media, Operation Firedamp revealed that Keating had met with Mitchell face-to-face, to discuss business. The question that perplexed the investigators, and later the public, was how could someone from Keating's background end up rubbing shoulders with the likes of Peter Bolger and George Mitchell.

* * * *

It had all been so much different a decade earlier when Michael Keating was seen as one of the country's most promising and talented young politicians. But an analysis of Keating's political career reveals a fickle and untrustworthy personality, with a propensity for corruption. Smartly dressed and articulate, he stood out as a welcome alternative to the grey old men who had dominated Irish politics before him. The charming chancer, who was born in Dublin in 1947, started his career as a secondary school teacher and later worked as a journalist, editing a number of weekly magazines. He also had a keen interest in politics and was elected to Dublin City Council in 1974, as a member of Fine Gael. Three years later, he and his Fianna Fáil arch-rival, Bertie Ahern, both won Dáil seats for the first time, in the Dublin North Central constituency.

Two years later Garret Fitzgerald promoted Keating to

the front bench, as the party's spokesperson on law reform and human rights. When Fine Gael returned to power after the General Election of 1981, Fitzgerald made him a Minister of State (Junior Minister) at the Department of Education, with Special Responsibility for Youth and Sport. He courted the media limelight and that same year a newspaper survey found that he had been the third most photographed politician, after Fitzgerald and Charles Haughey. But behind-the-scenes Keating was proving to be a troublesome Minister and had several run-ins with the party leadership. On one occasion, Keating decided, against the wishes of the Cabinet, that the State would buy a stately manor in Adare, County Limerick. The Minister of State travelled to Adare to address a meeting about the purchase even though Fitzgerald had ordered him not to do so. The Taoiseach reportedly dispatched a Garda car to stop Keating when he discovered the junior minister had disregarded his order. But Keating had taken a lift on an Army helicopter instead of driving, causing the Government serious embarrassment in the process.

After the Adare incident and numerous other spats with the party hierarchy, Keating found himself left out in the cold. He was relegated to the back benches after the February 1982 General Election which saw Fianna Fáil return to power. During the election he had ignored his party's instructions to support his running mate, Alice Glenn, who lost her seat as a result. In 1983 he took office for a year as Lord Mayor of Dublin. He later complained that his allowance as first citizen had been "woefully inadequate", to allow him to properly entertain his various guests.

Fed up with his exile from the Cabinet, Keating began to look around for another opportunity and found it in the new Progressive Democrats party. Fine Gael had described the PD's as a dissident Fianna Fáil group but he soon made them eat their own words. The opportunistic politician was a welcome defector for the PDs. However, before he finally agreed to make the move he insisted on being given the position of Deputy Leader. And even before he had officially moved, he was accused of double-crossing and lying to both Fine Gael and the media.

Controversy continued to follow Keating. In 1986, a newspaper revealed how he had used Department of Education funds to pay for his personal election leaflets and posters. Despite this, Keating was re-elected for the PDs at the 1987 General Election. But by then, the new party that campaigned for high standards in political life, considered him something of a liability.

With nothing much to do around the Dáil, Keating got involved in a publishing company with a friend called Jim Booth, of the Inner City Traders Association. Booth was subsequently convicted of receiving stolen goods and possession of a firearm. Keating denied that he had ever been involved in the company.

In 1989, he committed the ultimate act of political treachery when he announced his sudden retirement from politics, and the PDs, on the opening day of their general election campaign. After that Keating involved himself in a series of dodgy business deals and ventures, including a plan to import a "Chinese cure for baldness". He also wrote a thriller, aptly titled *Day of Reckoning*, which was launched by Charles Haughey. According to the publicity campaign it told the story of "a brave and cunning individual who takes the big institutions for a ride".

In 1992, he briefly emerged from the political wilderness again and re-joined Fine Gael to run in the General Election in south Dublin. But the public had grown tired of his fickle approach to politics and he received a paltry three per cent of the vote. He continued to flirt with various quick-buck business ventures most of which failed. One former associate said: "Michael is a born loser. He is always out to find the get-rich-quick stroke which is why he is so utterly untrustworthy." Keating went into partnership in one company which specialised in providing training services. But he was booted out when his partner discovered that he had been using company stationary for other, totally unrelated, business ventures.

In his best-selling book *GUBU Nation,* author Damian Corless related a strange story about how Keating had tried to con movie-maker Neil Jordan by pretending he had access to diaries containing sensational material about Michael Collins, the hero of Ireland's War of Independence. Jordan was making a movie about Collins at the time and Keating told him that the diaries contained claims that Collins had been an active homosexual, who preyed on young soldiers for sexual gratification. Then the conman admitted that he had never actually seen the diary. Jordan rebuffed the obvious chancer.

At the same time Keating was helping to launder Mitchell's money. Around the time that Operation Firedamp began in early 1997, Keating joined Bolger in a venture to export beef to West Africa. Bolger and an accountant called Michael O'Leary, a partner in the prestigious accountancy firm Simpson Xavier and Company, were named as the directors of a company called Louiseville Ltd., which traded as Eringold. Their plan was to open a factory making canned meat for the African market. Although Keating claimed to have been ripped off by Bolger in the past, he was still happy to get involved in the project. The CAB investigation would later discover that the Eringold project was a scam by Bolger to launder Mitchell's drug money. In the meantime, Keating used his political connections to get the project off the ground. He convinced Ivan Yates, the Fine Gael Agriculture Minister, to write a letter of recommendation for the Minister of Trade in Gambia, on Keating's behalf. In the letter Yates described Keating as being "well respected and highly professional" and Bolger's commitment and professionalism as "second to none". The Minister had no reason to suspect that Michael Keating had fallen into nasty company and took his former colleague's word on Bolger.

On March 17, Keating, Bolger and O'Leary arrived at Banjul airport on a Sabena flight from Brussels. It was the start of four days of negotiations for a €20 million deal. The three men were given VIP treatment and Keating was introduced everywhere he went with the title "honourable". Several meetings were held with the various government ministries and the Gambia Ports Authority. When the Eringold men returned to Ireland, they received visits from the Gambian officials in Dublin. Keating brought the guests on a tour of the Dáil to showcase his access to power. On August 21, the Gambian Cabinet sent a fax to the offices of Eringold confirming that it had approved a €2 million Government investment in the project. But by then the reputable Irish VIPs were in a spot of bother.

* * * *

As the Operation Firedamp investigation progressed, informants had pointed the team in the direction of an EBS branch in north Dublin, where Mitchell had held a number of accounts. In January the Bureau served production orders on the building society head office, demanding details of all accounts in the names of George Mitchell and David Doran, an alias that they believed Mitchell was using. The EBS head office furnished details of two accounts in the names of Mitchell and Doran. The records showed that, between January and March 1995, a total of IR£229,000 (€291,000) had been lodged in the two accounts. Intelligence sources revealed that Michael Egan, the car-lot owner who was jailed for the O'Connor's robbery, had lodged the cash for the Penguin. He had deposited the money in sums of around IR£10,000 (€12,700) each time.

A third account at the ESB was then identified as belonging to Robbie Murphy, a protégé of the Penguin and a well-known drug trafficker from Artane in north Dublin. Also known as the Technician, thirty-two year-old Murphy was a convicted armed robber who had moved into the heroin and cocaine trade with footballer Derek Dunne and another inner-city thug called Thomas 'the Boxer' Mullen. As the main suppliers of heroin in the north inner-city, the notorious trio had been targeted in street protests by anti-drug groups. Murphy had also fled the country in the summer of 1996 because of the pressure he was under from the Gardaí and the anti-drug movement. It was discovered that a total of IR£110,000 (€140,000) had been lodged to an EBS account, which was held in the name of one of his relations. As the Untouchables followed the money trail, it soon became apparent that the cash also belonged to Mitchell.

The CAB discovered that, between May and July 1996, just over IR£340,000 (€432,000) had been cleared out of the three accounts. The largest withdrawals occurred just after the murder of Veronica Guerin and the Government's announcement of a tough new anti-crime package. EBS cheques were issued, in the names of Mitchell, Doran and Murphy's relation. The withdrawal of the cash from the three accounts automatically fell into the category of a suspicious transaction and it should have been reported to the Money Laundering Investigation Unit (MLIU) but it wasn't. The investigators subsequently identified a corrupt official in the EBS who had been secretly working for the mobsters. The official, who was later arrested by the CAB, admitted to being an acquaintance of Robbie Murphy and moving money for him. At Murphy's behest, the contact ensured Mitchell had no problems opening his account or making lodgements and withdrawals.

Some of the EBS cheques were cashed and the rest were exchanged in another bank for drafts in smaller sums. Between the three accounts, four drafts worth IR£198,000 (€252,000) were then passed on to Peter Bolger. And it was at this point that Michael Keating's involvement in the money laundering conspiracy was confirmed. In July 1996, Bolger gave Keating the drafts in an envelope. Two of the drafts, for the total sum of IR£48,000 (€61,000) were in the name 'G. Mitchell'). The former Minister had suggested lodging them to his solicitor's client account for safe-keeping.

On September 30, 1996, Bolger instructed Keating to

withdraw the money from his solicitor's account. The former Mayor then lodged the drafts with the AIB branch in Terenure in south Dublin. He requested that the money be transferred to the client account of Bolger's solicitor, Gabriel Haughton at the Ulster Bank in Dun Laoghaire.

Of the IR£198,000 (€252,000) that was transferred, IR£143,000 (€182,000) was later moved from the Dun Laoghaire account to a company called Panorama Consultants, who had an offshore account in the Isle of Man. Panorama Consultants was a front company controlled by Bolger, on behalf of Mitchell. The last of the money was moved just days before Operation Firedamp was launched. Uplifted bank records subsequently showed that an additional sum of IR£75,000 (€95,000) had also been transferred from the Dun Laoghaire solicitor's client account to Haughton's reserve account, held in a bank in London. From there the money was also transferred to Panorama Consultants.

At the same time the investigation team was aware that Bolger had been having regular meetings with George Mitchell in Brussels. Undercover Belgian police had kept a discreet watch on the men's meetings, on behalf of the Irish authorities. At that stage the Penguin was also featuring in Dutch police investigations into organised crime. The investigators were also satisfied that, in the first half of 1997, Keating had travelled alone to Holland, on at least one occasion, to meet the Penguin.

By the beginning of July 1997, the Firedamp team was prepared to show their hand and make their move. Between July 21 and 24, O'Brien's team carried out a series of searches across Dublin, including at Bolger's home, the offices of Eringold, Keating's office and a number of legal and accountancy firms. In the offices of Bolger's solicitor in Dun Laoghaire on July 22, they found a number of files belonging to the conman. Most significantly they found a large folder labelled 'Bolger/Mitchell/Doran-Panorama Consultants'. In the file they found evidence that linked Bolger with the godfather and his alias. It stated in one entry on July 4, 1996, that Bolger was acting on instructions from George Mitchell and the non-existent David Doran. There was also correspondence relating to proposed property transactions in the UK, worth in the region of Stg£1 million (€1.45 million).

Detective Sergeant O'Brien informed staff at the legal firm of the serious nature of the investigation and his belief that the George Mitchell mentioned in the file was in fact the drug baron. The following morning, O'Brien received a phone call from Bolger's solicitor, Gabriel Haughton, informing him that he was holding another IR£300,000 (€436,000) in his client account for Bolger. O'Brien immediately returned to the solicitor's office. At the meeting Bolger's legal representative informed the Detective Sergeant that the money was soon to be loaned by Panorama Consultants to a company called Palfrey Estates. The money was to be a short-term loan to buy US Railroad Bonds. Haughton showed O'Brien a Memorandum of Agreement between the two companies, dated May 30, 1997. O'Brien informed Haughton that it was suspected that the IR£300,000 (€436,000) was the proceeds of crime and that Bolger was in the process of laundering it through the lawyer's client account.

The following day, Friday July 25, Bolger's solicitor sent two fax messages to the offices of the Criminal Assets Bureau. The legal representative stated he was under a legal obligation to follow his client's instructions until otherwise ordered by the High Court. He also demanded the return of the files seized during the searches. The CAB responded with a request that Haughton should not remove any monies belonging to Bolger, Mitchell or any other associated companies. It was late on Friday evening and it was obvious that the lawyer was under pressure from the Banker to move the cash before the CAB could take action.

At a conference in Harcourt Square, Det. Chief Supt. Fachtna Murphy decided that they had to move fast before, as with the previous sums, the drug money disappeared. But to do this they needed a High Court order to freeze the money, before the banks opened for business again on Monday morning.

The officers attached to Team Three worked through the weekend preparing affidavits for an early morning hearing in the High Court. The court documents outlined the reasons why the CAB believed the money was the proceeds of crime. The documents detailed Mitchell's connection to organised crime and Bolger's conviction for fraud in the UK. Fachtna Murphy retained counsel to present the CAB application and requested an early sitting of the High Court on Monday morning, on the grounds of the utmost urgency. This was typical of what the Untouchables termed the "fire brigade response". They often found themselves in a race against time to obtain freezing orders, just before criminal bank accounts were cleared out. In certain circumstances for example, where intelligence was received late in the evening that money was about to be removed the following morning, officers worked through the night to prepare for trying to obtain an injunction, before the banks opened for business the next day. This had happened successfully in a number of cases where foreign law enforcement agencies, such as the FBI, had requested urgent assistance.

On Monday morning at 9 am, Mr Justice Smyth heard the application for an interim injunction, freezing the money in Bolger's client account. As the clock ticked towards bank opening hours at 10 am, the court appointed Barry Galvin as the official Receiver and ordered him to locate the money, take it into his possession and lodge it to a special bank account, set up for that purpose. When the hearing was over, Det. Sgt. O'Brien, Det. Gda. Cliona Richardson and Barry Galvin jumped into a waiting squad car and sped to Haughton's office, through the rush hour traffic, with sirens blaring. On the way Paul O'Brien phoned the lawyer, informing him that the CAB had been granted a freezing order and telling him not to release the cash.

When they arrived at the offices, Gabriel Haughton brought Galvin and O'Brien to an office where he was presented with the High Court order. Bureau Legal Officer

Galvin demanded to know precisely how much money the solicitor had in respect of his client Bolger and where the cash was being held. The Banker's solicitor confirmed that some of it was in his Ulster Bank client account and the balance was in a solicitors' reserve account in the NatWest bank in London. Haughton asked to be excused for a moment while he checked the accounts holding the cash. While the meeting was taking place the CAB officers waiting in the squad car parked outside spotted Bolger leaving the building. He had been there to collect a cheque for the money when Galvin and O'Brien arrived. Bolger had underestimated his new enemies and hadn't expected them to move so fast. Another half hour and the Penguin's money would have been gone.

In the meantime, the lawyer returned to the office and informed Galvin that IR£118, 643 (€151,000) was in his client account in the Ulster Bank. The remainder, IR£181,357 (€230,500), had been lodged to the London account. Galvin requested Gabriel Haughton to sign a letter of authority to the NatWest, instructing them to furnish Det. Gda. Richardson with the balance, in the form of a bank draft made payable to Barry Galvin as the Receiver. As soon as the letter was handed over Richardson raced to Dublin airport to catch a flight to London to retrieve the cash. The lawyer then handed Galvin a cheque for the balance in the Irish account. By 3.30 pm Richardson had collected the draft in London and was on her way home. The mob had been completely out-manoeuvred.

The informants working for Team Three subsequently reported that Bolger, Keating and others, had had a long meeting the previous weekend to discuss the CAB searches and how they could get the IR£300,000 (€381,000) out of the country before it was seized. They were trying to work out exactly how much the Untouchables knew and, more importantly, how they had come by the information they obviously possessed. With the CAB moving so quickly, Bolger was now faced with the difficulty of explaining the origins of the IR£300,000 (€381,000) that had been seized. In the

meantime Det. Sgt. O'Brien was also tipped off that more
money had been stashed in Bolger's Templeogue home and
that he intended moving it out of the country.

On August 6, Team Three obtained a warrant to search
Bolger's home for the second time. The previous day they
had served him with a tax demand for IR£141,592 (€180,000),
based on earnings calculated for one year. Bolger was also
informed that the Bureau had become his new Inspector of
Taxes. As the officers began their search, Bolger's wife
grabbed a sheet of paper from a printer beside a computer in
an upstairs room. She was about to flush the page down the
toilet, when Det. Gda. Richardson stopped her and took
possession of it. The officers discovered that it was a false
document relating to the origins of the money. When Det.
Sgt. O'Brien asked Bolger why his wife had tried to destroy
the piece of paper he replied: "She's well-trained".

When the officers searched the computer room they found
a shredding machine which had been recently used to destroy
a large number of documents. When O'Brien examined the
computer he found a number of contract documents relating
to the sale of a Monrovian logging interest and a shipment of
Latvian furniture, which had been imported to Northern
Ireland. The documents, which had just been created, were
dated as far back as the previous April. Letters had also been
prepared in the names of foreign businessmen, to back up the
pretence that the money came from different business deals.

Bolger claimed that he had been preparing affidavits for
his defence and that they had no right to seize his computer.
The Untouchables suddenly found themselves in a tricky
situation. Seizing documents that formed part of an
individual's defence was potentially illegal. But O'Brien had
good grounds to believe that the Banker was preparing to
deceive the courts. He decided to seize the computer and the
shredding machine. The computer was later analysed by Garda
experts and then sent for further examination to the UK. It
was confirmed that all the documentation, which also included
correspondence from 'businessmen' in Sierra Leone and

Liberia, had been created on the day of the raid.

O'Brien's team spent most of a full week on their hands and knees piecing together the slivers of shredded paper they had seized. When they finished they had successfully reassembled 16 pages of the false documentation.

In the following days Gabriel Haughton, acting on Bolger's instructions, threatened to seek a High Court injunction against the Bureau, for contempt of court and an order seeking the return of the seized material. The lawyer also accused them of following and harassing Bolger, particularly Det. Sgt. O'Brien. They demanded the return of what they described as privileged court documents. The legal representative rather curiously claimed that the reason the draft affidavits and other material were found in Bolger's home was due to a shortage of secretarial staff in his solicitor's offices over the holiday season. The letter stated:

> 'Due to the holiday season this office was under severe secretarial pressure and this was the reason documents, prepared by ourselves in contemplation of these proceedings, were being typed up by our client at his premises.'

It was obvious that Bolger was anxious to stall the CAB investigation.

On September 16, Bolger flew to Brussels to discuss the ongoing situation with the Penguin. Undercover Belgian police secretly monitored his meeting. With the Banker safely out of the country, Det. Inspector John McDermott and Det. Sergeant Paul O'Brien arrested Michael Keating on suspicion of money laundering offences, under the Drug Trafficking Act. He was brought to Pearse Street Garda Station where he was questioned over a two-day period. His home, Silverdale House in Castleknock, was also searched. Keating was horrified that he had been arrested and he tried to convince the officers that he had been completely duped.

In a statement he admitted to receiving the cheques in the

name of George Mitchell from Bolger. He claimed that when he became "suspicious" that they belonged to the crime lord Bolger convinced him that it was not the same man. Keating said that he felt he and his solicitor had been "manipulated and abused" by Bolger. "In retrospect now I am very disappointed in myself, firstly for not keeping miles away from Peter Bolger, who has damaged so many peoples' lives and second for not acting with more responsibility," said Keating.

The detectives put it to the former politician that he had secretly met with Mitchell in Holland but he vehemently denied this. When they showed him a picture of the Penguin he turned his head away. "Get that picture of that evil man away from me," he declared in disgust.

Keating also denied that he was a director of Eringold and claimed to be in fear of his life. "I want to say at this point that I have a strong fear of Peter Bolger and his associates and I don't underestimate their capacity for inflicting harm on innocent people such as myself, who they have inveigled into their schemes," Keating added in an emotional performance.

At 10 am on the morning of September 18, 1997, Bolger was arrested under drug trafficking legislation, as he got off a flight from Brussels. He was also taken to Pearse Street Garda Station. The County Sheriff seized the Banker's black Mercedes car, to offset his tax liability. In the meantime Keating was released without charge. Bolger refused to make any statement and was also released after 48 hours in custody.

As soon as he was released, Bolger began an exhaustive series of legal actions, some of them purely vexatious, which were designed to tie the Criminal Assets Bureau up in knots. Every allegation and application he made to the court would have to be responded to by Bureau officers. The intention was to bog the Untouchables down in paper work. But over the next two years Bolger was repeatedly exposed as a liar by the courts.

Within days of his arrest, he took his first action. On September 23, Bolger sought a High Court injunction restraining the Criminal Assets Bureau from what his solicitor Gabriel Haughton described as, "threatening and intimidatory activities". Bolger was effectively seeking orders to prevent the Untouchables from going near him, or any of his associates, in the course of their investigation. The evidence was presented to the court in the form of sworn written affidavits, which were read before Mr Justice Smyth.

In Bolger's Affidavit, read out by Haughton, he outlined the activities of Eringold and the Gambia project. He claimed that the CAB had embarked on a campaign of vilification against him. Bolger also alleged that they had been tailing him, had illegally removed "documents" which he was preparing for his defence, and had beaten and abused him while in custody. The gangland Banker also claimed that the Untouchables had spread rumours that he was a major drug trafficker and an associate of the Penguin who, he said, "was known for complicity in unlawful killings". He singled out the officer who he saw as his biggest threat in the investigation – Det. Sgt. Paul O'Brien – and claimed that O'Brien had been "falsely and maliciously" telling potential witnesses that the Banker was engaged in money laundering. Bolger also alleged that the CAB had frightened and intimidated Michael Keating and Michael O'Leary and that they had been told that he was associated with drug importation and advised them to no longer associate with him. His company's business had been interfered with and Eringold might have to close down. Bolger said he feared for his safety and that of his family as a result of the "widespread false and malicious rumours". Knowing Mitchell's background he said he felt he had very good reason to be fearful.

Donal O'Donnell SC, who represented the CAB, then read an Affidavit from Michael O'Leary in which he denied that he held any directorship in Bolger's company Louiseville Ltd or that he had acted on his behalf as an accountant. O'Leary also stated that no one in the Criminal Assets Bureau had told him Bolger was a drug dealer or was an associate of Mitchell. Michael Keating also denied that he had ever been a director of Louiseville or that he had been intimidated or threatened. Keating admitted that Bolger had handed him the bank drafts in 1996 made out to George Mitchell.

Det. Insp. John McDermott "emphatically rejected" any wrong doing, assault or verbal abuse of Bolger while in custody. He said Bolger had received four visits from his solicitor and when released he had made no complaint of being assaulted or ill-treated. McDermott declared that the allegations were a "wrongful attempt to interfere or frustrate the Criminal Assets Bureau". At all times the inquiries were being carried out in a "conscientious, courteous, fair and reasonable manner". Det. Sgt. O'Brien's evidence revealed how the ongoing investigation had uncovered the financial links between Mitchell and Bolger. He also mentioned the discovery of the Bolger/Mitchell/Doran file during the search of Haughton's office. O'Brien also informed the court about Bolger's UK fraud conviction in 1995, which Bolger had omitted to reveal, and the discovery that he had been falsifying documents to explain to the courts the origin of the frozen IR£300,000 (€381,000).

In his submission Donal O'Donnell SC said that one of the orders being sought by Bolger was to restrain the Bureau officers from describing him as a criminal. "It appears Mr Bolger is indeed a criminal in that he has been convicted on charges of fraud and absconded from the courts of justice in the UK," he said. The counsel for the CAB said that it was impossible to see how any effective investigation could be carried out if the orders sought by Bolger were granted. "This application is an abuse of the process of the court. It appears to be an attempt to frustrate and impede and interfere with this investigation." O'Donnell added during the several hours of legal argument.

Mr Justice Smyth threw out Bolger's application. In reference to the affidavits of Bolger and his solicitor Gabriel Haughton, the judge remarked that "some of the facts deposed in those affidavits must have been known to be untrue". He was critical that the Banker had not mentioned his conviction in the UK and confirmed that the file found in the solicitor's office clearly showed that he was indeed connected to George Mitchell.

Mr Justice Smyth said that Bolger's claims were "clearly less than frank or straightforward. In short this Affidavit does not hold together."

In relation to the allegations made against Det. Sgt. O'Brien he said: "I feel that Det. Sgt. O'Brien would be failing in his duty if he failed to warn a potential witness that certain action may constitute a criminal offence."

With regard to the Bureau's role he ruled: "I do not think it [CAB] acted in any way oppressively, in this case, but pursued its investigations vigorously and determinedly. The Bureau has been given powers with teeth for very good reason. The firm, vigorous and thorough nature in which this investigation has been carried out has enabled the Bureau to come to court today with comprehensive arguments to countermand the unwarranted allegations of Mr. Bolger."

The Banker had lost the first round.

* * * *

Over the next several months Bolger became a thorn in the side of the Criminal Assets Bureau. He made application after application to the courts against the Bureau. It seemed that there wasn't a week that went by that the Banker was not in the courts. In October, he hired a team of top English lawyers, solicitor Charles Buckley and Queen's Counsel Douglas Hogg, the former Tory Agriculture Minister, who remained in the country for several months at huge expense. Behind-the-scenes, the Untouchables were informed that Mitchell and a number of other criminal figures were secretly bank-rolling the legal challenges in the hope of disrupting the CAB's activities and it also provided a useful smoke screen.

In the summer of 1998, the investigators discovered evidence that the gangland Banker had succeeded in moving large sums of drug money out of the country, from right under

their noses. Bolger secretly shifted large amounts of cash out
of Ireland through his old partner-in-crime, Edward Phelan.
In turn Phelan had been investing the cash for Bolger with
Englishman Chris Fallon, who was involved in a futures and
options investment company in London. Phelan met Fallon
in prison, where the investor was serving five years for
financial fraud. They had kept in touch when they got out.
Phelan had been back in Ireland for only a few months when
Bolger made contact with him. He had agreed to invest sums
of cash on Bolger's behalf with Fallon's company. In
December 1996, Bolger had given Phelan over Stg£50,000
(€73,000) to invest with Fallon. Bolger also dealt directly with
the London fraudster himself and was estimated to have given
him around IR£300,000 (€381,000). While the CAB were
breathing down his neck in August and October 1997, Bolger
gave Phelan a total of Stg£235,000 (€342,000) and $100,000
(€79,000) to deliver to Fallon. The money was then
redistributed to other accounts Bolger had set up on Mitchell's
behalf, in Liechtenstein and the Isle of Man, including the
Panorama Consultants. But while the Banker might have
evaded the Bureau, Fallon's company was later rumoured to
have ripped the mob off for several Stg£100,000 (€145,000).
The Bureau would later learn from reliable informants that
Mitchell's contacts in the London underworld had threatened
to murder Fallon as a result.

Lawyers acting for Louiseville Ltd, Bolger's company,
meanwhile, claimed that the Mercedes car seized in September
1997 was the property of the company and that it did not belong
to the Banker. The CAB on the other hand claimed that the
car was Bolger's personal property. To resolve the dispute,
the County Sheriff issued what are referred to as Interpleader
Proceedings in the High Court, for a ruling on who actually
owned the car.

The case began on February 4, 1998. During the four-
day hearing Bolger gave some extraordinary testimony. When
the Banker was quizzed about his liability to the Revenue
Commissioners he acknowledged that he "might owe some

money". He did not accept, however, that it was as high as the tax bill he had received from the CAB for IR£140,000 (€178,000). He indicated that he had availed of the Tax Amnesty in 1993 and claimed that he had instructed a firm of English lawyers to send "whatever sums" were due by him to the Irish Revenue.

Evidence was then produced that the solicitors had sent two cheques to the Revenue Commissioners in January 1994, for just over IR£14,000 (€18,000). But the cheques bounced and were returned to Bolger by the Revenue on May 16 of the same year. The fraudster claimed that he didn't see those letters and the bounced cheques until August 1997, over three years later. He said he had no idea as to why the cheques had bounced.

In relation to his failure to appear at the end of his trial for fraud in London, Bolger claimed that he had been advised by two doctors that he was too unwell to go back. But neither doctor was available to corroborate his story. He claimed that he had also instructed his UK lawyers to appeal the sentence he received but again he could not provide any proof that he had ever done so.

Bolger's evidence was peppered with inconsistencies and contradictions. He told an extremely confusing story of how he came to buy a Mercedes car from George Mitchell in September 1995. This was the same man who, a few months earlier, had told another High Court judge that he did not even know the Penguin. The car story had three versions which left Mr Justice Peter Shanley and everyone in the court utterly bewildered.

Firstly, Bolger said that he had agreed a price of IR£10,400 (€13,000) for the car and put down a IR£400 (€508) deposit and wired the rest of the cash to Mitchell's solicitors. The second version was that Mitchell offered to sell him the car for IR£1,500 (€1,900) and give him a car for his wife if Bolger could organise a IR£1 million (€1.27 million) loan for the godfather. The third explanation was the knock out. Bolger said he had agreed to buy the Mercedes and a Nissan Micra from Mitchell. Against this he traded in another car and paid Mitchell IR£1,500 (€1,900) and a further IR£2,300 (€2,900). And if he secured the IR£1 million loan (€1.27 million) for the Godfather he would not have to pay the outstanding balance for the cars. He also revealed how he had paid for the seized car with wads of cash he kept in the boot of his existing motor!

Mr Justice Shanley took two weeks to consider his judgement. On February 27, he ruled that the seized car was in fact Bolger's own property. The judge said that he viewed Bolger's evidence with suspicion. He said he found it "surprising" that the bagman did not call the doctors he named in court to corroborate his illness story. It was also surprising that he produced no evidence of having mounted an appeal against his UK conviction. In relation to his business dealings with George Mitchell, the judge said that he found the "differing accounts of the purchase of his first car impossible to reconcile". He ruled that Bolger had been purposely dealing in cash because he was trying to avoid paying tax and ordered that the car be transferred to the Criminal Assets Bureau.

Bolger had just lost round two.

* * * *

The ongoing CAB investigation had seriously disrupted the Penguin's huge money laundering operation in Ireland. He was also pumping funds into Bolger's campaign in the courts. As soon as he was alerted to the CAB investigation, Mitchell had taken several precautions. He dumped his credit cards and changed his mobile phones so his movements could not be tracked electronically. He maintained daily contact with Bolger and his other henchmen back in Ireland, so that he was briefed on what was happening. Mitchell then decided to take his own form of action against his new enemy – he ordered a contract to murder Barry Galvin. Mitchell and the rest of gangland were by now aware that Barry Galvin was one of the driving forces behind the Bureau. The fact that the Bureau

Legal Officer was not a cop made Mitchell consider that he could be got at. After all, the Penguin was no stranger to murder but even he should have realised that attacking Ireland's version of Elliot Ness would be a step too far, just like the Guerin murder. But, of course, in the aftermath of that outrage it had been Mitchell who had advised Gilligan to murder a cop, to throw the investigation into confusion.

And the Penguin wasn't the only criminal with the idea. English drug trafficker, John Morrissey, a business acquaintance of Mitchell, had also crossed swords with the campaigning lawyer. Galvin had made sure the gangster, who had been linked to a string of gangland murders in Europe and the UK, did not get a warm welcome when he moved to live in Kinsale, County Cork in 1995. Morrissey was also a close associate of the Penguin's sidekick Alan Buckley, whose Munster Mafia had been repeatedly targeted by the former State Solicitor for Cork.

Described as a giant – he stood 6ft 4ins – Morrissey opened an upmarket restaurant after reputedly spending IR£600,000 (€762,000) doing it up. The locals knew him as 'Johnny Cash', because he paid for everything in cash. Morrissey was among the first group of foreign criminals, such as David Huck *(See Chapter Seven.)*, who were targeted by the Criminal Assets Bureau. In December 1997, Morrissey had been forced to leave his beloved adopted home when the CAB moved against him, with an initial tax bill of IR£100,000 (€127,000). They also seized whatever assets and cash they could locate belonging to him. As a result, the Penguin's pal also harboured a major grievance against the Untouchables.

Garda intelligence sources and their colleagues in the UK, received information that Morrissey planned to fly in a hit team to attack Galvin and that Mitchell's men would supply the weapons to be used. A major security operation was put in place and armed bodyguards were assigned to the courageous legal officer. Extra protection was also placed at his home and offices in Cork. All Bureau personnel were also placed on a state of high alert, especially the team involved in

Operation Firedamp. As a result of the security scare, Commissioner Pat Byrne took the unprecedented step of issuing Barry Galvin with a Garda-issue revolver for extra protection. The Gardaí also made sure that the villains found out that the cops were aware of the plot, and it was aborted. At that stage the Penguin had other problems.

In March 1998, the Penguin's mob plotted to hijack a truck carrying IR£4 million (€5 million) worth of computer ink jet cartridges. The truck was transporting the cartridges from the Hewlett Packard factory in Leixlip, County Kildare to a customer in Holland. Unfortunately for the gang the National Bureau of Criminal Investigations had set-up Operation Wedgwood in 1997, to investigate a dramatic increase in well-organised computer chip robberies. Gangs had discovered that there was a huge market for parts, such as chips and disk drivers. And with so many international computer manufacturers based in Ireland, there was any amount of targets to hit. From the mid-1990s there had been a sharp rise in the number of delivery trucks and warehouses being hijacked and robbed. One truck load of parts could fetch anything from €1 million upwards. The parts were easy to conceal and to sell on the black market. Mitchell had begun organising the theft and re-sale of computer parts when he moved to his new home in Amsterdam. Gardaí got wind of the Hewlett Parkard heist and had the truck under observation from the moment it left the factory.

From information received the Gardaí knew that the original plan was for the gang to hijack the truck as it drove through the UK, but this didn't happen. Undercover police then kept tabs on the truck as it crossed by ferry to Belgium, where local surveillance cops were waiting for it. Dutch police took over the watch as the truck crossed the border and followed it to a warehouse near the town of Hoofddorp. In an amazing stroke of luck, for the police, Mitchell broke his most sacred rule. As heavily-armed cops burst into the warehouse they found the rotund Penguin sitting on a forklift as he removed the computer parts from the truck. It was about as hands-on as any villain could get. Mitchell, the truck driver Thomas Massey and three Dutch Nationals, were arrested in the swoop. The crime lord was charged with masterminding the robbery and held in custody until his trial. It was a major setback for the whole organisation.

Despite this, two weeks later, on March 23, 1998, the Penguin's bagman was back in court with yet another vexatious application. This time Bolger was seeking an order to have Barry Galvin and Paul O'Brien cited for contempt of court. He also sought an order prohibiting the CAB from prosecuting its case against him. He again claimed that the Untouchables had subjected him to a series of "dirty tricks" and that this had been carried on to frustrate a prosecution he was bringing against the CAB. In reference to the IR£300,000 (€381,000) which the Criminal Assets Bureau had frozen, he claimed that the money came from a Northern Ireland company and a "Liberian diplomat", for investment in US Railroad Bonds. Bolger also claimed that "anonymous faxes" had been landing on the desks of Gambian public officials, containing excerpts of newspaper reports on the dramatic case. Before the application was heard Bolger's counsel requested that it be heard in camera, away from the press. But Mr Justice Morris refused. "If this was an appropriate case I would have no hesitation to hear it in camera."

After an hour the Judge threw out the application. He ruled that Galvin and O'Brien were not in contempt of any court order, nor were they acting in an "unfair or oppressive manner".

The following day Bolger got another visit from his hated adversaries. This time he was served with an updated tax demand for IR£892,000 (€1,133,000) for the year 1996 to 1997, when he was involved in the movement of Mitchell's money. When interest was added the bill came to IR£1,198,374 (€1,522,000). By May 31, 2000, that figure had increased to IR£1,314,265 (€1,669,000).

Bolger also issued High Court proceedings to seek an order for compensation against the CAB, Barry Galvin and

Paul O'Brien, for IR£312 million (€396 million). He claimed
the sum covered the losses he had suffered in the Gambian
meat project, which was dropped after the money laundering
investigation began. Some time later this figure was reduced
to IR£68 million (€86 million) but the action ultimately failed.

* * * *

George Mitchell went on trial at Haarlem district Court near
Amsterdam in August 1998. The crime lord, who had been in
custody since his arrest, looked like a successful executive,
dressed in a dark grey tailored suit, with pale yellow shirt and
matching silk tie as he stood before the court. The prosecution
described him as the ringleader of the plot to steal the lorry
load of computer parts. When questioned about his business
he would only say that he was involved in "an import-export
company" and claimed he had been framed. He said he did
not wish to say anything about his role in the "affair". Mitchell
admitted that he had served four years in an Irish prison. "In
jail I furthered my education, doing business studies and
accountancy, but when I came out I was over the borderline
of 40 and couldn't find work easily. I arrived to start a new
life in Holland, I formed a company and was working every
day up to my arrest," he claimed.

Mitchell's lawyer, Rob van der Velde, said there was "no
evidence whatsoever from Ireland" to suggest his client
masterminded the robbery. But public prosecutor, ALM
Welschen, declared: "His role as the ringleader is crystal clear
– this was a careful and meticulously planned operation,
controlled at all times by George Mitchell."

Then turning to address Mitchell, he said: "You elected
to remain silent because you have so much to hide."

The prosecutor told the court that two of the three Dutch
nationals arrested with Mitchell had already admitted that
George Mitchell had recruited them to drive the truck to a
secret location.

On September 11, the court sentenced Mitchell to a thirty-month jail term. When compared to Irish courts, the sentence was incredibly light.

A month later, an officer from the National Crime Squad in Utrecht visited the Penguin in his cell in Amsterdam Prison. The Penguin was given a reminder that the dreaded CAB were still thinking of him. On behalf of the Irish authorities, the Dutch cop served George Mitchell with an initial tax demand for over IR£100,000 (€127,000).

* * * *

On October 20, 1998, Bolger was arrested at his home on foot of the fourteen outstanding extradition warrants issued by the London Metropolitan police. But the conman immediately claimed that his arrest was part of a Criminal Assets Bureau dirty tricks campaign. His lawyers went to the High Court for an inquiry into the legality of his arrest. Even though the arrest had nothing to do with the CAB, the Bureau found itself back in court, again. Lawyers for the CAB informed the court that they were not involved in the bagman's detention. In the meantime Bolger was freed on bail to pursue his ongoing cases against his Irish tormentors.

The High Court challenge to the Criminal Assets Bureau, which had been brought by Bolger, would be the longest and toughest case the Bureau would experience during its first decade in operation. Behind-the-scenes several criminal figures, including the Monk, Gerry Hutch, who was already in the wars with the CAB, were suspected of helping to bank roll the case. It was in every criminal's interest that the axe would fall on the Untouchables.

In early 1999, the case was heard over twenty-nine days in the High Court, before Mr Justice Kevin O'Higgins. The entire proceedings were held in camera and therefore could not be reported in the media.

Bolger's strategy was to attack the CAB's credibility on a broad front. A large part of the hearing was taken up with a challenge to the constitutionality of the Proceeds of Crime Act and the powers of the Criminal Assets Bureau. It also focused on Bolger's myriad allegations of threats, intimidation, assault, lies and press leaks. The officers attached to Team Three were subjected to the brunt of the barrage of accusations, including professional misconduct and corruption. Everything was used to attack the credibility of the individual officers involved. One retired member of the Bureau recalled: "We were aware that a lot of criminals had bank-rolled Bolger's case, especially George Mitchell and Gerry Hutch. While Bolger's allegations seemed ludicrous, the strategy was to throw everything but the kitchen sink at us to undermine the credibility of every officer in the Bureau. If the case had gone against us we would have been out of business."

But things did not go the way the mob wanted.

On June 4, 1999, Mr Justice O'Higgins delivered his judgement. He dismissed all of Bolger's accusations and applications. The court upheld the right of the Bureau to seek orders freezing money that it suspected to be the proceeds of crime, to prevent money laundering. He ruled that he was satisfied that the money seized in 1997, IR£300,000 (€381,000), was indeed the proceeds of crime. In the course of his long and comprehensive judgement the judge summarised the approach the Penguin's Banker took to the case: "I am quite satisfied that Mr Bolger was involved in a premeditated, calculated, sophisticated and outrageous attempt to mislead this Court. His explanation as to the genesis of the money, the subject matter of these proceedings, is in shreds …the view of the Court [that the IR£300,000 (€381,000) is the proceeds of crime] is reinforced and strengthened by the evidence proffered on behalf of the Respondents [CAB]."

In the meantime the Bureau had submitted a file to the DPP recommending that Bolger be charged with criminal offences under the tax laws.

In September 1999, on the instructions of the DPP, Detective Sergeant Paul O'Brien formally arrested Peter Bolger and charged him with a total of fourteen counts of failing to declare his taxes and make returns. Bolger was granted bail and ordered to surrender his passport to the Gardaí. At a subsequent court appearance Bolger told the court that he needed his passport for business purposes. During the hearing, Det. Sgt. O'Brien informed the court of Bolger's habit of not turning up for trials of serious crimes and recommended that the court should impose a large cash bail. Bolger was granted his passport request, on the grounds that he produce IR£50,000 (€64,000) in the form of a cash surety. But the bagman knew that there was a catch. If the CAB could show that the bail money was in fact his own property then they could seize it and use it to pay off some of his outstanding tax bill. So in order to outsmart his hated enemies, he pretended that the IR£50,000 (€64,000) was put up by yet another of his many mystery friends in Liechtenstein. In reality he moved the cash from one of his hidden accounts. At a further bail hearing, however, the court reduced the sum of bail and effectively released the IR£50,000 (€64,000). In the meantime Det. Sgt. O'Brien and his team had uncovered evidence that the cash belonged to Bolger. Within an hour of the bail conditions being changed, the Untouchables arrived at the solicitor's office with a High Court Order to seize the cash. The Banker was sick when he heard the news.

Undeterred by either the High Court judgement, or indeed the huge mounting costs on his case against the CAB, Bolger appealed to the Supreme Court. The hearing lasted four days and was also joined by John Gilligan's constitutional challenge to the same legislation.

On October 18, 2001 the Supreme Court unanimously dismissed the appeal and upheld the High Court decision. Chief Justice Keane said the "unquestionably draconian legislation" had been enacted by the Oireachtas because professional criminals had developed sophisticated and elaborate forms of what had become known as money laundering, to conceal the proceeds of their criminal activities. The Chief Justice said that the principal argument, on behalf of Bolger and Gilligan, was that the provisions of the 1996

Proceeds of Crime Act formed part of the criminal law and not the civil law, and that people affected by the provisions were deprived of some important safeguards which historically were a feature of the criminal law – the court dismissed this. It had been a good day for the Untouchables. Later Det. Chief Supt. McKenna said that he welcomed the judgement and that it clearly demonstrated that the civil confiscation process to tackle the proceeds of crime was warranted.

On February 15, 2002, Bolger finally gave up his fight and pleaded guilty to the tax charges in the Circuit Criminal Court. Judge Elizabeth Dunne said she regarded the amounts of money involved, IR£1.5 million (€1.9 million), to be at the "very serious end of the scale for crimes of this nature". The Bureau Revenue officer dealing with the case, identified only as "Tax Inspector A", said Bolger had not yet repaid any of the tax bills due. Det. Sgt. O'Brien confirmed that Bolger was under medication at the time of his arrest and that he was also aware that his wife, Pauline, suffered from leukaemia and had undergone a bone marrow transplant. The couple had two children in their twenties and one of them had recently given birth. Bolger's counsel said that he had fallen into "extremely hard times" and suggested that, "no public service would be served", by jailing his client.

Judge Dunne said that she had no choice but to impose a custodial sentence and she jailed Bolger for twelve months. If Bolger had not pleaded guilty, she said, she would have imposed up to three years.

Mitchell's Bagman served a total of nine months behind bars. A request to be transferred to the much more comfortable Shelton Abbey open prison in County Wicklow, shortly after he went inside, was turned down. In the meantime, however, his efforts to frustrate the legal process paid off when a court threw out the London extradition case, on the grounds that too much time had elapsed since the original offences.

But Bolger's war with the CAB, on behalf of organised crime, had been a costly one. In 2006, he still had a €2 million CAB demand for tax and VAT hanging over him. The legal bill for the High Court and Supreme Court challenges, paid by him and the other underworld "investors", was over €500,000. He had also been ordered to pay the State's legal costs of around the same amount. The Untouchables had also successfully seized over €413,000 and Bolger's car. But the story of the devious fraudster is far from over. In 2005, he opened a bathroom supply shop in Rathfarnham in south Dublin but according to intelligence sources interviewed at the time of this book's publication, Bolger is still classified as an associate of George Mitchell and several other criminal figures. Associates said that he was still involved in "international business" deals.

* * * *

Michael Keating had been keen to keep his head down after the Penguin affair. After his links to organised crime had been laid bare to the world, he had grown hoarse protesting his innocence. But in 1999, he suddenly became embroiled in another scandal – a Stg£20 million (€29 million) computer VAT fraud in the UK. Keating was implicated as a central player in the racket with forty-six-year-old Limerick playboy, Daniel O'Connell, and twenty-year-old Bernadette Devine from Sligo.

The scam involved creating a paper trail for the fictional import and export of computer chips between Ireland and the UK. The con, also known as Carousel Fraud, generated multi-million pounds worth of fake Vat refund claims. Two companies owned by Keating had been central to the scam and the UK authorities revealed that the former Lord Mayor of Dublin would be arrested, and charged, if he set foot in the UK. Tax and revenue crimes are not included in the existing extradition treaty between the Irish Republic and the UK. Following a request from HM Customs shortly after O'Connell and Devine were arrested in London, however, the CAB searched Keating's home looking for evidence.

In August 2000, O'Connell was jailed for eight years after

a twenty-seven-week trial, at London's Middlesex Guildhall Crown Court. It had taken the jury eleven days of deliberation to reach their verdict. During the hearing, the Prosecution described Michael Keating as a central player in the racket and O'Connell's "partner-in-crime". O'Connell claimed that Keating had blackmailed him and forced him into a life of crime. He claimed that the smooth-talking politician had threatened to put him in a wheelchair and to injure his girlfriend if he didn't do what Keating wanted.

In 2001, Bernadette Devine was jailed for six years for her part in the scam.

Although Keating pleaded his innocence and declared that he would have no problem going to the UK to face the music, he decided to stay put in Dublin. While the investigations in London were unfolding, Keating got another visit from the CAB, this time with a tax bill for over €1 million. In the same month that Peter Bolger went to jail, Michael Keating paid €266,600 in settlement of his outstanding tax liabilities. In the interim period he had been forced to sell his home in Castleknock and had moved to live in north County Dublin. He was said to be still "ducking and diving" in 2006. CAB officers suspect that Keating is not as poor as he maintains. It is believed that he has invested money with close associates in South Africa, Eastern Europe and South Africa.

As a direct result of Operation Firedamp, Alan Buckley also found himself receiving the attentions of the Criminal Assets Bureau. Buckley was eventually forced to pay €350,000 based on his earnings from criminal activity. The drug trafficker was forced to sell his family home to raise the money. At the time, the smooth-talking gangster claimed that he was no longer involved in organised crime. In an interview with this writer for the *Sunday World* in 2002 he said: "It is six years since I had any involvement in any of that [drug crime]. For eight years I was involved. It was pure greed mixed with the excitement. I have no need or desire to go near that life again. I want to forget all that. I don't need to do that [drug crime] any more. I paid the price by handing over a lot of money and I am still paying. My only work today is purely legitimate."

But like Bolger, police intelligence still considers Buckley to be a major player in international drug trafficking and he is still closely aligned to the Penguin. Two other associates of the Penguin, Stephen Kearney and Gerry Hopkins, were also forced to stump up over €1.5 million between them, on the foot of demands from the Criminal Assets Bureau and later settled for significant six-figure sums. Hopkins, like his brother-in-law the Monk, physically paid his money to the CAB in hard cash. Wearing a baseball hat and gloves, he handed over a briefcase to a Bureau officer to settle his criminal debt. Another associate of the gang also paid over IR£200,000 (€254,000). Also involved were two criminals who later featured in Operation Alpha against the monk and his mob and subsequently paid in the region of €1million between them.

In 2003, the dreaded Untouchables scored another major victory against the Penguin when his older brother, and partner-in-crime, Paddy, was jailed for two years for failing to make tax returns, worth over €1 million. Paddy Mitchell had always been his brother's eyes and ears. He was the only person that the Penguin truly did trust in the criminal underworld. He was involved in every class of racket, from importing firearms and drugs, to organising burglaries and selling stolen antiques and paintings. Mitchell had even been involved in organising "arranged marriages" between Irish people and wealthy Chinese and other non-Europeans. But Paddy Mitchell was made to pay up when he became a major target of Operation Firedamp.

The Untouchables suspected that over the years the Penguin's sibling had built up a secret portfolio of around fifty properties, renting rooms to drug abusers, alcoholics and criminals. After an exhaustive series of twenty-three searches, which included twelve solicitors firms, auctioneers and mortgage advisers, the CAB were able to prove that Mitchell owned eleven of these properties.

On April 10, Paddy Mitchell pleaded guilty in the Dublin Circuit Criminal Court. His two year sentence was later reduced to six months. Mitchell was also forced to sell six of his properties to pay the Criminal Assets Bureau bill of €1 million.

In May 2006, the Criminal Assets Bureau froze €153,000 which was the proceeds from the sale of a house which George Mitchell had owned, under an assumed name, for thirteen years. As a result of Operation Firedamp, the Untouchables discovered that the Penguin had secretly created an alternative identity for himself, using the name Michael O'Brien.

At the time this book went to print, George Mitchell was still considered to be one of Europe's most significant players in international drug rackets. In Dublin Johnny Doran and Paddy Mitchell still look after the Penguin's interests. By using the likes of Peter Bolger, and in order to get around money laundering legislation, Mitchell has established businesses and property portfolios, in several countries outside the European Union. A senior officer attached to the Amsterdam Serious Crime Squad told this writer that Mitchell had grown fatter and even more paranoid. He remarked: "Now he is so heavy that it is hard for him to even waddle. He also wears a belt around his body to carry up to twelve phones so that we cannot bug them. He really has become Mr Big."

Eleven

The General's Loot

Martin Cahill, the General, was the undisputed godfather of organised crime in Ireland – until a professional hit man ended it all with five well-aimed bullets from a .357 Magnum. Up to that moment Cahill had dominated gangland. To the Irish public the General was the hooded bogey man, an outlandish joker who always hid his face while having no compunction about dropping his trousers to reveal his *Mickey Mouse*® shorts. It was only after his death that the world finally got a glimpse of the man behind the grinning face of the universally feared crime lord.

The story of the General is well-known by now. But it is hard to write a book about organised crime in Ireland without referring to him. For three decades, Cahill was the brains behind one of the country's most ruthless armed crime gangs ever. He taught some of the best known gangsters in the underworld and was the Gardaí's 'most wanted' criminal for years.

When Cahill was murdered in August 1994, it seemed that his fellow gangsters had helped him to elude his most hated enemies – the Gardaí and the State – to the end. After twenty years, they still hadn't managed to secure the General, with a long-term stay in prison. In life, Cahill openly displayed his contempt for law and order and the wealth he had accumulated from scores of armed robberies. Unlike any other criminal, Cahill also purposely took his fight to the cops. Getting one over on the police was sometimes the sole motivation for his more mischievous strokes. At every opportunity he tried to humiliate them. For example, Cahill equipped his mob with an arsenal of weapons which he had stolen from the Garda depot where illegal firearms were stored. He even tried to plant some of the guns in the homes of well-known journalists and made it look like the work of the police. On one occasion he set fire to a court building to prevent a case going ahead and then stole the DPP's most sensitive crime files.

Gardaí responded by setting up the high profile Tango Squad, to specifically target the General and his gang. But that didn't stop Cahill. He dug holes in the Garda golf course and later joked openly to detectives about how he got a "hole-in-one" there. It also wasn't unusual for him to leave clues, which were not of a forensic nature, at the scenes of certain crimes, just to cajole them. But he also resorted to chilling crimes of savagery against defenceless State servants. As has already been documented in this book, he blew up the State forensic scientist, James Donovan and he shot Brian Purcell, a Social Welfare inspector. The General was one of the first criminals to illustrate the need for an organisation like the Criminal Assets Bureau.

By the time the Bureau was established, however, Martin Joseph Cahill had been out of the picture for over two years. But the Untouchables had long memories. And they were determined to make him pay – even from beyond the grave.

When the CAB went to war with the crooks, however, there was no time or resources to deal with dead villains. Nor was there a will to go in search of his assets. There was more than enough work targeting the live villains. But one man in the Criminal Assets Bureau had a different idea.

Det. Chief Supt. Felix McKenna had probably more experience of investigating the General than any other cop in Ireland. He was one of a handful of officers who could genuinely say that he knew the crime lord better than most. In fact, for almost thirty years, the careers of McKenna and Cahill had run side-by-side and had crossed each other many times. The quick-witted Monaghan man had been a cop for eight years when he began his career as a detective in 1973. At the same time the former burglar from Rathmines also decided on a change of direction in his 'career'. The early 1970s saw an explosion of serious crime, as armed robberies became the stock and trade of terrorists and villains alike.

McKenna was recruited as a member of the Special Task Force, or the 'Flying Squad', under the leadership of a tough Detective Inspector called Ned Ryan. Ryan would become such a thorn in the General's side in later years that the gangster tried to have him murdered. The Flying Squad consisted of thirty hard young detectives whose job it was to target the upsurge in armed heists. Within a short time they were specifically targeting Cahill and a group of his associates. Over the following several years, McKenna took part in covert and overt surveillance of Cahill. He arrested him several times and investigated many of his crimes. McKenna became an expert on the man who would become the country's most feared godfather.

In November 1974, the Flying Squad arrested Cahill, his brother Eddie and brother-in-law Hughie Delaney, following an IR£80,000 (€102,000) heist from a security van in Rathfarnham, South Dublin. Although they were charged, the three men got away on technicalities. Three years later, Cahill got his last significant jail sentence when McKenna and his colleagues secured a three-year sentence against him for stealing a car destined for use in an armed robbery.

After his release, Cahill continued his crime spree. Between April 1982 and July 1983, the General's gang stole cash, gold and jewels worth over IR£1,570,000 (€2,000,000) in a series of heists, including the O'Connors robbery in Harold's Cross. In 1987, McKenna was assigned as a team leader of the Tango Squad. One of his colleagues on the squad was John McDermott who joined the CAB as a Detective Inspector in 1996. Although the squad did not catch Tango One, they did manage to put most of the gang members behind bars over a two-year period.

In November 1993, McKenna again found himself as the lead investigator in another of Cahill's crimes. This time the General's mob kidnapped the family of bank executive Jim

Lacey and forced him to hand over cash to the gang.
McKenna's investigation team managed to convict gang
member Joseph 'Jo Jo' Kavanagh, who had pretended to also
be a hostage during the attack. During the inquiry, McKenna
experienced first hand the need for legislative change. While
investigating the Lacey kidnapping, McKenna had seized a
substantial sum of money from John Traynor, who had
masterminded the crime with Cahill. The future Bureau chief
was later forced to return the money, under a Police Property
Application. Traynor claimed that the money was from car
dealing and as it could not be proven that the cash was from
the proceeds of the kidnapping, the Gardaí had to give it back.
In reality it was drug money from the Gilligan operation but
no one knew that at the time. And even if they had known, the
police had no powers to do anything about it. It was hardly
surprising after that incident that Martin Cahill was never far
from McKenna's thoughts when he joined the Criminal Assets
Bureau. For the Chief Superintendent it wasn't just business
when it came to the General – it was also personal.

However, pursuing an investigation into Martin Cahill's
assets would not be easy. There was some reluctance within
the Bureau as it was felt that he had been dead too long to
bother chasing after his estate. And there was also the well-
known fact that the whereabouts of Cahill's fortune, built up
from the proceeds of the huge number of robberies the General
had orchestrated, had been buried with him. But McKenna
argued that they owed it to the scores of people Cahill and his
gang had terrorised, including the victims of his appalling
violence, to be seen to exact some form of recompense. The
discussion went on for some time.

It wasn't until McKenna's return to the CAB as the Chief
Bureau Officer in 1999, after the promotion of Fachtna
Murphy, however, that he was able to finally nominate Cahill
as a target. In early 2000, the Untouchables began investigating
the property portfolio of the dead gangster.

As part of a normal CAB investigation officers gather
background information and intelligence from colleagues

familiar with the particular target. But this time they had to go no further than the "Chief's" office. The investigation focused on Cahill's wife, Frances, and her sister, the General's lover, Tina Lawless, who between them gave birth to his nine children. The bank records in the names of Frances Cahill and Tina Lawless were uplifted from financial institutions. Solicitor's offices were also searched. Bureau members, who were colleagues of the Social Welfare officer who had been shot by the General, compiled details of all assistance payments made to the gang boss and the two women.

The earliest property transaction that could be traced was Cahill's purchase, in 1980, of a small grocery shop in the name of Tina Lawless. The following year Cahill used money he had stolen to buy the JetFoil pub with John Traynor. Situated in the old dockland area of Dublin, the pub was a dingy, rundown haven for drug dealers and drunks. Traynor later burned the pub down in an insurance scam and the money was divided between himself and the General. In 1991, they sold the site for IR£94,000 (€120,000) and again split the money. In 1983, Cahill paid IR£80,000 (€102,000) in cash for a four-bedroom detached house at Cowper Downs in a leafy upmarket corner of Rathmines. It was the last place that anyone expected Cahill to want to live. He despised his neighbours because they weren't his people. But he liked the area because it was near to the site of Hollyfield Buildings, the rundown slum where he had spent most of his younger life. "I know people who have had nervous breakdowns after being cut off from Hollyfield and their friends. I wanted to stay in the neighbourhood and here I am," he once remarked in a magazine interview a few years before his death. At the back of the house he built a large pigeon loft which Dublin Corporation tried to have knocked down a year later. Their action failed, however, because they couldn't identify the legal owners at the time. Although Cowper Downs was held in the name of a former gang member for Tina Lawless, it was Frances and Cahill's first family who lived there.

At the same time, Cahill and his wife were the registered

tenants of Number 21 Swan Grove, a small cluster of Corporation houses, a short drive away near the village of Rathmines. In fact Tina Lawless lived there with Cahill's second family. The General shuttled between the two homes every day, when he wasn't 'working'.

In February 1992, Cahill bought the house from the Local Authority in the name of his wife for IR£20,000 (€25,000). On February 25, a security camera in the AIB branch on Morehampton Road recorded the General doing something that he had never done before – lodging money. He wasn't wearing his customary balaclava or wielding a gun. Looking like a down-on-his-luck used car salesman, in a cheap polyester suit, he carried a plastic bag containing IR£19,500 (€24,500) which was mostly in used £50 (€65) notes. He exchanged the money at the counter for a bank draft made payable to Dublin Corporation.

A half hour after the General had left the bank, two armed men wearing motorbike helmets burst through the door and made their way to the hatch where Cahill had made the lodgement. They threw a bag at the teller, and ordered her to put all the cash into it. Just before the arrival of Cahill's men, staff had removed IR£8,000 (€10,000) of the money to the vault. The gangsters, however, knew exactly what they were looking for. "Where's the rest of the fuckin' fifty pound notes? There should be more here," one of them shouted. The raiders left with the remaining IR£11,000 (€14,000) in cash. Cahill had just got his house for a great bargain!

Within a few months, the CAB had prepared their case to seize the properties. They had ample evidence that they were bought with the proceeds of crime. In June 2000, the Untouchables cited Frances Cahill, Martin Junior and Tina Lawless in a High Court application, seeking an order freezing Cowper Downs, Swan Grove and a derelict store and yard at Dolphin's Barn. In a lengthy Affidavit, which was read to the court, Felix McKenna outlined in detail the career of his old adversary. He also recalled the attacks on James Donovan and Brian Purcell as part of his evidence of criminal activity.

The order was granted.

The Cahills, however, challenged the order and negotiations dragged on for over four years. Prior to the CAB's application, Frances Cahill had moved to live and work in the UK with her youngest children. In the meantime, the once close relationship between the sisters had deteriorated. They were soon anxious to do a deal. Behind-the-scenes McKenna was working to ensure that the women were not left homeless or destitute. Eventually a deal was hammered out.

On March 2, 2005 the High Court was told that the family had consented to the sale of Cowper Downs. Under the terms of the agreement the CAB dropped its claim to Swan Grove and the derelict site and agreed a payment of €175,000 to the wife, son and lover of the late gangster, from the proceeds of the sale.

In May a team of workers began the job of cleaning up Cowper Downs to make it presentable for auction. In the intervening years the property had fallen into complete disrepair, both inside and out. But even then there was to be more drama.

The builders and cleaners had already filled seven industrial skips with rubbish and debris from the garden and house when they began tearing down the ramshackle remains of the General's once prized pigeon loft. As they dug out the foundations they uncovered a buried sack. There was intense excitement that some of Cahill's infamous hidden loot had suddenly been found. The officer in charge of the case, Det. Gda. Henry Ainsworth, and a team of colleagues rushed to Cowper Downs to retrieve the bag. Work was halted on the site as the bag was taken away for examination. It would have been ironic if Cahill's most implacable foe, Felix McKenna, had ultimately found his treasure trove. But they were disappointed. When they searched the bag, the Untouchables found a quantity of silverware and a number of chalices. At first it was thought that this could have been the proceeds of one of Cahill's many burglaries but it was later discovered that the loot had actually been stolen from a local church in

Rathmines in 2001 – seven years after his death. Gardaí suspected that the culprit was a close relation of the fallen General, who was following in his footsteps. It was later learned that he had been chased on the night of the burglary but the stolen silver had never been found. The Church was delighted with the work of the CAB that day.

But the find had prompted Felix McKenna to leave nothing to chance. He ordered specialist Garda search teams into the house and garden to conduct a thorough search. Special scanning equipment was brought in to check for possible hidden cavities in the house.

After two days nothing was found and preparations to make the house presentable for sale continued. One Bureau source remarked with a smile at the time: "The house can go on sale now. At least the new owners will be able to rest easy at the thought that they are not living on top of Cahill's stolen treasure."

Two weeks later Cowper Downs was sold for over €900,000 at auction. The agreed amount of €175,000 was paid to Frances and Martin Cahill Junior and Tina Lawless. Det. Chief Supt. Felix McKenna, who had been on the General's case for three decades, had the money transferred to the Department of Finance. He and his Untouchables had finally made Martin Cahill pay up.

Epilogue

It was early on the morning of October 23, 1996 and the sense of anticipation and excitement was palpable around the High Court in Dublin as the word spread that the Criminal Assets Bureau had something big on. The media had heard that the Untouchables were about to make their first court appearance since receiving their statutory powers, eight days earlier. The Bureau was about to apply for the first order freezing a bank account belonging to a major criminal. The urgency of the early hearing was to get to the bank before it opened, so that they could impose the freezing order and stop heroin dealer Derek 'Maradona' Dunne, the CAB's first target, from withdrawing his money.

Barry Galvin, Fachtna Murphy, Felix McKenna and several CAB officers marched confidently into court with their counsel. When the Judge arrived on the bench he was informed that the Bureau were seeking an order, under the Proceeds of Crime Act, restraining the former League of Ireland footballer from withdrawing IR£53,000 (€67,000) from a bank account he held in Central Dublin. In an Affidavit, which was read to the court, Fachtna Murphy claimed that Dunne was "one of the leading suppliers of heroin in the inner-city of Dublin".

The Judge responded with a few pressing questions for the CAB. He wanted to know had Dunne been convicted of drug trafficking offences? He hadn't. Did Dunne have drug trafficking charges pending? Again the answer was no. Counsel also informed the Judge that Dunne had been acquitted of drug charges in Liverpool, two months earlier.

The judge seemed perplexed. This was the first time he had been asked for an order under the revolutionary new legislation. "I think I will have another read of the Acts," he told the Untouchables and announced a short adjournment.

Once the judge had satisfied his legal queries the order was granted and the CAB officers left for Dunne's bank. By the time it opened, the CAB had seized the first instalment in the fund of cash taken from criminals which, over the next ten years, would steadily grow to almost €100 million.

The Dunne case was a milestone for the new Bureau. Maradona, who was living with the Penguin's daughter, Rachel, had been high on the priority list of the new unit. During the previous three years, Dunne had been the target of repeated Garda investigations into heroin dealing in the inner-city. But he had proved an illusive prey and had managed to keep one step away from the actual product. Several of his mules and street dealers had been nabbed but he had escaped the net. In August 1996, Dunne had been acquitted, after a second trial at Liverpool Crown Court, of conspiracy to smuggle heroin into Ireland between July 1994 and March 1995. When the trial ended a smiling Dunne had taken a plane to Amsterdam, where he had resettled with Rachel. Mitchell himself had already moved his operation to Holland. Dunne had decided to leave Ireland because of the combined heat from the Gardaí and his problems with the Monk, after a serious assault on Hutch's nephew in 1995.

The CAB seizure order came as a total shock, not only to Dunne, but also to many of his cronies. It was the first time that many of them realised that just because they hadn't been convicted of drug trafficking, it didn't mean their money could not be taken away from them. Dunne was one of a group of five drug traffickers whom the CAB had intended to take on. The Bureau had already identified the accounts of the various drug traffickers and asked the financial institutions concerned to alert them if there was any attempt to move funds. When Dunne flew back on October 22, to close his bank account, the bank had stalled and asked him to return the following morning. In the meantime they tipped off the Gardaí. The CAB's hand had been forced and it had to urgently seek the

High Court application. For the rest of the evening and night the Untouchables put together pleadings and affidavits for the High Court to freeze the loot. One insider recalled: "This was our first case and everyone worked hard to make sure that we had everything in order for the courts. There was an air of excitement about the place and all the stops were pulled out to get it done."

The CAB's first operation was a big success and Dunne lost his money. Four years later he was murdered during a drug feud in Amsterdam.

In their first few years in operation the CAB hit several more major heroin dealers in the city, freezing and later selling off houses and other properties they owned. The Bureau also moved against members of the Travelling community and criminal gangs in Limerick and Cork. Among the targets was Limerick godfather, Brian Collopy, who was forced to sell a house to pay part of a €500,000 tax bill. Another former criminal, Mikey Kelly, who had been elected to Limerick City Council found himself arrested and charged with tax offences. Kelly, who ran a dodgy security company, which fronted a protection racket, was jailed for eight months after being convicted of twenty-six charges of tax and social welfare fraud. Kelly subsequently died following a shooting incident in his home, which was thought to have been suicide.

Through the years the Bureau also launched a major operation to target the proceeds of the prostitution and lap dancing industry. In the course of the investigations they sold off a number of brothels and collected millions of euro in taxes. Among those targeted was notorious pimp Tommy McDonnell, from County Clare, and Maltese Madam, Teresa Behan. Between those two targets alone, the CAB raised over one million euro, from the sale of three premises. They also prosecuted McDonnell for tax evasion offences and he was jailed for 18 months.

Another operation targeted the private security business. Two men who were in partnership together, one a former IRA member and the other an ex-Military policeman, were issued with tax demands in excess of €3 million for non-payment of tax and VAT.

Martin Cahill was not the only dead criminal who was made to pay from beyond the grave. In 2000, the MLIU received a suspicious transaction report from a post office after a relative of murdered drug lord PJ Judge withdrew IR£60,000 (€76,000) in cash. Judge, who was suitably nicknamed the Psycho, was shot dead in December 1996. He had been one of the most feared criminals in the underworld and controlled a huge heroin, hashish and ecstasy dealing operation. The cash was subsequently found hidden in a coal bucket during a search of his relative's home. A major Bureau investigation identified two individuals who had laundered Judge's money. As a result they were forced to pay €1 million in unpaid taxes.

In 2005 and 2006 the Criminal Assets Bureau began tackling a massive money laundering racket being operated on behalf of Sinn Féin and the IRA. The money came from extortion, smuggling and robbery and had successfully operated in Ireland for decades. The funds were being used to fund the political ambitions of Sinn Féin and the IRA's campaign of violence. In December 2004, Sinn Féin/IRA members robbed over €37 million in cash from the Northern Bank in Belfast. Following the robbery a large amount of the cash was moved south of the Border by prominent members of Sinn Féin and the IRA. Just over €3 million was recovered in Cork in 2005. The money was found hidden at the home of Cork financial consultant Ted Cunningham. A number of Sinn Féin/IRA members in Munster were also arrested, as part of the investigation that was spearheaded by the Criminal Assets Bureau. The office of former Sinn Féin Vice President and professional negotiator Phil Flynn was also searched in the same swoops. At the time of writing that investigation is still ongoing. A number of individuals are expected to face criminal charges for money laundering offences and also very large tax bills.

As has already been documented in this book, Republicans

control a vast smuggling empire along the border with Northern Ireland. The racket is so extensive that it has caused a serious dent in the coffers of the UK Revenue Collectors. The widespread racket has also created an environmental disaster, as the greedy 'patriotic' Republicans have dumped highly toxic waste into waterways along the border. The waste was the result of "fuel laundering" processes to take dye out of diesel oil in a bid to evade VAT payments. In March 2006, a huge joint-operation involving police and customs from both sides of the Border uncovered evidence of a multi-million euro organised crime network. The oil laundering and smuggling racket was controlled by Thomas 'Slab' Murphy, a member of the IRA Army Council and a senior figure in Sinn Féin. During the major search operation, the Untouchables and their northern counterparts, the Assets Recovery Agency (ARA), uncovered evidence of a hidden economy worth hundreds of millions of euro. Also discovered was a large purpose-built torture chamber that was being used by the Provos to interrogate and torture their victims.

A few days after the dramatic swoops, Sinn Féin/IRA President Gerry Adams described Slab Murphy as a "good Republican" who had been "important to the peace process". In a typically veiled and menacing threat, Adams warned that people should leave his comrade alone. He said the same thing when it was established that his own organisation had been responsible for the Northern Bank heist. In May 2006, Slab Murphy was served with a demand for €5 million by the CAB.

In February 2006, the Untouchables began an investigation into another aspect of Republican racketeering when they uncovered the existence of a vast property business controlled by the Republican movement in the UK and the Republic of Ireland. The investment in office blocks, houses, hotels and pubs had come from the criminal activities of the Republican movement and involved a number of prominent businessmen. The property portfolio was "conservatively" estimated to be worth €100 million. As a result of the money laundering operations, Sinn Féin has become one of the richest political parties in Western Europe, giving it the electoral resources to take power in Ireland. The discovery of this hidden cash machine prompted the Irish Justice Minister Michael McDowell to describe it as "a state within a state". The Republican crime empire is likely to occupy the Untouchables for many years to come.

****

In the near future a new group of individuals, including some of the country's wealthiest businessmen and builders, will find themselves under the CAB spotlight. An Amendment to the Proceeds of Crime Act in 2005 provided the Bureau with extended powers to investigate people who have benefited financially, as a result of paying bribes to corrupt public officials. Under Section 16 (B) of the Act, the High Court will have the power to grant the Criminal Assets Bureau what will be known as "corrupt enrichment orders". Many of the expected targets are individuals who have already been before the various Tribunals probing corruption in public life. Developers who have paid officials bribes, in the past, in order to get planning permission may have to repay every bit of money they made as a result. In order to achieve this, the CAB was in the process of recruiting forensic analysts and accountants, as it promises to be an extremely complex, and highly controversial, area of investigation.

Over the past ten years the Criminal Assets Bureau has proven to be a hugely effective law enforcement weapon. It has remained intact after a number of formidable legal challenges and the public have given the organisation its universal approval. The pan-European Financial Action Task Force (FATF), an inter-governmental agency established to combat money laundering, has consistently praised the Bureau for its effectiveness in the war against organised crime. FATF has recommended that other countries adopt the same multi-agency approach. Since 1996, CAB officers have travelled all over the world as invited guests of Governments and law enforcement agencies who want to learn from the Irish experience. In the UK the Assets Recovery Agency was specifically modelled on the Bureau. In 2003, on the initiative of Felix McKenna, the Camden Assets Recovery Inter-agency Network (CARIN) was established at an international conference hosted by the CAB in Dublin. CARIN was devised to facilitate greater cross border co-operation. Agencies from forty jurisdictions are now involved. Civil libertarians, members of the legal profession and, most significantly, CAB's targets, have criticised the "draconian" legislation used to pursue the proceeds of crime. The highest courts in Ireland, however, have found the legislation to be a proportionate response to the serious threat posed to society by organised crime.

In modern Ireland the Untouchables have a vital and absolutely necessary role to play. Long may they continue to prosper and seize.